A Grammar of Murder

# A Grammar of Murder

## VIOLENT SCENES AND FILM FORM

KARLA OELER

The University of Chicago Press   CHICAGO AND LONDON

**Karla Oeler** is associate professor of film studies at
Emory University.

The University of Chicago Press, Chicago 60637
The University of Chicago Press, Ltd., London
© 2009 by The University of Chicago
All rights reserved. Published 2009
Printed in the United States of America

18 17 16 15 14 13 12 11 10 09        1 2 3 4 5

ISBN-13: 978-0-226-61794-7 (cloth)
ISBN-10: 0-226-61794-7 (cloth)

ISBN-13: 978-0-226-61795-4 (paper)
ISBN-10: 0-226-61795-5 (paper)

Library of Congress Cataloging-in-Publication Data

Oeler, Karla.
   A grammar of murder : violent scenes and film form / Karla Oeler.
      p. cm.
   Includes bibliographical references and index.
   ISBN-13: 978-0-226-61794-7 (cloth : alk. paper)
   ISBN-13: 978-0-226-61795-4 (pbk. : alk. paper)
   ISBN-10: 0-226-61794-7 (cloth : alk. paper)
   ISBN-10: 0-226-61795-5 (pbk. : alk. paper) 1. Murder in motion
pictures. 2. Murder in mass media. 3. Motion pictures—Aesthetics.
4. Thrillers (Motion pictures)—History and criticism. 5. Detective
and mystery films—History and criticism. I. Title.
   PN1995.9.M835O45 2009
   791.43'6552—dc22

                                                     2009001193

♾ The paper used in this publication meets the minimum
requirements of the American National Standard for Information
Sciences—Permanence of Paper for Printed Library Materials,
ANSI Z39.48-1992.

To my mother, Elizabeth Margaret Oeler

I never saw that you did painting need
And therefore to your fair no painting set;
I found, or thought I found; you did exceed
The barren tender of a poet's debt;
And therefore have I slept in your report,
That you yourself being extant well might show
How far a modern quill doth come too short,
Speaking of worth, what worth in you doth grow.
This silence for my sin you did impute,
Which shall be most my glory, being dumb;
For I impair not beauty being mute,
When others would give life and bring a tomb.
    There lives more life in one of your fair eyes
    Than both your poets can in praise devise.

*William Shakespeare*

# Contents

# Illustrations

# Acknowledgments

I want to thank Matthew Bernstein, who carefully read this book and swiftly provided me with extensive, thoughtful responses at a key moment. Herbert Eagle's work on Russian formalist film theory and Soviet cinema has been formative for me, and he responded to the manuscript with many careful, crucial observations, which are deeply appreciated. I am grateful to D. A. Miller for writing criticism that often takes my breath away—and for his witty, incisive, and detailed response to my work. Galina Aksenovna, Joyce Jesionowski, and Russell Merritt, through their admirable scholarship and expansive cinephilia, were very important interlocutors and readers.

From the beginning, Shoshana Felman's scholarly work has been a touchstone; her incomparable pedagogy inspired and guided my thinking about the murder scene as a key narrative moment. I also wish to thank Michael Holquist; in both its genesis and final argument, this book is profoundly indebted to his work on Bakhtin. Throughout, I was able to rely on Marsha Meskimmon, my long-standing friend, for her rapid, nimble-minded, and always deeply resonant responses. Jay Fliegelman responded to a draft with a genial overflow of ebullient, irreverent intellectual energy for which he is well remembered and sorely missed. With their inspiring writing on, and conversations about, film history and criticism, and especially Soviet cinema, Katerina Clark, Charles Musser, John MacKay, Elizabeth Papazian, Masha Salazkina, and James Steffen provided an incredibly rich intellectual environment in which to work. I wish to express my appreciation for the late Josephine Woll. Her insightful comments and encouragement were essential.

I want to thank the following departmental colleagues and friends: David

Cook played a central role; this book depended on his interest and support and benefited enormously from our conversations. I also relied on Juliette Apkarian for enriching and sustaining a lively interdisciplinary environment in which to work on Russian and Soviet film at Emory. Nina Martin broadened my film-viewing horizons, challenged my critical assumptions, and boosted my energy and happiness with weekend movies (and pasta dinners). I want to express my deepest gratitude to my colleagues Dahlia Judovitz, Alex Hicks, Cathy Caruth, Elissa Marder, Yayoi Everett, Matthew Payne, Mark Jordan, Elena Glazov-Corrigan, Kevin Corrigan, Evan Lieberman, and Eddie Von Mueller for their invaluable engagement and friendship. In particular, I want to acknowledge the much-relied-upon camaraderie, intellectual and emotional, of Valérie Loichot, Jennifer Terni, and Elizabeth Goodstein. My friends Aidan Wasley, Sean O'Sullivan, Antonio Romero, Dan O'Neill, Philippe Rosenberg, Peter Wakefield, Kent Brintnall, Antje Ascheid, Charles Baraw, Tatjana Gajic, Elisabeth Hansot, and Annie Hall either read and carefully responded to parts of the manuscript or talked through various aspects of the writing process with me.

I am profoundly appreciative of the seriousness and intelligence of the Emory students who took Classical and Contemporary Film Theory and my graduate seminars. With them I worked out my ideas. In particular I want to thank David Fresko, Alexander Greenhough, Karen Kalb, Noriko Morisue, Elizabeth Lathrop, Jason Paul, and Jason Roberts for their research assistance.

The manuscript was fortunate to reach the desk of Susan Bielstein at the University of Chicago Press and I am very grateful to her for her fairness and consideration. I would also like to thank Megan Marz for her skill and dedication in shepherding the book through the publication process, and Erik Carlson, who has seen almost every film I discuss and did a meticulous job of copyediting.

I want to express my gratitude to the Institute for Critical International Studies at Emory University for twice providing me with funding to attend the Pordenone/Sacile Silent Film Festival. Much of what I learned at the festival went into this book. I also want to thank the Department of Special Collections of the Stanford University Libraries for permission to publish two pages of the 1929 edition of Lev Kuleshov's *Iskusstvo kino*. An earlier version of part of chapter 3 of this book was published in *Cinema Journal* 48, no. 2, "Renoir and Murder" (Winter 2009). Another part of chapter 3 appeared in *Film International* 5, no. 6, "André Bazin and the Preservation of Loss," edited by Jeff Crouse.

Fundamental to this book were the love, encouragement, and generosity of my mother and my aunts, Helen Ferketic, Kathryn Fagan, and Bernadette Oeler. Finally, I am privileged to acknowledge Alex Woloch. He read every word of this book at least once and responded to every draft with originality and acumen that consistently inspired, challenged, and delighted me. His multifaceted involvement in *A Grammar of Murder* goes beyond his superlative readings of the manuscript at all stages: he sustained the book's ambitions and provided me with time.

# Introduction

Consider the concluding sequence of *Strike* (1925), in which Sergei Eisenstein intercuts a massacre of workers with clips of the actual slaughter of a bull (figs. 1–2): Eisenstein himself notes that the sequence will not have the same meaning for all audiences; the killing of the bull will leave abattoir workers unmoved.[1] Even abattoir workers, however, would not interpret the juxtaposition of slaughterhouse and massacre as equating the killing of persons with the culturally accepted work of the butcher. There could be a perverse slippage of meaning here—except that something beyond the formal juxtaposition of massacre and slaughter coordinates our interpretation of the scene. We personify the bull; we do not taurify the people.[2] Representations of killing rely on our awareness of the irreducible human individual.

This example is not innocent, since it is the practice of montage, famously deployed through this kind of shot by Eisenstein, which lies at the heart of an areferential and sometimes antireferential film praxis that runs through twentieth-century cinema: here cinema does not primarily show phenomena; it produces signification.[3] The contiguity of the slaughter of the bull with the massacre of the strikers exists not within the story world, but on the level of discourse. Although the slaughter of the bull functions mainly as a discursive metaphor, its effect relies on photography-based cinema's power to reference actual objects and movements: Eisenstein inserts shots of the real killing of a bull because he wants the photographic registration of actual blood and violent death to produce a physiological shock.

In structuring the way the spectator sees, or fails to see, the staged massacre of the strikers through the real killing of the bull (or vice versa), Eisenstein's film thus confronts what, for twentieth-century film theory and aesthetics, is a central dialectic of cinema's representational practice:

1                                    2

photography-based cinema can function as a powerful tool for making meaning (particularly through montage or the arrangement of shots), but its attraction also lies in its ability to reference world and event prior to narrative or rhetorical meaning. If André Bazin provides one influential articulation of this dialectic—"the cinema's ultimate aim should be not so much to mean as to reveal"[4]—it does not, as this study will continually demonstrate, remain confined to his film criticism. In fact, we might say that it saturates film culture. Siegfried Kracauer, Maurice Caveing, Edgar Morin, and Georges Sadoul locate it at cinema's inception, in the divergent projects of Georges Méliès, who uses film to signify things that never took place, such as a trip to the moon, and Louis and Auguste Lumière, who show the world at hand (workers leaving a factory).[5] Retrospectively, at the end of the twentieth century and in the deep twilight of photography-based film, Mary Ann Doane can still describe "the project of cinema in modernity" as the dialectical synthesis of "endowing the singular with significance without relinquishing singularity."[6] Like Bazin, and in dialogue with critics such as Miriam Hansen and Paul Willemen, Doane associates cinema's power to capture singularity with the indexical quality of the photographic image.[7]

To "endow the singular with significance," for montage theorists such as Eisenstein, Lev Kuleshov, and Vsevolod Pudovkin, means to channel the potential meaning of a shot by juxtaposing it with other shots. Alone, the individual shot has a reservoir of potential meaning; inserted into a sequence, its signifying potential narrows. The surrounding shots function to pare away many *possible* meanings, transforming the individual photographic image into an explicit sign, its significance produced differentially in and through its relationship to other shots in the sequence. Pudovkin illustrates this process with an example that combines a close-up of a face and a close-up of a murder weapon:

Suppose, for example, we have three such pieces: on one is somebody's smiling face, on another is a frightened face, and on the third is a revolver pointing at somebody.

Let us combine these pieces in two different orders. Let us suppose that in the first instance we show first the smiling face, then the revolver, then the frightened face; and that the second time we show the frightened face first, then the revolver, then the smiling face. In the first instance the impression we get is that the owner of the face is a coward; in the second that he is brave.[8]

Pudovkin's example—with a pointing revolver, appropriately, at its center—echoes Kuleshov's legendary experiment, which gave empirical support to what has become known as the "Kuleshov effect." The experiment reveals that the juxtaposition of shots gives rise to meaning not inherent in the isolated image. Spectators watching a single image of an actor spliced together with a variety of shots, each calling for a different emotional response, claimed to perceive changes in the actor's objectively constant facial expression. The effect implies that the image, when inserted in a montage sequence, loses independent signifying—or referential—power.

It is no accident that our first two examples—the slaughter of the bull in *Strike* and Pudovkin's pointing revolver with faces—both represent killing, or the threat of killing. In classical film theory, a standard example for illustrating the process of montage—and a standard metaphor for its effect—is murder. Murder and montage intersect in the writing of such diverse and crucial figures as Hugo Münsterberg, Béla Balázs, Lev Kuleshov, Vsevolod Pudovkin, Sergei Eisenstein, Boris Bilinsky, Rudolf Arnheim—even Christian Metz. As early as 1929, when he is writing "The Dramaturgy of Film Form," the linking of murder and montage has become so ingrained that Eisenstein merely goes through the motions:

1. A hand raises a knife.
2. The eyes of the victim open wide.
3. His hands clutch the table.
4. The knife jerks.
5. The eyes close.
6. Blood spurts out.
7. A mouth shrieks.
8. Drops fall onto a shoe . . . and all that kitsch!"[9]

The repeated deployment of the murder scene as an example to illustrate the functions of montage might derive, in part, from the popularity of murder narratives within mass culture. Famous silent-era representations of

murder, or threatened murder, abound—the gun pointed at the camera in
*The Great Train Robbery* (Edwin S. Porter, 1903), the assassination of Lincoln
(Joseph Henabery) in *The Birth of a Nation* (D. W. Griffith, 1915), and the shooting by Chief Officer Giliarovsky (Grigory Alexandrov) of Vakulinchuk (Alexander Antonov) in *The Battleship Potemkin* (Eisenstein, 1925) are but a few
well-known examples. But the consistency with which the early film theorists all take up the same example calls for an explanation that goes beyond
the fact that it is a film spectacle readily at hand and easily recognizable: a
multitude of other events could have served as well.[10] The mere proliferation
of murder narratives in popular culture does not begin to explain yet another phenomenon: the ubiquitous and surprisingly persistent comparison
of montage to killing. Montage famously serves as a vehicle for conveying
violence (e.g., the shower sequence in *Psycho*). What often escapes consideration, however, is that the reverse is also true: deadly violence, throughout the history of film-theoretical writing, has, as we shall see, often served
as a metaphor *for* montage. This book argues that murder's demonstration
of the limited and disposable significance of the individual life intertwines
with that key dialectic of twentieth-century cinema that we have seen articulated by Bazin and Doane: between photographically showing particular
persons (as well as things and events) and delimiting or abstracting them
through framing, editing, lighting, and other cinematic and narrative techniques in order to produce meaning. Murder is such a foundational scene in
the history of cinema because the obliteration of life that it revolves around
dramatizes the way that cinematic representation—which shows the photographic trace of a now absent object—always is poised between conveying the reality of the object and registering the loss of reality, or disembodiment, intrinsic to representation itself.

*

The privileged status of murder for questions of representation has a long
history, but the popular appeal of the murder narrative developed in the
late eighteenth and early nineteenth centuries with the rise of mass culture.
While we can speak of a mass production of murder *narratives*, however,
we do not commonly speak of murder as an object of mass production, despite the proliferation of war and genocide in the twentieth century. "Mass
murder" has an oxymoronic ring. "Murder" names an individual act involv-
ing individual persons; on a mass scale we call it by another name such as
"massacre," "genocide," or "war." Murder, moreover, takes place outside the
law. "Execution," or "capital punishment" name killings done in the name
of the law. The distinctions among these terms, however, lack stability. For

those who oppose state-sanctioned killing, execution equals "murder." "Kill one man, and you are a murderer. Kill millions of men, and you are a conqueror. Kill them all, and you are a god." This quotation from Jean Rostand's *Thoughts of a Biologist* (1939) ironically observes that the sheer quantity of the act of killing can transform its perceived quality. Also, many would reject the stipulation that "murder" pertains only to human beings in order to condemn the slaughter of Eisenstein's bull. Despite the instability of the term, murder's essential individuality and extralegality counter the cold impersonality and might-is-right ethic of strategic mass killing. Murder produces a story; mass killing produces a statistic. Hence the tendency— from the Odessa steps massacre in Eisenstein's *The Battleship Potemkin* (1925) to the one-by-one killing of the American soldiers in *Bataan* (Tay Garnett, 1943)—to stage mass violence as a series of individual murders. This book takes such phenomena into account, broadly considering cinematic scenes that focus on the deliberate killing of—and, in some cases, merely the attempt to kill—an individual, even when this killing takes place in the context of war, or in conformity to a proclaimed law.

Scenes of murder and killing dramatize, on a thematic level (even as they entail, on a discursive level) a heightened tension between signification and reference. In the *act* of killing, the murderer violently asserts that the victim's life has but limited and disposable significance. This delimited significance can be enormous. We might think, for instance, of scenes showing the assassination or execution of public figures such as Abraham Lincoln, Joan of Arc, or Malcolm X. In other scenarios, the victim can have great personal significance to the killer, as when Michael Corleone (Al Pacino) has his brother Fredo (John Cazales) killed in *The Godfather Part II* (Francis Ford Coppola, 1974); when Maurice Legrand (Michel Simon) kills his mistress (Janie Marèse) in *La Chienne* (Jean Renoir, 1931); or when Ben Brigade (Randolph Scott) finally kills, in a shootout, a man named Frank (Lee Van Cleef) who, many years before, hanged his wife in *Ride Lonesome* (Budd Boetticher, 1959). In all of these instances, however, it is precisely the importance the victim has for the killer that delimits his or her significance: the victim comes to mean one big thing to the killer; the decision to kill entails divesting the person of irreducibility and flux.

*Killers* can reduce their victims, not simply by transforming them into corpses, but, prior to that, by seeing them as irredeemably connected with— and incapable of moving beyond—characteristics or actions that make it desirable to kill them. *Representations* of killing not only show, on the level of the story, the killer's reductive judgment of the victim; on the level of discourse, the violent eradication of the victim from the diegetic world renders conspicuous—even as it provides motivation for—the necessary abridgement of representation itself. Some character types are particularly easy to kill off—anonymous cowboys and Indians, hired guns, enemy soldiers. The mortality rate for minor characters engaged in violent activity is high.[11] Murder scenes entail not only the usual selections and omissions that accompany any discursive characterization; they more or less abruptly cut some characters right out of the discourse. The discourse often rids itself of the character even as the murderer annihilates the storied victim, signaling that the character is, at a given moment within the plot, dispensable to the narrative. Murder scenes thus can court complicity with the very act they represent.

And yet the question of a life's meaning can take on weight in the face of its negation. The represented character is potentially redefined in the act of being killed, and through such redefinition, murder can add to the representation of a person as much as it detracts. The brutal erasure of a character from the story world paradoxically holds the promise of more forcefully evoking his or her seeming reality. Indeed, the killing of a character often implies a person more powerfully than narrative realization through the presentation of a character's words, thoughts, and actions, or the description of her or his appearance. The sense of a gap left by a murder victim characterizes what Devin McKinney calls "strong violence"—the kind that "makes us cry over spilt blood." McKinney lists the following questions as the crucial ones by which we can identify "strong violence": "Do I care about this character? Will his or her passing leave a gap? Will I remember what I've seen?"[12]

Murder can produce a heightened realism, and heightened realism can, theoretically, produce murder. In a discussion of "a 'realist' theater, a kind of pre-cinema," Bazin writes that theater's ability to incite the audience to murder marks the apotheosis of realism, or the point where realism vanishes into the real: "We must first of all recognize that melodrama and drama stirred up a realist revolution at the very core of the theater: the ideal stendhalian spectator fires a revolver at the traitor in the play (Orson Welles was later to do the opposite on Broadway and turn a machinegun on the orchestra stalls)."[13] Murder can exert two diametrically opposed forces: it can convincingly reduce the significance of a life and, conversely, it can suggest a life's incomprehensible importance. This forking path presented by murder crystallizes a central problematic of characterization. It also renders the murder scene, like other cinematic objects par excellence such as the racing train and the romantic kiss, a site where cinema imagines and transforms itself.[14] Representing the act of murder has effects for film form that go far beyond murder scenes. In particular, the development of montage and Soviet "revolutionary" aesthetics and the crystallization of certain generic codes central to the Hollywood system are inconceivable without this scene, or narrative event.

Soviet montage stands out as a key historical moment in the development of a theory and practice of cinematic signification, and this moment arises in close conjunction with murder, both as an object of representation and as a metaphor for representation. Soviet filmmakers Lev Kuleshov, Vsevolod Pudovkin, Alexander Dovzhenko, and Sergei Eisenstein not only draw on the event of murder to elucidate their theoretical writing; they create intensely wrought film sequences of murder, massacre, revolution, and war.[15] Kuleshov's masterpiece, *By the Law* (1926), adapts Jack London's tale of murder in the Yukon, "The Unexpected" (1906). All of Pudovkin's famous early features—*The Mother* (1926), *The End of St. Petersburg* (1927), *The Heir of Genghis Khan* (1928, also known as *Storm over Asia*), and *Deserter* (1933)—feature crucial scenes of killing, as do Dovzhenko's *Earth* (1930) and *Arsenal* (1928). All of Eisenstein's completed features (as well as the incomplete *¡Que viva México!* 1931–32, and the destroyed *Bezhin Meadow*, 1935–37), with the exception of *The General Line* (1929), have at least one scene of deadly violence. And even *The General Line* playfully stages the killing of the bull Fomka as a mock murder mystery. Among films that he planned, but did not make, Eisenstein prepared a treatment of Theodore Dreiser's *An American Tragedy*, transforming the drowning of Roberta into an occasion for the cinematic realization of a Joycean interior monologue. In his theoretical writing Eisenstein often turns to well-known murder narratives such as Honoré de Balzac's "The Red Inn," Dostoevsky's *The Brothers Karamazov*, and Émile Zola's *Thérèse Racquin*. In addition, he famously led a seminar at the State Institute of Cinematography (VGIK) on "hidden montage," centered on the problem of filming the murder scene in *Crime and Punishment* with a single camera setup.[16]

The generation that gave rise to Soviet montage certainly had compelling reasons to show scenes of killing in representing their world. Grigorii Kozintsev writes of his school days:

> I was born in Kiev and attended the gymnasium there. It was a queer kind of education we had in the first years of the Revolution. Classes were frequently interrupted by artillery fire, and when I left school in the evening, with my satchel stuffed with books, you could never be sure who was currently occupying the town. The Austro-Hungarian occupiers had been replaced by Petliura's men. At Petchersk, not far from the gymnasium, the twisted corpses of shot men lay in the ditch. Our teachers described the flora and fauna of

Africa, explained the conjugation of Latin verbs; and meanwhile machine-guns chattered in the suburbs. In the night you heard the hooves of cavalry detachments trotting by; or the inky southern silence would be rent by shots; or by a cacophony of cries, bangs, gratings: thundering, drumming, echoing, howling. It was bandits trying to break down the gates of the house, and the guard pickets formed by the tenants shaking sheets of tin, hammering on stoves and brass plates, calling for help from goodness knows whom. Came the dawn. And again, satchel in hand, I would trot by broken windows, walls scarred with bullets, encountering armed men absurdly decked out in blue frock-coats. Death stalked the town. People spoke of death with no respect: 'They've stuck him to the wall,' 'he's done with profit and loss,' 'they've made small change of him,' 'they've done for him.' Distantly the artillery rumbled. The urchins would stop, listen, discuss the caliber of the guns.[17]

Kozintsev's experience was not unique: on the Eastern Front in 1918, Grigory Alexandrov worked in a frontline theater and Eduard Tisse headed the film crew on the first agit train (which was reporting on the Civil War); back in Moscow, Dziga Vertov edited Tisse's footage. Mark Donskoy and Friedrich Ermler were soldiers.[18] In her book on Kozintsev, Barabara Leaming quotes from the above passage and concludes: "In this remarkable sentence—a record of childhood experience—we detect that principle of montage, founded upon collision, which would play so important a role in the development of Soviet avant-garde art. Such experiential juxtapositions as Kozintsev records here might be taken to adumbrate a later taste for aesthetic juxtaposition, as evinced in his avant-garde efforts. Radical juxtaposition would become a fundamental tactic of Kozintsev's early work."[19] Making a connection between childhood experience and artistic proclivity inevitably entails speculation, but Kozintsev's juxtaposition of boyhood perceptions, the paratactic sentence structure he uses to convey their stark contrast, and the "collision" of images in montage exhibit a compelling affinity. Side by side, Latin conjugations and twisted corpses resist aggregation into a continuous, meaningful experience. The "collisions" of montage that Leaming detects here might produce new meanings in and through the shock of their contiguity, but at the same time they also suggest, like other modern modalities of representation such as cubism and interior monologue, a reflexive awareness of the limitations of representation, and a corresponding abrogation of meaning.

Even before the Soviets, beginning with D. W. Griffith, editing or montage techniques developed in tandem with the representation of violence. Historicizing this mutual friendship in "Dickens, Griffith, and Ourselves" (1942), Eisenstein, the most intensive theorist of montage, speculates that

Griffith's parallel editing reflects a specific social structure, the capitalist division between rich and poor. Griffith's films repeatedly feature conflict between the two: shots of vagabonds attempting theft and threatening women and children alternate with shots of men who race against time to protect their loved ones and their property, as in *An Unseen Enemy* (1912), *The Lonedale Operator* (1911), and *The Lonely Villa* (1909). And scenes of the decadent or frivolous wealthy appear crosscut with scenes of the oppressed poor as in *Orphans of the Storm* (1921), *Intolerance* (1916), and *Corner in Wheat* (1909).[20] These films mostly, but not always, keep poor apart from rich in both story *and* discourse. Confining the lower classes to their own shot segments, the discourse reinforces the stratification pictured in the story world. While acknowledging a debt to Griffith, Eisenstein claims that Soviet montage transcends this technique of parallel editing precisely because the revolutionary context replaces the simple polarities of capitalist society with a more complex set of coordinates. His implication: Soviet montage aesthetics, born in the crucible of revolution, reflect a Marxist politics and philosophy in their *dialectical* form; and only this dialectical context frees Soviet filmmakers fully to develop the potential of montage. Transcending parallel lines, montage, as form, realizes cinema's, and history's, ineluctable alternation between fixity and instability, opposition and merging.

Despite the different socioeconomic context in which they work, when Kuleshov, Pudovkin, and Eisenstein further develop the practice of montage, they, like Griffith before them, commonly turn to deadly violence as matter for their films—and as an example for their theoretical arguments. Surprisingly, although Griffith's politics differ from those of the Soviet montageurs, in both we find the same intersection of montage and murder—or attempted murder—in relation to class conflict. This formal and thematic convergence between the American and the Soviets reflects the way the Soviets build on Griffith's example, but it also suggests a reciprocity between form and event that extends from the Victorian sentimentalism of *The Birth of a Nation* to the dialectical materialism of *Strike*: murder, in these very different contexts, with their radically opposed understandings of class conflict, creates the cinematic grammar through which it is grasped.[21]

Let us consider the intersection of characterization, violence, and montage in two classic examples, one by Griffith, the other by Eisenstein. Griffith's parallel editing has the power to transform the implied human being who faces the threat of murder into an instrument for building suspense. Exhibiting the naked structure of this suspense mechanism, Griffith's *The Fatal Hour* (1908) concerns a heroine who faces a gun attached to a clock; a villain has rigged the gun to go off when the clock strikes twelve. For Tom Gunning, the scene exemplifies a key consequence of Griffith's integration of innovative editing and film narrative: the inscription of time.[22] To create suspense, Griffith's editing must construct, with or without the use of a clock, a linear time with an impending endpoint. *The Fatal Hour*, in its very title, suggests the mechanism by which such linear, bounded time structures the narrative: the phrase merges the concepts of death and time as the editing collapses the heroine's "life time," which seems to be running out, into clock time (and almost into the film's running time). The heroine, defined primarily by her vulnerability to murder, almost completely reduces to the narrative function of accentuating linear time; she embodies subjection to a visibly encroaching end. This near reduction of character to a span of time occurs throughout Griffith's oeuvre and continually recurs in various action genres. (Three well-known examples include the bus-bombing sequence in Alfred Hitchcock's *Sabotage* [1936], the race of the fatally poisoned hero Frank Bigelow [Edmond O'Brien] to punish his killer before dying in *D.O.A.* [Rudolf Maté, 1950], and the deadline for saving the life of Manni [Moritz Bleibtreu] in *Run Lola Run* [Tom Tykwer, 1998].)

Rendering the character's life legible primarily as quantity rather than quality, this form realizes an aspect of reification described by Marx: "Through the subordination of man to the machine the situation arises in which men are effaced by their labour; in which the pendulum of the clock has become as accurate a measure of the relative activity of two workers as it is of the speed of two locomotives. Therefore, we should not say that one man's hour is worth another man's hour, but rather that one man during an hour is worth just as much as another man during an hour. Time is everything, man is nothing; he is at the most the incarnation of time."[23] We might also think here of the metropolitan consciousness analyzed by Georg Simmel in "The Metropolis and Mental Life."[24] For Simmel, the money economy and the overstimulation of modern urban life can lead to the reduction of everything, including individuals, to quantities of time and money. The metropolitan consciousness protects itself from overload by developing a rational indifference to nonquantifiable particularities. Film characters reduced to spans of time by seemingly imminent violent death correspond to the perception of persons by the "rationally indifferent" consciousness that Simmel describes. But the reduction of character to time span is, of course, never complete: even with characterization as simple as that in *The Fatal Hour*, the human image resists reduction to the narrative function of inscribing time; the "wasting" of a character—even a character whose screen life is predominantly associated with the ticking of an on-screen clock—is always potentially more than the wasting of time. Murder scenes, insofar as they imply a human reference that exceeds a time span, subvert reification.[25] And if the reification of the human image can be subverted in the murder scene, then scenes of attempted murder may also confer a kind of authenticity that can then be manipulated, or that simply fades away, when the victim survives.

Clearly we can easily care—or imagine how contemporary audiences might have cared—about Griffith's potential victim. Gunning's powerful argument stressing the originality of Griffith's foregrounding of *narrative temporality* suggests an important difference between time as it might be experienced in life and in the movie theater. Cinema's ability to manipulate time in relation to character opens the possibility of experiences of time in modernity alternative to those shaped by the reifying effects of the factory clock and the train schedule described by Simmel and Marx.

The social groups that, according to Eisenstein, run parallel in Griffith intersect in the Soviet context, where the devaluation and evaluation of life implied by the murder scene fuse with the dynamics of striking and revolution—the focus of the early feature films of Pudovkin and Eisenstein. Eisenstein's *Strike* (1925), *The Battleship Potemkin* (1925), *October* (1928), and *¡Que viva México!* and Pudovkin's *The Mother*, *The End of St. Petersburg*, *The Heir of Genghis Khan*, and *Deserter* (1933) deploy montage rhetorically to confront capitalist or imperialist oppression. The films' heroes find themselves weighing the value of their very being against the good of the collective, or the claims of their generation against those of their children. Of greatest value are the martyrs and those who risk their lives for the revolutionary cause; these characters receive the most individualized narrative attention in all of the above films except *Strike*. But this attention comes at a fatal cost: "The one first raising the cry of revolt—he first fell to the hand of the executioner." This title commentary on the death of *The Battleship Potemkin's* Vakulinchuk, revolutionary cinema's most prominent martyr, reveals the inverse relation between, and paradoxical convergence of, tsarist and revolutionary points of view. In the story world, *and* in the discourse, Vakulinchuk's revolutionary importance requires his death. The discourse allows his implied life significance only in and through his martyrdom for a larger cause. The classics of Soviet montage identify the meaning of the hero's life with his or her self-sacrifice for the collective cause, immediately subsuming the particular into the universal. Formally and thematically, these films valorize revolutionary martyrdom; they frequently structure violent death not as the brutal end of a life meaningful in itself, but as a life's crowning significance within a progressive historical trajectory.[26]

The exploitation of the implicit reference, inseparable from the formal functioning of the murder scene, defines the martyr. The martyr is distinct from the victim in that our sympathy for the implied person is exhaustively converted into an aim. But while montage can forcefully channel the potential meaning of the filmed person, its power to reduce particularity is in tension with the murder scene's ability to evoke an irreducible life, which gives murder its affective charge. This tension can result in disjunctions, as when, in *Ivan the Terrible, Part II*, Eisenstein lingers briefly on a close-up of the neck of a Boyar who is about to be executed, and on a close-up of the executioner Malyuta's face. As Kristin Thompson points out, Malyuta's close-up suggests a "seme of sensitivity" that is otherwise entirely out of character: "In order to accomplish one purpose—a look at the Boyars as victims—the text must use a character in a way that is inconsistent with his other narrative functions."[27] Montage can, and often does, suppress such instants of "excess" with an ordering of shots that swiftly coordinates meaning. As Thompson notes, Malyuta's "pause has been short indeed."[28]

The conversion of murder into martyrdom intersects, in classical Soviet cinema, with the intensive development of a new form for representing human beings and their annihilation: montage. The genesis of montage in Soviet cinema and film theory is linked with a politics and with narratives that tend to reduce the individual life to abstracted significance. To dispense with individuality is to dispense with murder as a category. In the strictest extreme of class struggle, murder cannot take place because killing an oppressor is not murder, but rather the creation of a new social order, and killing the oppressed is always a matter of class violence in which the individual is irrelevant. Early Soviet cinema, in its most successful scenes of violence, evades both the rhetoric of martyrdom, which suppresses the individual by making him a political signifier, and the melodrama of "bourgeois individualism," which, casting the hero in relief, falsely disconnects him from the social. Scenes of murder—and even war—in films such as Kuleshov's *By the Law* and Pudovkin's *The End of St. Petersburg* serve as important examples of the promise of montage to negotiate between signification and reference, general and particular, in representing persons. Such scenes present a powerful way to investigate the intersection between the often violent historical reference of Soviet montage and montage as a form which works to harness, by arranging in signifying sequences, the potentially excessive meaning of photographic images.

The problematic articulated at the juncture of murder and montage touches numerous aspects of film syntax: framing, point of view, early conceptualizations of sound montage, and avant-garde theories of the actor developing in the second and third decades of the twentieth century (which, as Mikhail Yampolsky argues, are linked to the genesis of Soviet montage theory and practice).[29] A single problem of representation—the scene of murder—arises in many different places within the formulation of film aesthetics. Murder is central to both the theorization and practical development of these processes (camera distance, acting, etc.) and often provokes a conflict between theory and practice, as though film theory itself—like the screen—were unable fully to contain or absorb the excess that is implicit in the murder scene. Ultimately, this history of montage in relation to the murder scene collapses into a history of montage itself—as well as formal and theoretical opposition to it.

*

Montage is shadowed by murder. But can we fairly render montage "guilty"? Theorists and critics ranging from Walter Benjamin to Jean-Luc Godard have valued montage as a technique and aesthetic with rich potential for progressive political expression. The histories of film criticism and filmmaking suggest that the scissors of montage can cut two ways, both signifying reductively and showing the reductiveness of signification. Part 1, "Murder and Montage," pays close attention to the filmed person as he or she appears within the montage aesthetic. The "cutting" of the actor's body into tightly framed shots of body parts frequently suggested violence to filmmakers, theorists, and spectators. But this perception of violence depends on the convention of seeing images showing people from head to toe as whole. Any cinematic image of a person, even a long shot, can be no more than a sign of wholeness. Thanks, in part, to cinema's formative association with theater, and to its photographic base, we sometimes see in early film theory and criticism a tacit naturalization of the long shot as "the whole body" instead of a rigorous insistence on its status as a sign.[30] With its frequent recourse to tightly framed body parts shown from multiple angles, the montage aesthetic can act as a corrective to this naturalization of what is only a sign of wholeness. Montage can function like cubism to achieve a new realism through emphasizing the partiality of any one view. The shock effect, abundantly documented in early film critical writing, of "disconnected" body parts potentially generates a sense of the body as something real. At the same time, severed heads, hands, and feet, arranged in signifying sequences, can turn the person they synecdochically imply into abstracted signification. Montage thus exhibits a tension similar to that of the murder scene, which remains poised between making its victim seem like someone real (whose destruction, and, retroactively, whose life, we cannot confine to a narrative meaning) and treating the victim as information that has importance for the plot, but not in itself.

The murder scene, which comes with such strong, and potentially contradictory, assertions about the meaning of a life, lends particular urgency to the question of how a film should show a person. How do films negotiate ethically, politically, or ideologically the limits of what they are able and willing to reveal about an individual? How should a filmed human being be made to mean? What constitutes showing too much or too little? If we often see in early writing on the cinema an anxiety about the film frame's seemingly violent disregard for bodily integrity, we need to remember that the concern for "wholeness" also presents problems. Indeed, both suture theory and feminist film theory have made spectatorial discomfort with partiality, or lack, their object of analysis and critique.[31] The breakdown of *women's* bodies into fetishized close-ups and the consequent flattening of female characters as subjects typify Hollywood editing—not the films of the Soviet montageurs. But even as it takes the bodies of women and turns them into signs of, and distractions from, lack, Hollywood draws on techniques that also belong to Soviet montage. Examining the murder scene's historical centrality to such a fundamental category of film aesthetics as montage discloses profound connections between film styles, and critical discourses, too often seen as merely opposed.

We perceive the partiality of any shot of a person not only when we compare the close-up to a long shot, or the absent film actor to the present stage actor, but when we raise the question of a film character's thoughts and sentiments, unrealized in word or action, inaccessible to, or unrecognized by, others. Regardless of the extent to which it is expressed in the discourse, the subjectivity of the victim is crucial to the murder scene, since murder is, precisely, the destruction of this point of view. No discourse can realistically show the point of view that murder negates; every murder scene has an ineluctable blind spot. This feature of the murder scene, however, makes it a useful prism through which to consider the status of inner life and its representation. Murder posits and enforces the fixity of the victim. But this extreme assertion of stasis leads to its antithesis: the person, or world, that murder seeks to annihilate retains a quality of contingency, or irreducibility.

Mikhail Bakhtin and Emmanuel Levinas have considered this inner world as it pertains to judging a life's meaning, particularly the most acute form of such judging: murder. In *Problems of Dostoevksy's Poetics*, Bakhtin valorizes Dostoevsky's aesthetic assertion that characters are entitled to the last word on themselves rather than being defined from outside or above. Murder realizes such an outside judgment—that a person is dispensable, killable, disposable. But interiority, precisely insofar as the "I" is *not* fixed but defined by the continuous possibility of change and difference, resists such a pronouncement. Thus, a common theme running through the multiple tales of execution and aborted execution in *The Idiot* (1868) is the condemned man's conviction that if he could live, he would be different. Bakhtin calls this resistance "inner unfinalizability" and defines it as the "capacity to outgrow . . . and to render untrue any externalizing and finalizing definition."[32] Levinas writes in response to the violence of totalitarianism in *Totality and Infinity*: "Interiority as such is a 'nothing,' 'pure thought,' nothing but thought. . . . For the totalization of history to not be the ultimate schema of being, it is necessary that death which for the survivor is an end be not only this end. . . . Interiority is the very possibility of a birth and death that do not derive their meaning from history. Interiority institutes an order different from historical time in which totality is constituted, an order where everything is *pending*, where what is no longer possible historically remains always possible."[33] Both Bakhtin and Levinas describe an inwardness that resists murder's assertion of life's finite, reified meaning. But while Bakhtin is writing literary criticism and focusing on the self-consciousness of characters, Levinas is writing an ethical philosophy and reflecting on people as subject to history. The resonance between their concepts of interiority demonstrates the referential ground against which characterization takes place; it also suggests the paradox that murder, and its representation, can evoke a subjectivity impervious to finalizing, or totalizing judgment.

Murder puts an end to the victim's subjective experience, but the murder *scene* can imply interiority, or even set it in relief, precisely through negating it. No medium can wholly and positively represent something that is "unfinalizable." Given the impossibility of positive representation, negation emerges as a powerful means to suggest the ineffable. It is not cinematic signification that is required, but that which eludes or exceeds it. A paradigmatic site of tension between signification and excess is the facial close-up.

For Kuleshov and Pudovkin, the film image that most emblematically *lacks* independent signifying power is the human face. In Pudovkin's example of three shots—a smiling face, a frightened face, and a revolver—the differential, paradigmatic relationship between the smiling face and the frightened face and the syntagmatic ordering of these shots in relation to a shot of a revolver produces signification: bravery or cowardice, depending on the ordering of the shots. The face—a site where inner, subjective experience is traditionally thought to be externalized—attains its expressive force not in itself, but through the external manipulation of montage. Moreover, this external manipulation determines—and can easily reverse—our perception of character traits such as courage and fearfulness.[34] Soviet montage theory notably dispenses with the notion that human sentiment reliably manifests itself in facial expression, for the Kuleshov effect undermines the notion of interiority as readable in the isolated image of the filmed face. Insertion into a montage sequence channels the meaning of the face. Placed within a chain of images, it loses its wider array of potential meanings. Indeed, Kuleshov at one point claims that an ensemble or montage of bodily gestures can enable both film and theater to dispense with the living face: "If we mask the actor and force him to strike a sad pose, the mask will express sadness: but if the actor strikes a joyful pose, it will look to us as if the mask is joyful too."[35] The fragmentation, reconstruction, and juxtapositions of montage—and of body parts—call into question the traditional role of facial expression as the central signifying force that renders interiority visible.

Writing in the same year (1921) that Kuleshov speculated on the effects of an actor's pose on a hypothetical mask, Jean Epstein claimed: "The close-up is the soul of the cinema. . . . Even more beautiful than a laugh is the face preparing for it. I must interrupt. I love the mouth which is about to speak and holds back."[36] In Epstein's examples, the face, notably, has not quite yet assumed a readable expression—it remains just on the verge of signifying. Bazin explicitly criticizes the montage aesthetic for overriding such instances of ambiguity: "Montage by its very nature rules out ambiguity of expression. Kuleshov's experiment proves this ad absurdum in giving on each occasion a precise meaning to the expression on a face, the ambiguity of which alone makes the three successively exclusive expressions possible."[37] For Bazin, the way montage "rules out ambiguity of expression" paradoxically *demonstrates* the ambiguity of the individual shot or image.[38] From these divergent arguments, we might conclude that images of faces can both sustain the montage chain's process of abstracted signification and resist it. The close-up of the pointing revolver, whose central position determines the significance of the face, smiling or frightened, in Pudovkin's hypothetical scene, is an apt example of the power of montage both instantaneously (photographically) to register and immediately destroy the ambiguous singularity of the image in the production of explicit, syntagmatic meaning. In this sense, the negation of a referential plenitude is implicated into the very logic of montage (and of cinematic signification). And it is not surprising that this intricate formal relationship would be particularly important in scenes within films—and indeed moments within film history—that in one way or another reference negation, particularly murder itself.

Photography and photography-based film have long suggested to theorists and critics not murder, but death. As early as Maxim Gorky's 1896 article "The Lumière Cinematograph," we can find connections made between cinema and death—most famously Bazin's "The Ontology of the Photographic Image," more recently Garrett Stewart's *Between Film and Screen: Modernism's Photo-Synthesis* and Laura Mulvey's *Death 24 × a Second*. Unlike death, murder entails an intentional reduction of an individual subject to a killable, or disposable, person—and, ultimately, to a corpse. A consideration of cinema through the prism of murder begins to emerge in the frequent comparison of cameras and guns, which share common technologies.[39] But the intersection between lethal violence and the cinema goes well beyond the intertwined technological development of their respective tools. Cinema is at once a mechanism for revelation and recognition—and for obscuration and eradication. The negating agency implied by murder makes the murder scene a privileged site for reflecting the way that photography-based filmmaking intentionally cuts the world it registers.

*

If we've watched films, we've watched bodies fall; in certain Hollywood genres, the very absence of murder would be most conspicuous. To understand murder's profound and far-reaching consequences for film form, part 2, "Murder and Genre," moves beyond the montage breakdown and construction of the murder scene to the placement and function of this scene within classical Hollywood genres. We have seen how montage entails a tension between individual and series (shot versus sequence). This tension between part and whole also informs Hollywood genre films on several levels. Studio craftsmanship emphasizes the construction of the film out of scenes into which the shooting script has broken down the story. This means that within such films we have a tension between the individual scene and the series of scenes. Like the individual shot, the individual scene partially derives its significance differentially, in and through its relation to the other scenes that make up the series to which it belongs. And in many Hollywood genres, it is precisely a scene of killing—the showdown, the death-in-the-gutter sequence, or the last stand of a few outgunned soldiers—to which the meaning of every other scene might be referred, even as the scene of killing acquires meaning from the scenes that surround it.

Scenes of killing not only help to determine the significance of all the other scenes that lead up to or result from them: they are often crucial in giving definition to character. The shootouts of the Western, according to Robert Warshow, occasion "a certain image of man, a style, which expresses itself most clearly in violence."[40] The moral qualities of the characters in a murder mystery often emerge in the course of the homicide investigation.

And the fighting of combat films often provides untested soldiers and men who have been discredited—for example, Joe Winocki (John Garfield) in *Air Force* (Howard Hawks, 1943), or Barney Todd (also known as Dan Burns, played by Lloyd Nolan) and Leonard Purckett (Robert Walker) in *Bataan*—with a chance to prove, or reclaim, their latent mettle, or honor. Such characters, seen across several films of a particular genre, metamorphose into types almost as easily recognizable as Harlequin, Pierrot, and Columbine of commedia dell'arte. Thus, Jeanine Bassinger, in her analysis of the World War II combat film, can construct a table listing the following character types: "inexperienced youth," "high-ranking leader who dies," "comedy relief," "cynic," "Quirt/Flagg," and so on.[41] Her table demonstrates that, in addition to the tension between the individual scene and the series of scenes, genre films entail a productive contrast between particular realizations of a character type and the type in general, which is so often defined in terms of its relation to violence.

More broadly, the individual genre film exists in tension with the cycle to which it belongs. In order to survive as a memorable film rather than as a forgettable and disposable cultural artifact, the genre film must distinguish itself from others of its kind even as it must to an extent repeat their conventions in order to draw its audience. Part 2 reads these various instances of tension between individual and series through mass culture's broader imposition of a "culture of sameness,"[42] or serial anonymity, which, as Paul Fussell documents in *Wartime*, can quite literally transform the individual members of a mass society into dispensable units, or, quoting Randall Jarrell, "just collective Objects . . . or Killable Puppets."[43] The murder scene starkly crystallizes the stakes of this formal tension between individual and series, for it pivots on the tension between asserting an individual's discardability and emphasizing his or her singularity. The tensions between scene and story, film and genre, refract the stakes of the murder scene, even though, in some genres, they have nothing to do with murder: they are the lineaments of form as such.

\*

To juxtapose montage and genre as they articulate murder scenes, we must juxtapose classical Soviet and Hollywood cinemas. The murder scene, in both cinemas, often echoes the same "primal" scene: the fight to the death at the heart of Hegel's dialectic between lordship and bondage. By invoking Hegel, I do not mean to subscribe to his totalizing view of history; instead, I read his dialectic as an influential modern narrative about the subject's struggle for recognition that specifically addresses the tension between individual and community. Both classical Soviet and Hollywood films repeatedly dramatize this tension, but in very different ways. Hegel's narrative, moreover, has played a role in the historical context that produced both cinemas. Soviet montage theory and practice clearly has a profound relation to the philosophy of the nineteenth-century's most prominent "left" Hegelian, Karl Marx.[44] And analysis of the Hollywood Western by critics such as Robert Warshow, Richard Slotkin, Jane Tompkins, and Gilberto Perez point up, even if they do not explicitly articulate, a resonance between the national myths that sustained the development of the United States and the narrative of political conflict articulated by Hegel.

To associate Hegel's dialectic of the fight for recognition with Soviet montage and Hollywood genre is important to the consideration of murder and cinema: it is an illuminating angle from which to view the assertion that the murder scene is a crucial site where cinema reflects upon itself. Murder is the negation of a point of view. And cinema, a series of chosen points of view, is also, necessarily, a series of exclusions: to assert one point of view in, say, a shot, means, at least momentarily, to negate all the possible others. Photography-based cinema perceives, shows, and signifies while more or less following various political, social, and cultural patterns of recognition that can (as in Hegel's paradigmatic fight to the death in the struggle for recognition) entail violent exclusions of points of view. Film cultures regularly define and deny otherness. It is at the site of the murder scene that some of these struggles for—and denials of—recognition most intensely play out. But if A *Grammar of Murder* illustrates the way that cinema's distilled formal categories are charged with sociohistorical necessity, it is conversely the case that the scene of murder is most legible not as a directly referenced event, but in relation to the formal strategies and problems that cluster around it.

# Murder
# and Montage

PART ONE

Murder
and Montage

# 1 Framing for Murder: Cut-Ins and Close-Ups

## The Human Face, the Murder Weapon, and the Close-Up

The close-up can both draw attention to singularity and transform it into a generalized, abstracted sign. In classical film theory, discussions of the close-up tend to revolve around two primary examples: close-ups of the human face and close-ups of murder weapons. Theoretical discussions of facial close-ups exhibit a tension between describing the enlarged face as a site of signification and seeing it as ambiguous. Sometimes this tension appears in the work of a single critic, even in a single essay. In "Magnification" (1921), Jean Epstein rhapsodizes about close-ups of faces that are on the verge of resolving into a definite expression; these faces are not fully legible. But he also revels in the possibility of "reading" faces in close-up: "I can see love. It half lowers its eyelids, raises the arc of the eyebrows laterally, inscribes itself on the taut forehead, swells the massiters, hardens the tuft of the chin, flickers on the mouth and at the edge of the nostrils."[1] Epstein's description articulates the face as a montage sequence of extreme close-ups that together signify "love." Similarly struck by the expressivity of the face in close-up, Balázs writes, "The film has brought us the silent soliloquy. . . . In this silent monologue the solitary human soul can find a tongue more candid and uninhibited than in any spoken soliloquy."[2] And Bazin, in an essay on Carl Theodor Dreyer's *The Passion of Joan of Arc*, calls the face "a privileged area of communication" and writes, "We are indebted to Dreyer for his irrefutable translation direct from the soul. Silvain's wart (Cauchon), Jean d'Yd's freckles, and Maurice Schutz's wrinkles are of the same substance as their souls."[3] Unlike Epstein, Balázs and Bazin, while claiming that the face expresses, do not specify what it says. For Epstein, the face in close-up can signify explicitly ("love"), but for Balázs and Bazin it suggests a meaningfulness that remains irreducible to words.

Ambiguous *and* communicative, expressive but not necessarily explicit, the face in these varied reflections on the close-up displays still another tension: Epstein analyzes the face as areas of muscle and cartilage; Bazin focuses on skin. They identify the face as flesh. Both Balázs and Bazin, however, also speak of the face as integrally connected with the soul. Elaborating on the tension between these ways of seeing the face, Anne Nesbet writes:

> The face is that part of the body we try most fervently to exempt from corporeality: to render, as far as is possible, *immaterial*. . . . The real depths of the human face revealed to us by violence or disease reduce the human being to flesh, which in the metaphysical sense amounts to being reduced to mere surface. And if the face is part of the body traditionally linked to individual identity and the "false depth" of spiritual *trompe l'oeil*, then the eyes may be said to be the "face" of the face. They are . . . that part [of the body] that must remain least tainted by signs of fleshliness . . . and, as Luis Buñuel would show the world in *Un Chien andalou* (1928), the place where a single pass of a razor blade, reasserting the eye's identity not just as machine or "spirit," but as meat, is able to inspire the most horror and disgust in the viewer.[4]

For Nesbet, the human eyes, which appear in extreme close-up at the end of Eisenstein's *Strike*, are "haunted" by the eye of the slaughtered bull, or "meat," that precedes their screen appearance: the man risks being taurified, or reduced to meat, unless he adopts the proper political consciousness. The workers struggle to realize themselves as political agents; the owners treat them as animals, reducing them to their biological being. The tension between understanding the face as meat and interpreting it as a manifestation of the spirit corresponds to murder's demonstration of the finite "thingness" of a human body and the way it can also provoke resistance to, or denial of, that demonstration.

Potentially implying both finitude and excess, the murder scene resonates with the power of the close-up to both cancel and reveal singularity. Gilles Deleuze recognizes this paradox of the close-up in the erotic, sometimes violent relationship between Bibi Andersson and Liv Ullman in Ingmar Bergman's *Persona* (1966): "The close-up has merely pushed the face to those regions where the principle of individuation ceases to hold sway. . . . The facial close-up is both the face and its effacement."[5] But long before Deleuze's declaration that the close-up can lead to loss of individuation, the recurring pairings of enlarged murder weapons and faces in early film theory and practice suggested the latent violence of the magnified image. Examples of revolvers and other weapons in close-up abound in theoretical and critical writing. We have already seen Pudovkin's hypothetical example in which he arranges and rearranges two facial expressions around a close-up of a gun. For Münsterberg, as we shall see, the close-up of a hand on a murder weapon instantiates the distinction between cinema and theater; for Kuleshov, it marks the difference between a well-crafted scene and an "old-fashioned" one that uses a single, wide framing and an excessively detailed set.[6] Eisenstein repeatedly describes shot breakdowns of murder scenes with their close-ups of knives and guns in his writing of the1920s.[7] Bazin writes that the "specific illusion" of the screen "is to make of a *revolver* or of a *face* the very center of the universe."[8] And as late as 1964 in "The Cinema: Language or Language System?" revisiting Kuleshov's claim that the individual shot functions as a word, Christian Metz turns to the example of a close-up of a revolver: "A close-up of a revolver does not mean 'revolver' (a purely virtual lexical unit), but at the very least, and without speaking of the connotations, it signifies 'Here is a revolver!'"[9] Through these two typical objects of the close-up—the face and the weapon—emerges a dialectic of the registration and destruction of the individual life.

**How Guns Get Attention in Film Theory**

Film theorists such as Hugo Münsterberg, Lev Kuleshov, Sergei Eisenstein, and Vsevolod Pudovkin declared editing to be a distinguishing feature of the cinema; and for them, a central device of this process was the cut to the close-up. The often-repeated example of the close-up of a hand on a revolver appears as early as Münsterberg's *The Photoplay: A Psychological Study* (1916). Münsterberg argues that the close-up mimics the act of directing attention. To make his point, he turns to a scene of murder, contrasting the drawing of the revolver on stage with the same scene as it would appear in film: "Suddenly we see not Booth himself as he seeks to assassinate the president, but only his hand holding the revolver and the play of his excited fingers filling the whole field of vision."[10]

For Münsterberg this "close-up" crucially distinguishes film art from theater. In theater, "the attended hand [clutching the revolver] must grow and the surrounding room must blur. But the stage cannot help us. Here begins the art of the photoplay. That one nervous hand which feverishly grasps the deadly weapon can suddenly for the space of a breath or two become enlarged and be alone visible on the screen, while everything else has really faded into darkness."[11] Münsterberg emphasizes the dual action of the close-up, which carves a small fragment from a larger scene: the close-up heightens perception of the particular through obscuring the whole. In this example, the pistol-wielding hand that will assassinate Lincoln fills the frame, crowding out other details ("Booth himself") and reducing the visible story world to a hand and a weapon. This simultaneous reduction and enlargement of the world, for Münsterberg, is the defining moment of the cinema: "Here begins the art of the photoplay." The camera takes aim, and in aiming, it both focuses and blinkers our vision.

For Münsterberg, the close-up harmonizes with the intention of the spectator, reinforcing natural cognitive functioning. In contrast, Kuleshov emphasizes the close-up's coercive aspect. Again focusing on hand and revolver, he describes a hypothetical suicide scene as it would be filmed in both pre-revolutionary Russia and in America. Mocking early Russian cinema's Balzacian attention to detail,[12] Kuleshov concludes that the spectator "sees a tiny actor among a large assortment of things, and while the actor is performing the juiciest psychological suffering, the viewer might be examining the leg of the writing table. . . . The spectator receives an extraordinarily distracted account of what is taking place on the screen." American cinema, according to Kuleshov, cuts out all such "inessential" detail: "Everything was shot in what is called close-up, that is, when it was necessary to show the face of a person suffering, they showed only his face. If he opened the drawer of a desk and took a pistol from it, they showed the desk drawer and the hand taking the pistol. When it came to pressing the trigger, they filmed the finger pressing on the trigger, because other objects and the surroundings in which the actor worked were irrelevant at that particular instant."[13] Kuleshov's montage channels the attention of the unruly spectator who would focus on the table leg and ignore the actor; the edit does not realize the natural movement of the spectator's consciousness—it determines it. The difference between Münsterberg and Kuleshov's theories of the close-up as it relates to spectator attention emerges out of the more general difference between the philosophical contexts in which they work. A neo-Kantian, Münsterberg insists on the apoliticism of art and emphasizes the disinterested quality of aesthetic experience, which entails a harmonious relationship between art and human cognition. In contrast, Kuleshov is working in a milieu that sees art—and especially the new art of film—as a political weapon.

For Eisenstein, as for Münsterberg, the example of the editing of "montage fragments"[14] in a murder scene helps to distinguish film from theater. In "The Montage of Film Attractions" (1924) he writes:

> Whereas in theatre an effect is achieved primarily through the physiological perception of an actually occurring fact (e.g. a murder), in cinema it is made up of the juxtaposition and accumulation, in the audience's psyche, of associations that the film's purpose requires, associations that are aroused by the

separate elements of the stated (in practical terms, in "montage fragments") fact, associations that produce, albeit tangentially, a similar (and often stronger) effect only when taken as a whole. Let us take that same murder as an example: a throat is gripped, eyes bulge, a knife is brandished, the victim closes his eyes, blood is spattered on a wall, the victim falls to the floor, a hand wipes off the knife—each fragment is chosen to "provoke" associations.[15]

For Eisenstein, the series of close-ups (gripped throat, bulging eyes, brandished knife, etc.) do not, like Münsterberg's example of Booth's gun, simply focus spectator attention. Each close-up provokes associations beyond itself, and together these associations produce a specifically cinematic effect. Cinema depends on these connections between the screened image and the spectator's memories and experience, thoughts and feelings. This degree of dependence distinguishes film from theater, which can physically confront the spectator with actual bodies whose sheer presence, particularly in scenes of violence, can produce in spectators an answering physiological response similar to what one might experience witnessing, from nearby, real violence. We might think, for instance, of the charged atmosphere at a boxing match, where it is not uncommon for spectators to cringe or to throw imaginary punches as they watch. (Eisenstein actually included a boxing match with the audience seated around the ring, in his theatrical production of Jack London's story "The Mexican.")[16] The different referential ground of film and theater (bodily trace versus bodily presence) necessitates, for Eisenstein, different methods for showing violence. Cinema, which relies on the trace of absent bodies, must make up for the charged atmosphere of a present violence by aggressing the viewer's psyche. Notably Eisenstein, in his early writings, deploys ferocious metaphors when describing the effect he wants his films to have on his audience:

a series of blows to the consciousness and emotions of the audience . . .

For us it is the next consecutive change of attraction—the next tactical manoeuvre in the attack on the audience under the slogan of October.

> It is not a "Cine-Eye" that we need but a "Cine-Fist."
> Soviet cinema must cut through to the skull! It is not "through the combined vision of millions of eyes that we shall fight the bourgeois world" (Vertov): we'd rapidly give them a million black eyes!
> We must cut with our cine-fist through to skulls, cut through to final victory and now, under the threat of an influx of "real life" and philistinism into the Revolution we must cut through as never before!
> Make way for the cine-fist![17]

These violent metaphors demonstrate that Eisenstein is aiming not primarily to produce signification, but to produce a physiological or emotional response that precedes intellectual grasp. This response can vary from spectator to spectator—or at least from social group to social group: "It is not in fact phenomena that are compared but chains of associations that are linked to a particular phenomenon in the mind of a particular audience. (It is quite clear that for a worker and a former cavalry officer the chain of associations set off by seeing a meeting broken up and the corresponding emotional effect in contrast to the material which frames this incident, will be somewhat different.)"[18] At this crucial moment in his early writing, where he addresses the power of the image to produce unpredictable and heterogeneous associations in various spectators, Eisenstein distances the phenomenon in an image from the associations it produces, arguing that primarily the associations, and not the phenomenon, produce the cinematic effect. In addition, not only the images, but their sequencing can trigger the associative or physiological response. Eisenstein expresses a desire, for instance, to complicate the chronological order of the murder scene: "(I do not, for example, use the chain: the gun is cocked—the shot fired—the bullet strikes—the victim falls: but the fall—the shot—the cocking—the raising of the wounded, etc.)"[19] This second murder scene in the same essay expresses Eisenstein's dissatisfaction with conventional cause-and-effect plot; he calls for an illogical, temporally out-of-order sequence that recalls Freud's description of the way shock, or traumatic experience, results in a confused ordering of events.

The sheer unpredictability and heterogeneity of the associations provoked by a phenomenon within the shot suggest the inherent ambiguity of anything that appears on a film screen. But Eisenstein did not want to leave this ambiguity intact: he aimed to condition audiences to make specific associations. Inspired by the work of Pavlov, he wanted to make the audience his "dogs." Correspondingly, he views the close-up as a device not for directing attention to an object per se as it does for Münsterberg and Kuleshov. Rather, it transforms the object into a signal so that ultimately, the object itself will be bypassed on the way to associations that lie beyond or outside of the image in the mind of the trained spectator.

Enacting, coercing, or redirecting spectator attention, the cut to the close-up of a weapon early on constitutes an emblematic formal paradigm of montage technique. Several well-known early films, most notably Griffith's, feature a cut-in to, if not a close-up of, a gun: Porter's *The Great Train Robbery*, Griffith's *The Fatal Hour*, *The Lonedale Operator*, *An Unseen Enemy*, *Thou Shalt Not Kill* (1913), *The Birth of a Nation*, and *Intolerance*. (In *The*

*Lonedale Operator*, the close-up reveals that what, relying on convention, we have assumed to be a revolver in the heroine's hand is really just a monkey wrench; the "punchline" relies on the power of the convention. In what may well be unintended irony, the robbers, despite the dimness of the room [the heroine has turned out the light to aid her ruse], are close enough to discern that she is not holding a gun, but they only "discover" this along with the audience when the cut-in appears. In the robbers' defense, it must be admitted that this cut-in coincides with the illumination of the room when the rescuer turns on the light. But it still seems as though the villains require, as much as the film audience, the *device* of the close-up, which *signifies* the act of attention, in order to pay attention to what the heroine is holding. Appearing to provide the same narrative knowledge to both character and spectator, this close-up almost collapses the divide between story and discourse.) This early conventionality of the murder weapon in close-up may help to explain film *theory's* turn to the close-up of the revolver as a paradigmatic example of a basic montage structure. The unanimity, however, with which so many early theorists reach for a gun (and, in some of Eisenstein's examples, a knife) to embark on a theoretical discussion of the cut to the close-up suggests that it is not the close-up per se that distinguishes the new art form, but, specifically, the monumental image of a deadly weapon.

### Case Study: Vsevolod Pudovkin's *The Heir of Genghis Khan* (aka *Storm over Asia*, 1928)

In practice, close-ups of revolvers do more than direct attention. Pudovkin's *The Heir of Genghis Khan* (1928) realizes cinematically—and almost point by point—the theoretical examples of the cut to the hand on the revolver used by Münsterberg and Kuleshov. Pudovkin, in addition to making such cuts, prescribes a technique for them: "If as detail concerned is selected a hand drawing a revolver from a pocket during the conversation, the scene must infallibly be shot as follows: the first long-shot ends with a movement of the hand of the actor reaching for his pocket; in the following close-up, showing the hand alone, the movement begun is completed and the hand gets out the revolver; then back to the long-shot, in which the hand with the revolver, continuing the movement from the pocket begun at the end of the close-up, aims the weapon at its adversary."[20] In Pudovkin's example, as in classical Hollywood editing, continuity of motion (the match on action) eases the discontinuity of the cut that so abruptly reduces the amount of space that appears in the frame. By his very concern with finding ways to soften the transition to the close-up, Pudovkin betrays the sense that without such techniques to assimilate it into the narrative, the close-up, coming in the midst of a scene, could confuse the audience.[21] The match on action provides a link to the vastness cast away in the close-up, insuring, through its continuous motion, that what has been cut from the frame has not inexplicably vanished, that it stays anchored to the magnified scrap of space that remains on the screen. Pudovkin's choice of words demonstrates the impact of eliminating space from the frame: it is the "hand" and not the person who has an adversary. The part displaces the person. Through the dynamic juxtapositions of its close-ups and long shots, *The Heir of Genghis Khan* realizes thematically (the cession of space to a colonizing force), and formally, a dialectic of loss and retrieval. The film develops and complicates the theories of Münsterberg and Kuleshov in regard to spectator attention and the cut to the close-up of the hand on the revolver.

*The Heir of Genghis Khan* tells the story of a young Mongolian, Bair (Valerii Inkizhinov), who gets into trouble with British colonialists for resisting fur buyer Henry Hughes (Viktor Tsopi) when Hughes attempts to take from him a valuable pelt for a ridiculously low price. The hero flees to the mountains where he joins a Bolshevik partisan force. Captured in a skirmish with the colonizing forces, he is condemned to execution, but at the very last minute (after he has already been shot and left for dead), the British commandant (A. Dedintsev) orders that he be kept alive. Discovering, in a sequence edited parallel to the execution scene, that a document borne by the hero declares him, falsely, a descendant of Genghis Khan, the commandant contrives to use the cachet of that name to set the hero up as a puppet ruler and thus disguise the exercise of British imperial power. In an extended surgery sequence, doctors transform the half-dead hero into a living mummy. After the bandages come off, the British further groom him to be a figurehead who will obscure their colonialist pilfering. While the British draw up a treaty in which Bair, who speaks no English, has no voice, he witnesses the murder of a fellow countryman by British soldiers. This killing transforms him into a warrior who ironically proves to be, for the British, too much like Genghis Khan. The film ends with a figurative storm—standing for the uprising led by the hero—which blows the colonizing army, like tumbleweed, off of the land.[22]

Pudovkin edits the execution sequence parallel to the scene in which the British commandant learns of Bair's "ancestry." Through this parallel structure, shots narrating the British construction of the identity, and use value, of the hero appear next to shots narrating their near annihilation of him. The execution scene features two cuts to a hand on a gun, one in medium shot, the other in close-up. Although the British bullet never literally kills the hero, Pudovkin's poetic montage implies that it does so metaphorically: the hero passes through a "living death" before his final revolt.

The occupying force attempts to control the story of the hero—first by condemning to death, shooting, and wounding him; then by forcing on him a puppetlike existence in which others control his identity and speak in his name. The film contrasts the story the imperialists tell about the hero with its own framing story. On a formal level it realizes the curtailment of the protagonist's freedom and, by extension, that of his land, through the interplay between the long shot and the close-up, particularly the close-up of the executioner's hand on the gun and, following that, the multiple close-ups of the resultant hole in the flesh which reduces the visible story world to a wound. Whereas the film *theory* of Münsterberg and Kuleshov implies that the cut to the close-up blocks attention to all else, Pudovkin's film *practice* suggests that in its dynamic relation to the long shot, the close-up can evoke the expanse of the diegetic world precisely through figuring its loss.

In *The Heir of Genghis Khan*, the close-up of the hand on the gun both denotes and enacts reduction: it signals the hero's impending demise and it reduces on-screen space. Through montage, the film deliberately contrasts this reduction of space, and the threatened reduction of Bair's lifetime, with their extension. The first time the film cuts in (not to a close-up, but to a medium shot) of the executioner (Boris Barnet) pulling a gun from his pocket, we see that he draws his weapon only to remove a pouch of tobacco; he fills his pipe and offers the condemned man a cigarette (figs. 3–5). The tobacco tease serves as an apparent reprieve, suggesting an illusory extension of the hero's time by exposing and then repacking the very weapon that threatens him; the revolver momentarily looms and recedes in the puff of a smoke.

Parallel editing severs the second close-up of the gun from the shot of its firing. After the close-up of the drawn weapon we return to the commandant in his office, reconsidering the hero's fate. This structure delays, for the spectator, the execution, again appearing to lengthen the hero's narrative time, which the gun threatens. The film cuts to this second medium close-up of hand and gun from a high-angle extreme long shot of executioner and condemned man standing on a sandy cliff overlooking a river far below (figs. 6–7). The cut reduces the vast space framed in the extreme long shot to the span of a hand and a gun. The film uses such sharply contrasting camera distances to associate the gun and, metonymically, the violence of the colonialist force, with the curtailment of open space (figs. 8–9). Several shots show Bair falling through space (over and down the cliff). The first part of the film accumulates extreme long shots as if to heighten the

contrast with the markedly tighter framing that commences after Bair is shot. After the British retrieve him from where he lies, nearly dead, at the base of the cliff, the film rigorously avoids extreme long shots and exterior settings. There are two exceptions: a flashback to a religious ceremony exploited by the commandant as a tool to help the British to control the populace, and the return, by car, of Henry Hughes, intercut with shots of the "wild steppes," which serve to mock the false romantic mystique in which this rapacious fur buyer wraps himself. Neither of these exceptions presents the "authentic" Asia with which Bair is associated. Indeed, they are presented, through montage, as colonial perceptions of Asia. Bair's wounding casts "his" Asia out of the frame until the closing sequence, when he escapes and leads an uprising. From its initial framings of open spaces, the film turns to an extended surgery sequence, dominated by the close-up, and a recovery sequence set in interiors. The film renders these interiors claustrophobic by frequently placing the camera so that the corner of the room occupies the center background: at least two walls appear in most shots that are not close-ups. In addition, in the mise-en-scène, multiple frames—doorways, the backs of chairs—echo the enclosure of the film frame.

The film intercuts shots of the hero's surgery with scenes of the commandant discussing the transformation of his wounded captive into a puppet ruler. Through parallel editing, the stitching of the wounds comes to suggest, metaphorically, the imperialist fabrication that brings the dead body of the colonial subject—a puppet—to life to perform the requisite show. The British draw back from murdering the hero's body, but the images suggest that the colonel and his men effectively kill him in order to reconstruct him as their own. From a medium close-up of the surgeon's hands and forearms as he scrubs (fig. 10), the film fades and cuts to a close-up of the colonel's hand reaching for the document that declares the hero a descendant of Genghis Khan and thus a viable figurehead (fig. 11). The surgeon's hands, preparing to stitch Bair, are matched with the hand holding the object the British will use to define the hero, bypassing his agency and tailoring him to suit their interests.

The surgery sequence features close-ups of both the entrance and exit wounds in the hero's shoulder (figs. 12–13). Two medium shots in succession show the turning of the unconscious hero onto his side, drawing attention to the exit wound, which, after a close-up of hands washing themselves in a basin and a close-up of surgical tools, appears a third time just before the surgeons lower the hero onto his back.[23] After the British commandant announces that Bair "is a tremendously lucky find" because the name of Ghengis Khan still inspires the Mongols, the entrance and exit wounds in

6

7

8

9

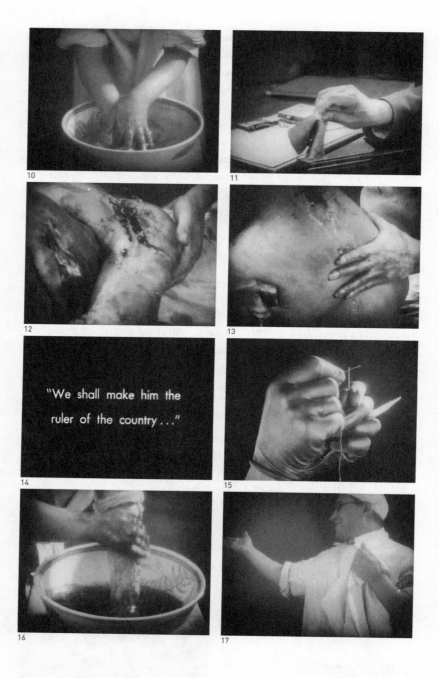

"We shall make him the
ruler of the country..."

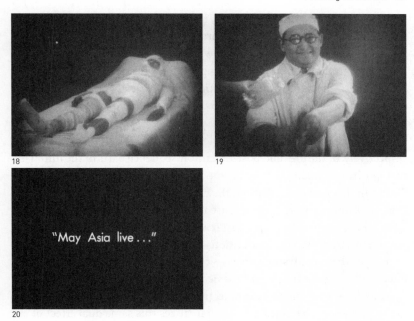

18

19

"May Asia live..."

20

the shoulder reappear in a series of rapidly edited shots. The screen then goes completely black for a barely perceptible instant and two rapid medium close-ups show the wound again as the hero is rolled onto his back.

Emphasized by the close-up, the overlapping edit and the fade, the lingering image of the almost screen-sized wound exceeds informational narrative significance. The bullet hole extends beyond the hero's flesh, stopping not only Bair, but the momentum of the film itself. From the title "We shall make him the ruler of the country," the film cuts to a close-up of surgically gloved hands threading a needle and holding a pair of scissors (figs. 14–15). The British cut and sew the hero's body in their attempt to kill and remake the man. A close-up of the surgeon scrubbing his forearms emphasizes the bloodiness of this makeover (fig. 16). The surgery sequence ends with the following images: a medium shot of the Doctor Frankenstein–like surgeon proudly gesturing at his work (fig. 17); a long shot of the hero, bandaged like a mummy, lying motionless on the gurney (fig. 18); a medium shot of the smiling surgeon (fig. 19); and, finally, the title "May Asia live" (fig. 20). The British recreate a mummified hero who stands for his colonized people; his wound is "Asia's" wound. (If cinema is "change mummified,"[24] this sequence reminds us that mummification entails destruction as well as preservation.)

Münsterberg and Kuleshov argue, respectively, that the cut to the close-up—a paradigmatic montage structure—imitates or compels human attention, making the object fill the frame while rendering everything else invisible. This argument implies that cutting an object from the frame effectively removes it from the spectator's attention, but *The Heir of Genghis Khan* complicates this assumption. Twice Pudovkin cuts to a hand and gun, the "textbook case" of Münsterberg, Kuleshov, Eisenstein, and Pudovkin himself. But Pudovkin deliberately contrasts long shot and close-up as dominants, respectively, of the pre- and post-execution-sequence parts of the film. This juxtaposition transforms the close-up into a negating device that displaces "Asia." In this mode of negation, the close-up does not solely direct attention to its object; it produces a sense that something has been lost. Eisenstein's theory of the close-up—that it achieves its effect not by directing attention but by provoking associations that are as important as, if not more important than, the framed object—comes much closer to describing the effect of Pudovkin's framing in *The Heir of Genghis Khan*.

The film frame can exclude objects and, at the same time, imply them in their absence. The murder scene dramatizes this same dual effect of exclusion and presence-in-absence: it typically cuts the victim from the discourse (and film frame) as well as the story world; but in his absence, the victim can come to seem less like a formal construction and more like an absented human being. Bair's "execution" is not a murder scene. We can call it an attempted "murder" rather than an attempted "execution" since the film makes clear the sheer arbitrariness and injustice of the British rule that mandates the hero's death. But Bair, though gravely wounded, does not die. Nevertheless, *The Heir of Genghis Khan*, though an idiosyncratic example, illustrates how murder, or attempted murder, can evoke a referentiality that exceeds the victim's visible manifestation in the frame, or the filmic and narrative cues used to construct him. The power of the murder scene comes from the way the victim and his world, eradicated from story and discourse, paradoxically develop a more insistent presence precisely as they vanish. Pudovkin's film relies on the way that the curtailment of space can make us miss the vastness that occupied, and was occupied by, the colonial subject before his brutal repression. Instead of cutting the victim from the frame, the film cuts his world, evoking it all the more powerfully in its absence.

\*

The metaphors of film theorists and critics reveals the resonance between violence and framing. Eisenstein compares the frame to a guillotine: "If . . . in

a well-defined characterization the figure's headgear [*golovnoi ubor*] happens
to be irrelevant, then it can simply be guillotined by the edge of the frame
[*Krai kadra dlia nego okazhetsia gil'otinoi*]."[25] The metaphor turns back on the
sentence, suggesting the cut that would transform "headgear" into "head."
Jacques Aumont maintains that Griffith's framings suggest the threat of
death: "Leaving the scene signifies at least potentially the death of the character. What closes the scene, via the frame, is in a sense this threat of death,
always implicitly and metaphorically proffered from beyond the frame. The
revolver of *An Unseen Enemy* can, God knows, be read in more ways than one,
but . . . can we not still see in it the literal agent of this threat, openly articulated in this way?"[26] And Bazin writes of the camera in Jean Renoir's *The
Rules of the Game* (1939), "This invisible witness is inevitably made to wear
blinders; its ideal ubiquity is restrained by framing, just as tyranny is often
restrained by assassination."[27] For Eisenstein and Aumont, framing implies
violence done to persons and things cut from the frame. Bazin, on the other
hand, suggests the camera's potentially violent tyranny over that which is
caught in the frame. The difference between Bazin's understanding of the
site of the frame's "violence" and that of Eisenstein and Aumont crystallizes
the problematic of murder and representation. The murder scene can function, like the film frame in the metaphors of Eisenstein and Aumont, as the
apotheosis of representation's own necessary abridgements: a violent cut
that eradicates a character from story and discourse. But murder scenes can
also indicate, through the negation of the victim, the reductiveness of the
camera's "tyrannous" gaze, which constitutes, like any subjective gaze, an
ineluctably partial vision.

## Murder and Perspectival Scale: Eisenstein's "Hidden Montage"

The dialectical subtlety of Pudovkin's film practice requires revision of sim-
pler, theoretical characterizations of the close-up as a tool for directing attention. The dynamic interplay between presence and absence that Pudovkin
achieves through framing echoes the thematics of the hero's brush with violent death: the loss of Bair is the loss of Asia; the loss of a man is the loss
of a world. The tension between inclusion and exclusion that structures the
close-up (and framing more broadly) also fundamentally structures the murder scene. But cinema does not arrive at close-ups solely through cutting,
and close-ups need not completely crowd everything else out of the frame.
Eisenstein's conceptualization and practice of montage within the shot allowed the juxtaposition of close-up and extreme long shot within a single
frame. In the unfinished fragments of *¡Que viva México!* in his seminar on

Dostoevsky's *Crime and Punishment* at VGIK, and in the final *Ivan* films, the drama of killing is also, blatantly, a drama of perspectival scale.

In his notes from the famous VGIK seminar devoted to solving the problem of filming, with a single shot setup, the scene of Raskolnikov's murder of the pawnbroker in *Crime and Punishment*, Vladimir Nizhny transcribes Eisenstein's reading of the scene: "The murder of the moneylender—this is the outer subject of the scene. The real, inner, subject—is the 'fall' and dethroning of Raskolnikov. 'Freedom and power—power above all. Power over all the trembling vermin, and over all the ant-hills'—that is his motto. It is precisely in this passage we are treating that he himself becomes one of the 'trembling vermin.'"[28] Eisenstein's interpretation of the scene suggests a drama of scale taking place in the mind of the murderer—a drama of scale associated, ultimately, with the popular concept of a superman, modeled after Napoleon, who exercises a bird's-eye view of history and possesses the will and strength to speed it, through violence, along its progressive trajectory. Against such a superman, Raskolnikov sets out to measure his own stature. The standard of measure is the ability to disregard "ordinary" human life as far below one's purview; the test is murder. Eisenstein— and Dostoevsky—give relatively little attention to the pawnbroker; for Eisenstein, her death is less significant than Raskolnikov's "dethroning." But his "mise-en-shot," through "hidden montage,"[29] ironizes any hierarchy between victim and murderer by taking the elevations and "anthills" in Raskolnikov's mind and subjecting them to a critical perspective. According to Nizhny, Eisenstein tells his students: "It is important for us that the old woman, as also the actor who plays Raskolnikov, shall be able to be shown in contrasts—close-ups and long-shots—within one and the same editing-piece without changing the camera set-up. This is the basis of our selection of the given camera-angle and given optical conditions."[30] One of these "optical conditions" is the use of a 28 mm, or wide-angle, lens, which exaggerates the difference in scale between objects in the foreground and background. The shot setup that Eisenstein's seminar finally resolves upon juxtaposes the pawnbroker in close-up with Raskolnikov in medium long shot; for much of the scene, the victim, not the murderer, dominates the screen space. Eisenstein makes a mountain out of an "anthill." Indeed, because the pawnbroker so powerfully dominates the frame, the seminar students must formulate a plan to pry the viewer's attention away from her. But Eisenstein critiques a student suggestion that, to draw attention away from the pawnbroker, her head must move entirely out of the frame; he insists that the drama of her removal from screen space be reserved for the instant when Raskolnikov hits her with his ax. When the human image takes up a large proportion of screen space, its sudden removal makes its absence felt more forcefully. Whereas *The Heir of Genghis Khan's* tight framing communicates the virtual annihilation of Bair through an absence *of* space, here, an absence *in* space, the gap left behind when the pawnbroker falls, conveys the shock of murder.

In his afterward to Nizhny's transcription of Eisenstein's seminars, Jay Leyda suggests that consideration of the seminar on *Crime and Punishment* can provide insight into the analysis of Eisenstein's final films, *Ivan the Terrible, Parts I and II*.[31] I would further suggest that Eisenstein's great unfinished film, *¡Que viva México!* on which he worked in 1931 and 1932, *foreshadows* the pedagogy we see in the 1933 seminar. This film juxtaposes a series of vignettes set along a time line of Mexico's past; it begins with the pre-Columbian and ends with an epilogue set in the twentieth century. The vignette "Mexico Fermenting" culminates in a shootout and an execution, both of which are visually realized through a drama of perspectival scale.[32] "Mexico Fermenting" refers to the making of pulque through fermenting the juice of the cactus maguey, and to the "fermenting" of social tensions that serve as prelude to revolution. Through framing and frequent use of a wide-angle lens, Eisenstein and cinematographer Eduard Tisse accentuate the maguey, which is the classic Hegelian "object to be worked on" that forms the pivot of the seesawing dynamic between master and slave. From this giant cactus the hacienda workers, including Sebastian, suck the juice. Several shots feature the towering maguey, which often frames the workers with its arms (figs. 21–22). Visually dominating the film's landscapes, the cactus figuratively dominates the characters' lives: workers depend upon it for their livelihood; the hacienda owner derives his wealth and power from its juice, but the alcohol also makes him brutish and weak, characteristics which in turn spark discontent among the workers. Before marrying, the hero of the vignette, Sebastian, introduced as a "peon" who works harvesting the maguey juice, must present his fiancée, Maria, to the owner of the estate where he works. In this feudal, colonized Mexico, the hacienda owner still exercises his droit du seigneur and allows a drunken guest to rape Maria with impunity. Sebastian, who immediately seeks revenge, is flung down the hacienda stairs and Maria imprisoned. In an effort to free Maria, Sebastian, his brother, and friends steal the hacienda owner's guns and set fire to his stable to create a distraction. Unable to release Maria and forced to flee from a shoot-out, they regroup in the maguey fields where they engage in a gunfight that results in the death of, among others, one of Sebastian's friends and the hacienda owner's daughter, Sara, who joins the posse that hunts them down. In this battle between the peons and the posse, the giant cactus

is a large cactus named maguey.

21                                                  22

shelters Sebastian and his friends. Located at the center of the relationship between worker and owner, the maguey dominates the scene of their violent clash. (Beyond the maguey as "object to be worked on," the film loosely suggests the trajectory of Hegel's Absolute Spirit, complete with skulls at the end, imposing a European pattern of national *Bildung* on Mexican history). In punishment for the death of his daughter, the owner has Sebastian and his remaining two friends executed, while Sebastian's brother, who escaped the posse, watches from a distance, protected by the branches of a maguey. Throughout the vignette, a crowd of other peons, in serapes and sombreros, witnesses the injustice. In Alexandrov's construction of the unfinished film, the vignette serves as a prelude to the final section, "Soldadera," about Mexico's revolutionary women in their struggle against dictator Porfirio Díaz.

Foreshadowing the seminar on the murder of the pawnbroker in *Crime and Punishment*, dramatic relations of scale figure prominently in multiple shots of the violent confrontations. Location within the frame and the occupation of screen space signify the shifting dynamics of domination and submission among the characters. Deep-focus shots show foregrounded figures observing, threatening, and/or obscuring the background figures who appear in extreme long shot. Returning to the historical context in which Eisenstein developed his montage aesthetic, we might draw a parallel with striking and revolution, which also entail dramas of scale, as it takes many proletarians to confront towering, and obscuring, figures of authority. The opening of *October* makes this parallel explicit, when comparatively tiny people topple a giant statue of Tsar Alexander III, casting ropes around his head and boots to dismember him, tearing off booted legs three or four times the size of a human being.[33] What initially appears as a close-up—the head of the statue—turns out to be a long shot once people enter the frame from behind and below, crawling upon it to cast their ropes over its face (figs. 23–24). In this trick of cinematic perspective, a long shot might be taken for a close-up, the dimensions of a giant bronze head potentially mistaken for human size. The film narrative simultaneously reveals and subverts the head's immensity as several people, relatively small within the frame, dismantle the huge statue. The trick of cinematic perspective simultaneously signifies a trick of political perspective, where, on the one hand, the tsar, as figurehead, is made of falsely human dimensions (a paternal figure), while on the other, the tsar as human is made to appear falsely imposing, massive, invulnerable. The image realizes perfectly the sudden historical diminution of the once-imposing figure of the ruler.

Similarly, in *¡Que viva México!* fiesta celebrants don giant conquistador masks, the immensity of which contrasts, even "collides," with the relatively small human bodies beneath them (fig. 25). Through these particular instances of what might be called a "conflict between volumes,"[34] Eisenstein finds one of his many formal methods for realizing on-screen a drama of scale expressive of class conflict. The interplay of relations of scale works simultaneously to express and subvert the staged grandeur of the powerful, shifting the emphasis, instead, to the importance of the collective. This drama of scale takes place in both temporal and spatial dimensions. Eisenstein frames the significance of the individual deaths occurring in the collective struggle in relation to a larger historical trajectory that delimits the negativity of

23

24

25

26          27

violent death. In *¡Que viva México!* the shifting of perspective from the individual to the collective, and from the human life span to centuries, transforms the negative of the individual tragedy into the positive of historical
progress.

In a particularly violent episode of this unfinished film, the story of
Sebastian and Maria in "Mexico Fermenting," Eisenstein and Tisse employ
sharp contrasts of scale to signal the vulnerability of the couple when they
first approach the hacienda owner with their plans to be married. They appear in a high-angle extreme long shot at the foot of the hacienda stairs
while in the foreground, filling a quarter of the frame, a man with a rifle,
in long shot, his back to the camera, descends, simultaneously framing and
dominating the small figures of the vignette's heroes (fig. 26); the man with
the rifle allows only Maria to pass. Maria again appears tiny juxtaposed with
the enormous image of the hacienda owner: he appears in close-up in the
foreground, drinking, his huge head dwarfing Maria, who appears in long
shot with her armed escort (fig. 27). Other leering faces—the hacienda owner's intoxicated guests—also appear in close-up.

Perspectival relations within the frame are the formal dominant in the
violent scenes of "Mexico Fermenting." Low-angle shots suggesting domination and high-angle shots suggesting subordination, which Pudovkin famously deploys so rigorously in *The Mother*, here have less potency in comparison to extreme contrasts in the sheer size of various human figures
within the frame. Often, camera angle and contrasts in size work in tandem to signify power relations. Generally, in the footage included in Alexandrov's reconstruction, low-angle shots frame the owner's lackeys; high-
angle shots frame Sebastian and Maria. When Sebastian and Maria approach
the foot of the hacienda stairs, for instance, they appear not only in extreme
long shot, but also in a position well below that of the camera. Similarly,
when the hacienda owner's lackeys throw Sebastian down the stairs, three

sombreros fill the foreground of the high-angle shot and the barrel of a gun juts out from beneath the middle sombrero while Sebastian, again in extreme long shot at the foot of the stairs, is helped off by two friends (fig. 28). But in the low-angle reverse shot, the camera angle shifts from complementing to counterpointing contrasts in the size of the human figures, and the crude power structure, realized graphically by the exaggeration of scale and angle in the previous shot, undergoes a spatial and dramatic reversal. Here three sombreros, Sebastian's fellow peons, appear in close-up at the foot of the stairs while the four armed lackeys at the top appear in an extreme long shot (fig. 29). Despite the low angle from which they are filmed, the men at the top of the stairs are dominated by the much larger sombreros that fill the bottom of the frame; indeed, as if perceiving a threat from the seeming giants at the foot of the stairs, they turn and slink off. Here the contrast between close-up and long shot within the frame overrides the more conventional deployment of camera angle to connote power relations.[35] The relative immensity of the three sombreros that seemingly repulse the owner's lackeys suggests a latent, powerful outrage and revolt against feudal injustice, but the low angle from which the camera shoots the lackeys still serves as a trace of the old power relations that remain in place. The counterpoint between camera angle and scale in this shot constitutes a formal tension which reflects the diegetic, and dialectic, tension between owners and workers. Formal "conflict" realizes, graphically, the class conflict that ultimately leads to murder.

After Sebastian's failed attempt to free Maria and the subsequent shootout in the desert, Sara and one of Sebastian's friends are left dead, Sebastian's brother has been wounded, and Sebastian and his two surviving comrades have been captured. Eisenstein, in Alexandrov's reconstruction, reprises the drama of scale that took place on the hacienda stairs, now substituting the dead Sara for the lackeys. A high-angle shot shows Sara laid on her funeral

28

29

bier in medium close-up at the top of the stairs while in the courtyard below, Sebastian's two friends appear in extreme long shot, guarded by a man
with a rifle (fig. 30). Sara's giant dead face dominates both the frame and the
tiny figures of the prisoners, just as, in the story, her death at their hands
spells their doom. Here the large-scale image of the face of the owner's dead
daughter literally and figuratively overwhelms the peons who will be murdered in revenge. In the execution scene, Eisenstein must reverse the dwarfing of these peons while simultaneously locating them as elements in the
much larger trajectory of Mexican history; he achieves this again by juxtaposing the large-scale and the small-scale. The owner's men bury Sebastian
and his two friends up to their necks in sand and set horses to trample their
heads. The camera remains near the level of the heads. The victims graphically assume greater size relative to their killers.

In its establishing shots, the execution scene, through use of the wide-
angle lens, appears minute on the vast Mexican plain. In long shot, slightly
to the right of center frame, stand, prior to their burial, Sebastian and his
two friends, in a triangular formation similar to images, common in Western painting, of Christ and the thieves on Calgary (fig. 31). Eisenstein uses
the Christological motifs that enter the film with the conquistadors to signal an important reversal: the Spanish colonizers in this film do not bring
Christ to the new world; they treat the people of the new world as a Christ-
like sacrificial victim.[36] Correspondingly, when one of Sebastian's friends
is killed in the shoot-out, he falls back, arms outstretched on his rifle,
the brim of his hat forming a halo in an upside-down crucifixion tableau
(fig. 32). Sebastian and his two friends, buried and trampled, are like the
proverbial seeds that must fall to the earth and die in order to bring forth
fruit—fruit here being the revolution. Marie Seton writes of Eisenstein's
plans for the scene:

30

31                                    32

The festival at Tetlapayac, which, in 1931, culminated with one of the Indian peons of the hacienda "going out of himself" into a state of penitential ecstasy, was to be intercut with the enacted death of the peon, Sebastian, and his two friends. Eisenstein's plan for the montage of simultaneous action was intended to reveal on the screen the concept that the symbolic ceremony was made manifest in the "reality" of the hunting down and trampling to death of the peons. Their bodies and their blood were Christ's body and blood as symbolized in the Corpus Christi ceremony. Intersecting this mystical concept was irony: the formal, or Church side of the "mystery," running parallel with the living mystery.[37]

Christological motifs imply an interplay between the grand and the humble that thematically corresponds to the film's formal juxtapositions of the large-scale and the small-scale: the first shall be last; the last, first. The Christological motifs work together with the contrasting close-ups and long shots within individual frames to suggest a rubric for determining the importance of the individual life. In the "Maguey" vignette, featuring Sebastian and Maria, the individual life's value, aesthetic and social, is rendered not as a static identity, but as a shifting play of differences realized primarily through montage juxtapositions of scale. Human figures, with their specific emplacement in the progressive historical trajectory overarching the film, reflect, through the amount of screen space they occupy in comparison to one another and the landscape, the vicissitudes of class struggle as it determines individual social position. When the dramatization of this struggle reaches its culminating scenes of killing—the gunfight in the desert and Sebastian's execution along with two of his companions—the montage juxtapositions of scale help to suppress individual loss in order to emphasize the scenes' progressive historical significance.

Other graphic details of the execution scene also work to frame, within a larger spatial and temporal context, the significance of the violence.

33                                              34

Eisenstein organizes the mise-en-scène in a triangular composition: the bodies of the three prisoners, and then just their heads, when they are buried up to the neck, form triangles which the snow-capped, triangular peaks in the background echo (fig. 33). These shots rhyme with a shot of three cacti before a mountain peak (fig. 34), suggesting a convergence between Sebastian and his friends and the plant they harvest: just as the cactus's fermented juice will eventually weaken the ruling class, so, too, will the blood of their martyrdom. In the shootout scene, we see the cactus "bleed" as bullets hit its branches. Sebastian's wounded younger brother drinks this "blood" as he sits under a maguey, witnessing the execution. This Christological draught suggests that the martyr Sebastian's legacy lives on in his brother.

In "The Cinema: Language or Language System," Christian Metz, perhaps in response to Eisenstein's own stated fascination with the "primal form" of the triangle,[38] interprets ¡Que viva México!'s triangular compositions as a connotative meaning that overlays the denotative: "The denotative relationship yields a signifier (three faces) and a signified (they have suffered, they are dead). This is the 'subject,' the 'story.' . . . Over this is superimposed the connotative relationship, which is the beginning of art: The nobility of the landscape as it is structured by the triangle of the faces (form of the image) expresses what the author, by means of his style, wanted to 'say': The greatness of the Mexican people, his certainty of their eventual victory, a kind of passion in that man from the North for all that sunny splendor."[39] In "The Semiology of the Cinema" Peter Wollen criticizes Metz's interpretation of Eisenstein's triangular composition, writing, "There is no objective code; therefore there can only be subjective impressions. . . . There is no way of telling what an image connotes in the sense in which Metz uses the word."[40]

But Eisenstein's intrashot juxtapositions of the large-scale and the small-scale, a formal dominant of "Mexico Fermenting," support Metz's interpretation of the image's connotative meaning even as they meet Wollen's demand for an objective code: it is precisely in terms of the juxtapositions of perspectival scale that the scene's triangular graphics lend a mitigating contextualization to its violence. The triangular peaks in extreme long shot graphically rhyme with the triangular spacing of the three large, foregrounded, brutalized heads of Sebastian and his friends. The depth of focus juxtaposes the echoing immensity of the Mexican landscape with the minuteness of the execution scene, which is, nevertheless, so momentous within this vignette (and so large within this particular shot). The signal events within the lives of these three characters—their revolt against injustice and their execution—appear at once grand and minute. Analogously, the film frames the individual lifetime in relation to historic time. The filmic discourse emphasizes shifts in temporality, setting defining moments of individual lives within the frame of Mexican history from the pre-Columbian to the present. In the Mexico traversed by Eisenstein, Alexandrov, and Tisse, vast temporal shifts coincided with simple movement through space. In his introduction to the reconstructed version of the film, Alexandrov recollects: "We were struck by a surprising feature of this enchanting country: one hundred kilometers meant the separation of one epoch from another— the ancient pre-Columbian era from the time of the Spanish conquest, the Mexico of feudal rule from modern Mexico."[41] The effect of these juxtapositions of temporalities widely differing in scale is reminiscent of the one Flaubert achieves when he places Frederic Moreau outside Paris, meditating on ancient rocks during the uprising of 1848 in *L'Education sentimentale*. But whereas the tenor of Flaubert's juxtaposition is decidedly apolitical, that of Eisenstein's is pointedly Hegelian and Marxist: the individual drama appears minute compared to the vast historical process of which it is, essentially, a part.

Spatial and temporal immensity work together to frame the scene of Sebastian's execution within a larger and grander historical narrative, which places its violence "in perspective." Such perspective, however, depends upon the deindividualization of the characters. The juxtapositions of scale, the Christological motifs, and the thematics of martyrdom and historical progress produce an explicit ideological meaning that diminishes the particularity of the individual. The very lucidity of the film's message ensures that the spectator does not get too distracted by the tragedy of Sebastian, his friends, his fiancée, Maria, and his brother Felicio. Montage here functions to contain the potentially bottomless negativity of murder in order to construct a narrative of historical necessity. Characters are defined primarily by where they fall (and die) along a historical trajectory. In individual scenes the aesthetic and social weight of particular characters is frequently rendered through shooting in depth with a wide-angle lens, which results in vast differences in the size of human figures within the same frame, allowing an ever-shifting domination of screen space by one set of characters, then another. In the film as a whole, however, the representation of human beings—and their violent ends—is stabilized and fixed to fit the film's collective, progressive, historical narrative. The montage of Mexican history "sums up" the meaning of the victims' lives outside themselves. A forceful revolutionary message is purchased from the murder scene's dialectic between affective reference and narrowed signification.

In the Eisenstein of ¡Que viva México! the *Crime and Punishment* seminar, and *Ivan the Terrible*, the morally legible tableaux of nineteenth-century melodrama attains new force: the wide-angle lens Eisenstein uses to achieve his "hidden montage" emphasizes the murder scene's shifting terrain of "anthills" and mountains that dupes Raskolnikov. This montage within tableaux veers sharply from the rapid, rhythmic editing, more commonly associated with the term "montage," which characterizes most contemporary film violence. Unlike rapidly passing, fragmentary images that call our very ability to perceive into question, the sharp contrasts within Eisenstein's tableaux not only assist our perception; they also demand our judgment. Thus, Joan Neuberger can point to a telling visual rhyme that extends across twenty-odd years and captures the striking difference between Eisenstein's early films, with their decentered, collective protagonists caught up in revolutionary violence, and his last two films, with a murdering autocrat as their hero: in *The Battleship Potemkin*, a long, snaking line of mourners pays its respects to the murdered Vakulinchuk, "killed for a bowl of soup." No one foregrounded individual looms over this line of people (the dead man lies in a tent on the ground). A similar line extends again, in extreme long shot, across the screen in *Ivan the Terrible, Part I*, but now that crowd, a long line of Muscovites who journey to the tsar to beseech his return, are dwarfed by their bloody ruler who, in close-up above them, indeed possesses a bird's eye view of his people, like ants, below.[42]

In these examples culled from Eisenstein's films and seminar, we see how simple, even crude, details such as the size of a human figure in the frame, or brute presence in, or absence from, the frame allow for a complex realization of the simultaneous devaluation and evaluation of individuals in violent scenes. ¡Que viva México! uses wide framing and deep focus to produce shots not dissimilar to those made nearly a decade later by Gregg Toland in collaboration with Orson Welles. Bazin famously champions such shots for allowing the spectator greater freedom to make sense out of them. But as we can see here, despite Bazin's claim that deep focus fosters a liberating ambiguity, Eisenstein's "montage within the frame" hastens signification, swiftly transforming Sebastian into a martyr. Indeed, under the Soviet montage aesthetic, in all its permutations, martyrdom is the ontological status for all photographed reality, as referential plenitude is systematically transformed into meaning.

## **2** Acting in Silents: Murder, Montage, and the Film Actor

**The Body in Pieces**

A wealth of early writing on the cinema discusses how the breakdown of the body through framing and acting technique produces cinematic signification. This breakdown legendarily appeared violent to some viewers. Balázs, for instance, tells the anecdote of a well-educated Siberian girl who had never seen a motion picture until she visited Moscow:

> The Siberian cousin came home pale and grim. "Well, how did you like the film?" the cousins asked her. She could scarcely be induced to answer, so overwhelmed was she by the sights she had seen. At last she said: "Oh, it was horrible, horrible! I can't understand why they allow such dreadful things to be shown here in Moscow. . . . Human beings were torn to pieces and the heads thrown one way and the bodies the other and the hands somewhere else again."
>
> We know that when Griffith first showed a big close-up in a Hollywood cinema and a huge "severed" head smiled at the public for the first time, there was a panic in the cinema. We ourselves no longer know by what intricate evolution of our consciousness we have learnt our visual association of ideas. What we have learnt is to integrate single disjointed pictures into a coherent scene, without even becoming conscious of the complicated psychological process involved.[1]

Balázs's Siberian girl furnishes the classic alienating perspective; like Lev Tolstoy's adolescent Natasha Bolkonsky at the opera, she "makes strange" the habituated spectator's automatized apprehension of the spectacle—specifically the spectacle of the human body in fragments. "Making strange" (*ostranenie*), as conceived by Victor Shklovsky in *Theory of Prose*, is a function of art. Ironically, here it is Balázs's anecdote of the naive spectator found in his *criticism* that makes the art strange, bringing out its seeming violence. Confronted with pictured body parts, the Siberian cousin persists in imagining intact human beings implied by (and suffering through) their disintegration into screen images. An uninitiated film spectator, she does not automatically grasp the meaning produced through shot juxtapositions; her lack of cinematic experience reveals the violence within the process of abstracted signification.

The montage aesthetic, with its revolutionary concept of the film actor's body as an assembly of signifying parts, certainly does not fit Metz's comparison of cinema to a mirror, where the spectator projects onto the screen—and has reflected back at him—his ego ideal, his better coordinated and more powerful self. The segmentation of the body in the process of cinematic signification complicates secondary identification—Metz's term for spectator identification with characters—and even thwarts primary identification with the camera, since the shots often flaunt the daring with which the frame lops off a remarkable portion of a person or scene. For its accession to the symbolic and its Brechtian refusal to remain in the "illusionistic" imaginary, European and American film theorists have historically commended Soviet montage, but they have given less attention to the anxiety that tight framing and disjunctive editing produced in spectators, theorists, and critics of early narrative cinema.

Why is bodily integrity so closely associated with a subjective, empathic sense of self that the mere image of the body's fragmentation produces the unease evident in early film theory and criticism? Jay Bernstein provides an explanation for why, even on the plane of aesthetic representation, bodily integrity matters, and imaged bodily fragmentation can disturb. Elaborating on work by Axel Honneth and Jürgen Habermas, he writes:

> Our organic makeup is completed, to the extent that it ever is, through socialization. Physical maturation, gaining control of our bodies in relation to the physical and social environment, occurs in tandem with socialization; hence through socialization we become the bodies we already necessarily are. Human beings not only are their bodies but, as self-conscious beings, have or possess their bodies; subjectivity is rooted in our simultaneously being the bodies we have or possess, where our having a body is 'the result of the capacity of assuming an objectivating attitude toward the prior fact of being a body.'[2] . . . So, on the one hand, the human body, as body, is from the outset socially constituted in its being and integrity; while, on the other hand, the symbolically constituted subject that has this body is itself written in the language of the body: the social subject is, minimally, a body in symbolic form. . . . Personal identity, as Habermas and Honneth use that phrase, is

the social inscription of bodily integrity, whilst intact bodily integrity is achieved by becoming a self-conscious agent.[3]

The profound connection between the recognition of the body as a discrete whole and the constitution of the subject helps to explain why a poetics of bodily fragmentation can have a disturbing power. If the sense of one's body is inextricable from one's sense of self, then, even in aesthetic representation, it is difficult to dissociate the image of the body from the self it implies. Pictured bodily fragmentation, as in Picasso's *Guernica*, can powerfully convey violence. Of this painting, Eisenstein tells the following anecdote:

> The Germans, looking at *Guernica*, asked the author:
> "Did you do this?"
> And proudly the painter answered:
> "No—*you!*"[4]

Picasso's retort points up the mimetic force of the painting: the imaged violence of "human beings . . . torn to pieces . . . the heads thrown one way and the bodies the other and the hands somewhere else again" shows, for Picasso, the Germans' violence. If the fragmentation of *Guernica* memorably evokes the violence unleashed against 1,600 Spanish citizens, it does so partly through refraining from any pretension fully to represent them. Similarly in Soviet montage, scenes of great violence can prompt a reflexive recognition of representation's limits. To awaken us from the convention of seeing wholeness in long shots and long takes, montage, like cubism, can insist, through the juxtaposition of several angles, the partiality of all of them. But by making parts of the body function as signs, montage can also obscure the body, and person, as such.

*

For many critics, cinema, and the montage aesthetic in particular, undercut notions of the body as integral and distinct from things. Maurice Merleau-Ponty writes: "If my arm is resting on the table I should never think of saying that it is beside the ash-tray in the way in which the ash-tray is beside the telephone. The outline of my body is a frontier which ordinary spatial relations do not cross. This is because its parts are interrelated in a peculiar way: they are not spread out side by side, but enveloped in each other."[5] Montage of the silent era systematically destroyed this integrity: film viewers and filmmakers perceived the body part as one object among others. The body appeared to lose some of its life while objects gained it. Writing in 1929, Boris Bilinsky remarks, "On the screen, no longer dead nature, it is as much the revolver as the hand and the cravat of the murderer that commits the crime."[6] Similarly, Jean Epstein, in "On Certain Characteristics of *Photo-génie*," writes, "And a close-up of a revolver is no longer a revolver, it is the revolver-character, in other words the impulse toward or remorse for crime, failure, suicide."[7] Pudovkin echoes Bilinsky and Epstein, "A revolver is a silent threat."[8] For Bilinsky and Pudovkin, the gun acquires living status even as it threatens to take away life. Of animate and inanimate alike, Pudovkin claims "that every object, taken from a given viewpoint and shown on the screen to spectators, is a dead object, even though it has moved before the camera."[9] In a montage of close-ups, the fragment of the body—the hand of the murderer, the face of the victim—appears on an equal footing with the inanimate object, the gun. In Balázs's terms, "in the silent film both man and object were equally pictures, photographs, their homogeneous material was projected on to the same screen, in the same way as in a painting, where they are equally patches of color and equally parts of the same composition. . . . Men and things were thus brought onto the same plane."[10] According to Yuri Tsivian, Eisenstein goes even further, arguing, in Tsivian's words, that "props work better than characters,"[11] and causing Victor Shklovsky to call *The Battleship Potemkin* "a Baroque film about the uprising of dishes."[12] Marie-Claire Ropars corroborates Tsivian's claim that Eisenstein found props more congenial than characters. Her groundbreaking reading of *October*'s opening statue sequence traces the gradual exclusion of living people from the frame and their replacement by things. Even as the sequence lends an uncanny animation to the statue by showing it rock on its pedestal, it deanimates living people, transforming the persons responsible for the stone tsar's demise into objects. Ropars analyzes the steps of this transformation: the people of the crowd surrounding the statue "mak[e] way for . . . figurative representatives (. . . scythes and rifles)."[13] Tools and weapons displace agents, discursive abstraction displaces a story world locatable in continuous space and time. (In key shots, the crowd's tools appear in "abstract space," which Ropars defines as space lacking people or other objects that lend a degree of temporal and spatial particularity to the symbolic objects shown.[14] Ropars demonstrates that "the space of the crowd becomes that of its objects" and concludes that "by repeating and reconstructing the shift from man to his objects, the discourse of montage finishes by inscribing these objects in a space whose abstraction rejoins the abstraction of the very first shots of the statue."[15])

\*

The perception of an uncanny equivalence between on-screen people and things does not end with the silent era. Not merely a critical perception, but a deliberate mode of stylization, the refusal, facilitated by the screen, to

35

privilege people over things stamps some classical French cinema through the work of émigré German expressionist cinematographers such as Eugen Shüfften, Keith Courant, and Rudolph Maté. Colin Crisp describes Shüfften's work as tending "to produce a representation of human beings as themselves no more than objects, driven by inexorable forces."[16] For Bazin, writing twenty years after *October*, cinema's inherent ability to realize a non-anthropocentric seeing constitutes one of its important potentials: "Man himself is just one fact among others, to whom no pride of place should be given *a priori*."[17] The opening shot of Michelangelo Antonioni's *The Eclipse* (1962) wonderfully recaptures the surprise of seeing the body part as equivalent to a discrete thing: it frames an arm resting on books on a table in a way that recalls, and counters, Merleau-Ponty's passage about the unique integrity of the body (fig. 35). Detached from any body, the shirt-sleeved arm appears almost unrecognizable as an arm until it moves and the camera pans right to show also the head and shoulder of the man (Francisco Rabal) to whom it belongs. The movement of the arm, and the film frame, which surprises by revealing the arm as attached and recognizable, enhances the uncanny severing of the arm that begins the shot. Antonioni's moving frame asks us to see anew the equivalence between persons and things revealed by the camera. In contrast, the montage in films such as *October* and Kuleshov's *By the Law* (1926) does not ask us to give particular attention to the equality between animate and inanimate, but to read it. In the most radical manifestations of Soviet avant-garde theories of the actor, such equality was a given: man was a thing, a machine.

## Man, Montage, and the Machine Aesthetic

In an important article, "Kuleshov's Experiments and the New Anthropology of the Actor," Mikhail Yampolsky traces the path by which the breakdown analysis of the actor's body in avant-garde theater of the second and third decades of the twentieth century provided inspiration for montage theory and practice. Yampolsky focuses on the influence of former director of the Imperial Theaters, Prince Sergei Volkonsky. Volkonsky popularized the ideas of the musicians François Delsarte and Émile Jaques-Dalcroze. Delsarte's contribution to acting theory consisted in developing a lexicon of gestures that corresponded to psychological states. Dalcroze invented eurhythmics, a system for experiencing and expressing elements of musical form through bodily movement.[18] Yampolsky demonstrates that while theorists such as Volkonsky and Vsevolod Meyerhold saw the "mechanics" of acting as a tool to communicate human thought and feeling regardless of whether the actor's subjective state matched that of the character he or she played, the cult of the machine led some theorists to push the comparison between the actor's body and a machine to its limits, reducing both actor and character.[19]

Adopting a Delsartian approach, Kuleshov saw fit to train the film actor, or *naturshchik*, to master a vocabulary of legible muscular movements. He inserts a chart showing the basis of such movements in *Art of the Cinema*, listing the various parts of the actor's body and their possible types of motion (fig. 36).[20] Like Kuleshov, Eisenstein rejects the actor's inner experience as productive of characterization: "The effect of the affective movement is achieved by the artificial mechanical setting in motion of the body as a whole and must in no way result from the emotional state of the performer."[21]

We can see resonances between Kuleshov's and Eisenstein's conception of film acting and other silent cinema. James Agee's famous description of slapstick, for instance, lists the exaggerated movements of articulated body parts. According to Agee, the slapstick actor "gave us a figure of speech, or rather of vision, for loss of consciousness. . . . The least he might do was to straighten up stiff as a plank and fall over backward with such skill that his whole length seemed to slap the floor at the same instant. Or he might make a cadenza—look vague, smile like an angel, roll up his eyes, lace his fingers, thrust his hands palms downward as far as they would go, hunch his shoulders, rise on tiptoes, prance ecstatically in narrowing circles until, with tallow knees, he sank down the vortex of his dizziness to the floor, and there signified nirvana by kicking up his heels twice, like a swimming frog."[22] This partition of the actor's body into eyes, fingers, palms, shoulders, toes, knees, and heels signifies a loss of consciousness; the disjoint of the body implies the breakdown of the mind. But like a well-crafted shot sequence, Agee's sentence unites these articulated gestures with an exuberant fluidity. This tension between articulation and flow is the very essence

основным осям: по вертикальной—вправо и влево, по горизонтальной — вверх и вниз и по попереч-ной — в стороны. Пример: движение головы: 1) по первой оси — жест, соответствующий отрицанию, 2) по второй оси — жест, соответствующий утвер-ждению, 3) по третьей оси — жест, соответствую-щий сомнению и порицанию (ну!.. ну!..).

Все остальные движения по этому сочленению будут комбинациями из трех основных осей. Дру-гих движений быть не может.

Составим таблицу осевых движений для главных частей человеческого тела.

| Сочленения. | Ось № 1. | Ось № 2. | Ось № 3. |
|---|---|---|---|
| 1. Глаз . . . | Вправо, влево. | Вверх, вниз. | Нет, есть ком-бинация № 1 и № 2, круговое движение. |
| 2. Нижняя че-люсть . . . | Вправо, влево. | Открывание и закрывание рта. | Нет. |
| 3. Шея . . . | Отрицание. | Утверждение. | Сомнение. |
| 4. Ключица . | Движение впе-ред и назад. | Нет. | Вверх, вниз. |
| 5. Плечо (рука от плеча до кисти) . | Скручивание всей руки. | Вперед (перед собой), Назад (от себя). | В бок, в сто-рону. |
| 6. Локоть (ру-ка от локтя до кисти) . | Скручивание (мнимаете ло-мок). | К себе. | В бок, в сто-рону. |

| Сочленения. | Ось № 1. | Ось № 2. | Ось № 3. |
|---|---|---|---|
| 7. Кисть . . . | Нет. | К себе. | В бок. |
| 8. Таляш . . . | Поворот кор-пуса. | Наклон корпу-са вперед, на-зад. | Наклон корпуса в бок. |
| 9. Бедро . . . | Повороты всей ноги (скручи-вание). | Жест вперед, назад. | Жест в бок. |
| 10. Колено . . | Скручивание. | Вперед, назад. | Нет. |
| 11. Ступня . . | Развернутая, свернутая. | Выступпый и собранный под'ем. | Ступня на ребро, внутрь, наружу. |

Натурщик должен строить свою работу по основ-ным осям или по их комбинациям, а располагать их—в пространстве по метрической пространствен-ной кубатуре. Возьмем для примера движение на сочленение талии по оси № 2.

В таблице мы видим, что это будут наклоны всего корпуса от талии вперед. Какие же положе-ния корпуса, двигающегося по второй оси, будут самыми четкими? Те, которые займут простые, ясно читаемые положения по стенке плоскости, идущей по направлению движения, т.-е. ясно прямое поло-жение человека, ясен наклон корпуса под углом в 45 градусов, ясен наклон корпуса, образующий прямой угол корпуса и ног по отношению к полу. Промежуточные положения будут трудно воспри-

36. Lev Kuleshov's chart from *Iskusstvo kino*, 1929. (Courtesy Department of Special Collections, Stanford University Libraries.)

of cinema, from the fixity of the individual frames underlying its illusory movement to the "intervals" and "sutures" of its discourse. In a different way, such tension also underlies slapstick performance, which commonly takes the most athletic bodies and puts them at risk of serious injury, juxtaposing lively movement with the threat of paralyzing rupture.

Vigorous American stunts inspired the practitioners and theorists of Soviet montage. American critics characterized Douglas Fairbanks (who visited the Soviet Union in the twenties) as more athlete than actor;[23] Kuleshov declared that cinema needed athletes as actors.[24] His privileging of the mechanics of bodily motion over psychological expression follows his larger aim of turning the body into a plastic signifier through framing, editing, and an acting practice that conceives the film actor's body as an assembly of parts, each possessing a repertoire of legible gestures.

An anxiety about the mechanization of the living body in and by the film medium still informs, over three decades later, "The Cinema: Language or Language System" (1964), Christian Metz's critique of structural linguistics, which he associates with montage:

The *machine* has ground up human language and dispenses it in clean slices, *to which no flesh clings.* . . . It is a great feast for the syntagmatic mentality. . . .

The natural object . . . is analyzed, literally and figuratively, and its constituent parts are isolated; this is the moment of *breakdown analysis*, as in the cinema. Then the parts are distributed into isofunctional categories: straight tracks to one side, curved to the other. This is the paradigmatic aspect—and it is only preparatory, as was the filming of individual scenes for Eisenstein. The grand moment . . . is the syntagmatic moment. One reassembles a duplicate of the original object, a duplicate which is perfectly grasped by the mind, since it is a pure product of the mind. It is the intelligibility of the object that is itself made into an object. . . . The goal of the reconstruction . . . is not to reproduce reality: the reconstruction is not a reproduction . . . but a simulation. . . . As the structural *skeleton* of the object made into a second object, it remains a kind of *prosthesis*.[25]

Metz's figurative language—"flesh," "skeleton," "prosthesis"—certainly suggests that life itself is the central "casualty" of the montage aesthetic's structural approach. His association of montage (and découpage) with a death-dispensing machine that produces segmented, legible code out of continuous living bodies depends on a unique aspect of twentieth-century cinema: while other media such as painting and prose may make use of the montage aesthetic, only twentieth-century cinema combines the indexical nature of photography and the illusion of recorded movement and time. Like the hero of Pudovkin's *The Heir of Genghis Khan*, whom surgery transforms into a mummified figurehead, the actor's body, in twentieth-century cinema, leaves a photographic trace that undergoes cutting in its transformation into cinematic signifier.

### Case Study: Lev Kuleshov's *By the Law* (1926)

On a formal level, *By the Law* abstracts the body parts of its actors, along with props, into a system of cinematically signifying relations just as it carefully marks out its characters' positions in a system of social relations (national identity, religion, economic structure, law). But in and around its scenes of murder and execution, the film also suggests that the people implied by its characterizations exceed these discursive and social systems of signification. Here, as in other murder scenes, montage, a crucial modernist aesthetic, paradoxically achieves reference, right at the point where it would seem to evade it.

The film concerns the deadly violence that erupts among five gold prospectors in the Yukon. Michael Dennin (Vladimir Fogel), poorly treated by his fellow gold miners, grows enraged and kills two, Harkey (Piotr Galadzhev) and Dutchy (Porfiry Podobed). The pair who survive his rampage and restrain him, Hans Nelson (Sergei Komarov) and his wife, Edith (Aleksandra Khokhlova), cannot take him back to civilization for a proper trial, so they try him themselves, condemn him to death, and hang him. Apparently, the noose breaks, and Dennin returns, takes his bags of gold, and leaves.

In describing his work on *By the Law*, Kuleshov indicates his dissatisfaction with acting and characterization in the avant-garde cinema of his time:

> Since, for a number of natural reasons, *we did not pay sufficient attention to the individual*, our acting standards have deteriorated. Even in Eisenstein's film, the human dimension, i.e., the work of the models, is mediocre.
>
> That is why we put so much care and effort into the filming of Jack London's story "The Unexpected," called By the Law in Victor Shklovsky's script.[26]

What does it mean for Kuleshov to "pay sufficient attention to the individual" in "the filming of" *By the Law*? His emphasis on the individual runs counter to Eisenstein's insistence, in his early writings, on filming the crowd as hero; it also suggests a tension between the individual and cinematic signification as practiced and theorized by Kuleshov up to this point.

Kuleshov attempts to give "sufficient attention to the individual" by minimizing stylistic devices that call attention to themselves: "Naturally, all the complex formal methods—intricate shots, unusual camera angles, American montage—had to be abandoned in this film. *Simplicity* ordained by human *reality* and drawn from observation is the only solution for this kind of modern picture and the key method in *By the Law*. . . . Neither the number of characters nor the scenery nor montage should be felt by the viewer."[27] What should be felt by the viewer is the film's dark vision of people acting unselfconsciously as objects of social forces that render them cruel:

> This scenario . . . is about a person, a bourgeois, whose suffering seems genuine enough and who tries to be heroic, but for all the wrong reasons, acting upon the maxims of middle-class morality. People's inhumanity covered up by sincere religious feeling, and the ensuing brutality, is the subject of our new film.
>
> . . . All that should get across is the truth about these people in Alaska, people who suffer and end up doing horrific things because of the obtuse and inhuman notions imposed on them by God and Her Majesty's Justice.[28]

Kuleshov emphasizes the way individual consciousness is always already determined by a grid of social signification imposed by systems such as class, nationality, religion, and law. His very objective requires that his characters' gestures and actions be marked, unnaturally, with the signs of the dehumanizing social systems that determine them. This marking finds its formal expression in montage. Kuleshov certainly does not retreat from his concept of the "model actor": props, bodily gestures, and close-ups of various body parts equally function as signs of character traits and emotions. But Kuleshov's vision of a benighted inhumanity can only emerge in and through its contrast with an imagined human potential to exceed or resist social determinations. Correspondingly, *By the Law* must move beyond the formal and thematic abstraction of the individual in social and discursive systems. This transcendence occurs most starkly around the scenes of murder and attempted execution. Returning the poetics of montage, as formal strategy, to its thematic grounding in the destruction of persons "outside the law," the film challenges, in its praxis, some of the director's most extreme theoretical statements.

Kuleshov concentrates on the inner life of his characters, but it is an inner life largely determined by class and national identity: "We may be accused of being morbid or misanthropic, but please do not forget that our film is about the modern English middle class—surely the most inhuman of all."[29] Pairing images of the individual characters with titles that emphasize their nationality, the opening credits imply the importance of national identity: "The Irishman, Michael Dennin," "Leader of the enterprise, the Swede Hans Nelson," "Nelson's wife, the Englishwoman Edith." The film plays on national stereotypes, in particular placing Dennin's Irishness in opposition to Edith's English middle-class status.

Like many silent films, *By the Law* repeatedly uses inanimate objects to signify interior states, creating an illusion of continuity between images of things and the thoughts, emotions, or traits of characters. Shots of Dennin frequently either contain objects or are juxtaposed with shots of objects that smoke and steam: in the credit sequence, an extreme close-up features his hands fumbling with a bag of tobacco and a long shot shows him by the camp kettle, which again appears in the murder scene, boiling over, as a visual metaphor for anger and turmoil. Dennin's angry suspicion that his fellow prospectors are trying to double-cross him dawns as he stands over a tub of steaming camp laundry. Hans first appears shaving (figs. 37–38). Consistent from start to finish, he follows the forms of civilization in a wilderness where they have lost all relevance: at the film's end he and his wife Edith follow the empty rituals of British law courts to put on the charade of a fair trial that results in Dennin's death sentence. Edith's introductory shot reveals not her face, but a prayer book and comb, resting on her knees in an

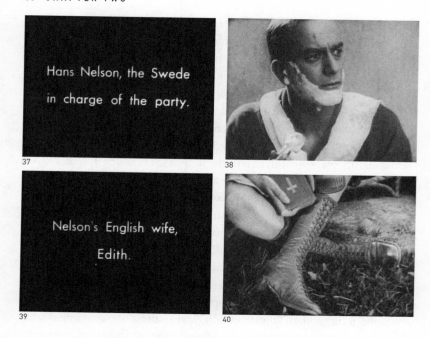

Hans Nelson, the Swede in charge of the party.

37

38

Nelson's English wife, Edith.

39

40

ironic juxtaposition of religiosity and vanity (figs. 39–40). Whereas for Bilinsky, cinematic animism endows props with souls, for Kuleshov, in *By the Law*, props stand for soul or, more precisely, for soullessness.

Parts of the actors' bodies share the frame with props, both functioning equally as signs. After the credit sequence, Dennin prepares breakfast for his fellow gold miners. Before he can join them in eating, Hans announces that they are breaking camp and sends Dennin off to collect the mining equipment. Dennin exits, and a high-angle shot shows hands stealing food off his plate (fig. 41). The plate of unfinished food, subject to grasping hands, graphically matches the bowl in which the miners swirl the waters of the Yukon in the hopes of sifting gold from its sediments. When Dennin brings this bowl containing the gold he has just discovered back to the breakfast table, an overhead close-up shows two pairs of hands on either side of the bowl, then the shadow of a hand—Edith's—over it (fig. 42). Bowl and plate stand metonymically for the objects of desire, gold and food; the grasping hands signify—and, indeed, externalize—the inner greed. Similarly, as Edith, seeking pieces of ore, swirls water in the bowl, a close-up of the eddying water shows the reflection of her face growing bigger and smaller, bigger and smaller, its image distorted by the material pursuit of gold (fig. 43). A perfect example of how reflection can be intertwined with distortion, this grotesque mirrored image suggests the spiritual deformation of greed, even

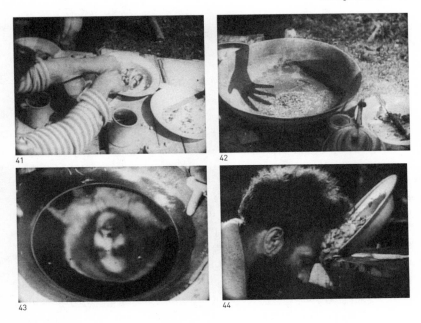

41

42

43

44

as it operates within the larger "distortion" of montage, which transforms implied human beings and the indexical trace of the living body into an explicit, narrowed set of characteristics. In the film's murder scene, which takes place at dinner, Dennin's empty plate signifies his absence and alienation from the group and rhymes visually with both the overhead shot of his plate in the early breakfast scene (where Harkey and Dutchy steal his food) and with the bowl of gold nuggets. Dennin bursts in and fires a rifle at Harkey and Dutchy. Harkey falls face down into his plate of food, literally drowning in the fruit of his greed (fig. 44). In the ensuing struggle, spilled coffee bubbles like blood on the dusty floor.

Smoke and steam, the divided "pie," the spilled drink standing in for blood—it is precisely a montage of prefabricated symbols that Jean Mitry critiques in *Aesthetics and Psychology of the Cinema*, arguing that new symbolic meanings ought to accrue to objects uniquely in the course of the film rather than being associated with those objects beforehand. Mitry would, however, approve of the fact that all these objects are part of the story world. As an example of the ideal production of symbolic meaning, Mitry turns to the ship doctor's pince-nez, caught in the hawser of the battleship *Potemkin* (fig. 45). Mitry shows how the film forges synecdochic (and syllogistic) connections between the pince-nez and the doctor, and between the doctor and the bourgeoisie, so that when the doctor's role ends with a shot of his

45

pince-nez dangling above the waters, the spectator understands that not only doctor and pince-nez have been tossed overboard, but the bourgeoisie as an entire class.[30] But the doctor's pince-nez, like Kuleshov's smoke and steam, the divided circle of the plate, and the spilled drink, also suggest a ready-made, metaphoric meaning: they suggest a point of view, however flawed, that has disappeared. The point of view implies a consciousness, even if "false." The doctor's glasses signify both a seeing and a myopia, just as they allow us both to see and not to see the doctor. Narrowing the potential meaning of the doctor's point of view, which is signaled, finally, by the pince-nez, Eisenstein's montage associates it strictly with the universal traits of its class—a deceitful and repressive brutality, whose toss overboard can only be welcomed. *The Battleship Potemkin*, like most Soviet avant-garde films about striking, revolt, and revolution, never shows the death of the oppressor at the hands of the oppressed. If it is a structural cliché in many violent Hollywood films to whet audience appetite for violence, and satisfy it, by showing the hero suffering all kinds of indignity before finally giving in to the need for revenge, it is likewise a cliché in many Soviet agitprop films to show all the indignities suffered by proletarians, the colonized, and so on—and to leave this outrageous injustice unanswered, at least within the central action of the film. In the story world, *Potemkin*'s doctor appears to suffer no more than a dunking, but discursively, his symbolic value overwhelms his implied humanity, stripping his narrative significance to his role as a to-be-dispensed-with member of a dying class. Finally indicated by a prop rather than by his own bodily form, the doctor, in "his" final scene, cedes his place to his pince-nez, which signifies his shortsightedness and marks the self-conscious curtailment of the discourse as it stops well short of representing a person.

The power of montage to signify character traits through highly legible shot sequences of body parts and objects can facilitate social critique. Such legibility led early Soviet filmmakers to see the cinema as a powerful revolutionary tool for addressing illiterate and non-Russian-speaking populations. But the drive toward greater legibility as cinema's primary goal, from Kuleshov's shot-sign to Hollywood's classical découpage, eventually led to a backlash, perhaps most famously articulated by Bazin. Bazin privileges instances of cinematic ambiguity, lauding such forms as the sequence shot and depth of field precisely for their partial *illegibility*, or the way they mimic the opacity of the world by, according to Bazin, refusing to reveal their meanings at a glance. The tension between legibility and illegibility, which structures both film and theory, and their interrelation, is crucial to characterization in murder narratives. Murder scenes excite because a human subject, even when only implied, and distorted, by the forms and media of narrative representation, is compelling, and not quite graspable. This special quality of subjectivity, cast into relief by the threat of annihilation, gives the murder scene its unique potential to forge a link between form and reference. Like the swirling waters that simultaneously mirror and alter Edith's face, montage reflects and distorts both the actor and the person implied through performance and characterization. But if *By the Law*, through montage, constructs its characters as a series of highly legible traits that are linked with larger social systems such as nationality, class, and religion, the film also subverts its own system of signification by suggesting a partially illegible subjectivity that is in excess of the grid of social significations imposed on it. As in many films that involve murder, the actual story inscribes these problems of reflection and distortion, apprehension and cancellation that already inhere in the filmic discourse.

For example, once Harkey and Dutchy have been buried, a flood ensues, preventing Hans and Edith from bringing Dennin before the law. Long shots of the cabin surrounded by floodwaters alternate with long shots of the flooded interior, where the inhabitants perch on pieces of furniture, separated from one another by gulfs of water (figs. 46–47). These shots of the interior, with Dennin, Hans, and Edith literally rendered islands, rhyme with the exterior shots that show the cabin to be an island. Visually rendering his "models" islands, Kuleshov makes them simultaneously both vehicle and tenor of the metaphor. An archipelago, literally and figuratively, they appear absurd in their flooded abode. "No man is an island," John Donne wrote, but a sea of dehumanizing *social* institutions and hierarchies separates this threesome. Divided by national prejudices, an unyielding and misguided religiosity, and a rigid, misunderstood, and misplaced code of law, Hans and Edith ultimately resolve their differences with Dennin through attempted hanging. The tragedy lies in the way that despite their

46                                          47

hesitations, the characters finally give in to the inhumanity of their social conditioning.

The dialogue suggests a voiding of human agency. Edith asks Dennin to explain his murderous rampage, and he replies, "Dumalos'" (It occurred to me.) His use of the impersonal construction implies that he was acted upon rather than decisively acting. The trial scene suggests that Hans and Edith, too, lack agency, as they automatically impose an irrelevant legal framework on their unique situation. The discourse undermines the legitimacy of their wilderness court. Three ironic titles, intercut one at a time with the same two-shot of Edith and Hans, inform us that they are "lawyers," "judge," and "jury." To lend the process an aura of authority, the "court" hangs a portrait of the queen on the cabin wall. But the queen's "justice" is inappropriate to the situation. In ironizing the authority of the portrait, the film self-reflexively alludes to the Kuleshov effect, where the context of an image determines its otherwise arbitrary significance. In the context of the wilderness court, as Hans and Edith construe it, the portrait of the queen is a sign of legal authority. Alter the context, and the meaning of the queen's portrait changes: beyond the story world, on the level of the film's discourse, the trial, far from deriving authority from the image of the queen's face, makes the face appear absurdly arbitrary as a symbol.

We have seen how, in their theoretical writing, both Kuleshov and Pudovkin concentrate on the power of montage to determine the significance attributed to the human face. In *By the Law*, the lineaments of Harkey's dead face, when covered by a makeshift burial shroud, complicate this argument. Until this point, the film uses the human face interchangeably with other body parts and inanimate props to signify character traits and motivations. The shrouded face reserves its unknowability (fig. 48). A secondary personage, Harkey has never been characterized by more than lineaments—those of a cheerfully selfish gold seeker. Ironically, the shots that imply his hu-

48

manity most fully are those where the legibility of his face and character are most obscured. The shroud, in obscuring the face, renders it suddenly unreadable, placing it beyond the parameters of the cinematic and social significations that heretofore have structured the character discursively and led to his demise.

The hiding of, specifically, the victim's face at the site of his or her annihilation again occurs in the hanging scene when a close-up of Dennin dissolves into a graphic match of the noose. The empty oval of the rope displaces the oval of the face, realizing the impending absence of that face from the story world. The close-up of the noose then dissolves into an extreme close-up of Dennin's eyes, then to a close-up of Dennin (figs. 49–52). The sequence (a close-up of Dennin's face, its displacement by the noose, an extreme close-up of Dennin's eyes) forms a chiasm.

The actual hanging appears metonymically in a high-angle two-shot that features not the heads, but the feet of Hans and Edith struggling for traction against the loose earth in order to push the support out from under Dennin so that he hangs (fig. 53). We then see the feet of the hanged man (fig. 54).[31] At the opposite end of the body from the head, or seat of consciousness, the feet, as a metonymic sign of the hanging, again call attention to the mechanized, rote nature of this killing. But the feet and legs also lead upward toward the characters' eyes, excluded from the frame. What is seen is continuous with what is not seen. The part calls to mind the whole while at the same time drawing attention to the absence of the whole from the screen. Similarly, the lynching of the Landrys (William Stark and Mattie Edwards) in Oscar Micheaux's *Within Our Gates* (1920) shows only the ropes (fig. 55). In telling contrast, when, in the same film, Efrem (E. G. Tatum) *imagines* his lynching, we see his face in close-up, noose around the neck, tongue out, eyes wide—an image that makes a mockery of him (fig. 56). But when he is

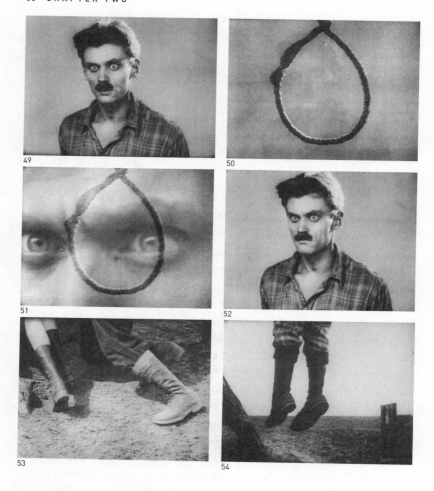

49

50

51

52

53

54

actually murdered, the film uses the mob to obscure his body (fig. 57). In *The Virginian* (Cecil B. DeMille, 1914), when the title character hangs his friend, the camera points at the ground to capture the gently swinging shadow of the hanged man. Stephen Prince identifies this tactic of "spatial displacement" as one of the visual codes that "provide the foundation for the poetics of violence in classical Hollywood cinema."[32] He writes:

> The code marks . . . violence as being beyond the bounds of what is acceptable. Doing so, it necessarily reminds viewers of the act of suppression that has called it into existence.
>
> I'm not suggesting by this that the viewer's awareness of spatial displacement works in any kind of intellectualized Brechtian sense. The code doesn't

55

56

57

break the illusion of the film narrative or even remind viewers that they are watching a movie. Conventional film theory has grossly overstated and mystified the mental conditions that accompany film viewing. Movie viewers in the 1940's, seeing spatial displacement, simply understood what it was and what it signified: that there was violence in the story they were not permitted to see.[33]

Spatial displacement is at least as old as *Oedipus Rex*, when Jocasta kills herself offstage. With the hanging of Dennin, we see it in a 1926 Soviet film, as well as in the classical Hollywood cinema Prince describes. Prince rightly suggests that this very conventionality makes the elision of the sight of violence appear so ordinary that viewers may scarcely notice it. But the very fact that spatial displacement in violent scenes is so conventional begs the question of why discourse, confronted with the problem of showing murder, gave rise—and continues to turn—to this convention. In *By the Law*, the shroud over Harkey's face, the dissolve from a close-up of Dennin to the empty noose, the silhouettes of Dennin and his executioners (backlit against the horizon as they approach the hanging tree), and the shots of feet metonymically call attention to what is obscured in the frame or excluded by it. By drawing attention to what is missing or absent from the frame, these positive representations also draw attention to their own inadequacy; they exhibit a reflexive awareness of their own mimetic limits. The character

traits signified through Kuleshov's montage lose importance as these images of murder and execution gesture toward a humanity that exceeds discursive (and, in Dennin's case, legal) representation.

Kuleshov's early writing on film valorizes simple, rapid, and powerful
"shot-signs": "You will not come away with the same impression from [a]
landscape as you would, for instance, from the view of a bullet fired from
a pistol. The shot should act as a sign, as a letter of the alphabet, so that
you can instantly read it, and so that for the viewer what is expressed in the
given shot will be utterly clear. If the viewer begins to get confused, then the
shot does not fulfill its function—the function of a sign or letter. I repeat,
each separate shot must act as each letter in a word. . . . The shot is a complete conception, and it must be read instantly."[34] Kuleshov's film practice,
however, in *By the Law*, partially confounds this ideal of bulletlike signification; here the obscuring of the human figure (and its downright removal
from screen space) around scenes of murder, and attempted murder, subverts, through visual negation, the film's positive, abstractive representations of its characters.

### *The End of St. Petersburg* (1927): Bringing Life to a Statue

Kuleshov's *By the Law* features a montage style that animates the inanimate,
editing props in such a way that they come to stand for soul. Pudovkin's *The
End of St. Petersburg*, his second full-length feature, reverses this process, giving an inanimate appearance to the animate. Commissioned ten years after
the October Revolution, along with Eisenstein's *October* and Esfir Shub's *Fall
of the Romanov Dynasty*, *The End of St. Petersburg* commemorates the Revolution from prewar strike agitation through World War I, culminating in the
1917 attack on the Winter Palace. The film bears some similarity to *October*
in its treatment of statues.[35] Rhetorically, through explicit montage juxtapositions, *The End of St. Petersburg* explodes one set of monuments—those of
tsarist St. Petersburg—replacing them with the revolutionary proletariat,
which it literally transforms into living statues.[36] Like the monuments they
replace, these celluloid "statues" imply, despite their newness, the death of
the object they commemorate, even as they preserve it in visual representation. Pudovkin directorially imposes stillness on the body of the performer
in an extreme transformation of "actor" into "model" or even mannequin.
This formal stillness, this monumental weight imposed on the human figure, constitutes a representational force that suppresses anything which
does not correspond to its static symbolism.[37]

58                    59

Pudovkin's montage initially associates the reactionary forces with the monuments of the imperial city. A shot of Lebedev, a factory owner (V. Obolenskii), appears juxtaposed with a shot of the Bronze Horseman (figs. 58–59). A living—but immobile—policeman on horseback rhymes with a shot of another equestrian statue (figs. 60–61). These types—the factory owner, the policeman—parody the statues they resemble, and this parody rhetorically, and iconically, clears the ground for the erection of new monuments. Similarly, the Peasant Lad (Ivan Chuvelev), whose experiences make up the film's central narrative (he leaves the poverty-stricken countryside to search for factory work, naively betrays his urban acquaintances who are organizing a strike, learns from his mistake, and atones for his error), initially appears juxtaposed with the backside of an equestrian statue (figs. 62–63). This juxtaposition mocks his haplessness, or even associates him with a horse's ass until he develops a revolutionary consciousness. Upon his arrival in the city, he and the elderly woman who accompanies him appear in a high-angle extreme long shot (made with a wide-angle lens) so far below an equestrian statue that they seem antlike in comparison to the gigantic hindquarters (fig. 64). But by the end of the film, he has become one of the many heroes of the Revolution, and low-angle shots show him exercising greater dominance over the screen space.

The new workers' monuments, like the old equestrian statues, also feature immobile human figures. We see, for instance, low-angle, large-scale images of striking workers standing perfectly still. Their frozenness literalizes their strike action, or inaction. And toward the end of the film we see shots of victorious revolutionaries in resolute poses.[38] The wind may ruffle their hair or garments, but it does not disturb their theatrical motionlessness. In addition to these workers and revolutionaries, there is a third group of unmoving human figures in tableaulike shots: corpses on the

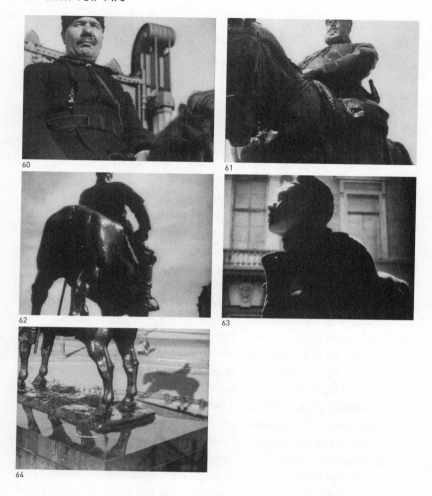

60

61

62

63

64

battlefields of World War I. From shots of soldiers' bodies, arrayed in and around a flooded trench or jutting out over a ridge against the sky, a spectator can recuperate some narrative significance: these tableaux signal the broader international context to which the 1917 Revolution responded. But they feature no central characters or plot lines. Contrasted with the frenetic motions of hawkish stock traders, or war profiteers, these arrays of corpses function not so much narratively, to provide plot information, as rhetorically, to emphasize the causal connection between capital and warmongering and ultimately to figure capitalists as mass murderers. The repetitive, frantic movements of the stock traders also appear juxtaposed with shots of utterly still workers. The tableaux of the immobile workers are not mimetic:

they do not *show* revolutionary proletarians refusing to work—they *signify* this refusal. Narrativity dissipates as the duration of these shots extends. Shot in close-up and medium shots, the workers appear monumental in size and freighted with historic significance. Their immobility abstracts them from the story world. In showing the destruction of tsarist monuments while placing large, immobile revolutionary proletarians on the screen, the film heralds a change not simply in the content of the monument (replacing persons of the ruling class with proletarians), but in the medium, replacing granite, marble, and bronze with more "democratic" celluloid, accessible to the masses. Turning its heroes into monuments, the film abstracts them not simply from the story world, but from the very history it has them making.

Pudovkin could well be describing such images when he writes, "The director never sees the actor as a real human being. . . . The same disintegration as with everything in film. Not for one moment is the director presented with live men. Before him he has always only a series of component parts of the future filmic construction. This does not necessitate a sort of killing and mechanicalisation of the actor. He can be as spontaneous as he likes . . . but the director, controlling the camera, will, owing to the nature of the cinematographic representation, himself pick out from the entire work of the living man the pieces he requires."[39] In Pudovkin's description, the actor does not rate as a film worker; he is "a series of component parts." How could this theoretical film actor *not* experience alienation from the product of his labor? Pudovkin's disavowal of violence draws attention to itself. The very denial that montage theory entails "a sort of killing" of the actor betrays a concern that violence may appear implicit in the revolutionized concept of the film actor's body as a series of abstractly signifying parts.

While Pudovkin deadens the quick to create celluloid statues, his tableaux of war corpses quicken the dead. Titles provide directions for understanding the battlefield tableaux, suggesting that a barren landscape with a dead hand sticking out over a ridge stands for "the people of Penza, Novgorod, and Tver" (figs. 65–66). Or that a high-angle long shot of a soldier lying face down in a creek stands for the war experience of soldiers from "Saxony, Württemburg, and Bavaria" (figs. 67–68). The silhouette of the tiniest fragment of a corpse and the image of a single dead soldier thus evoke the deaths of many. The limited visibility of these bodies—and particularly the dead hand, which appears center frame, but little, almost lost in the barren landscape—reflexively draws attention to the hopelessly incomplete nature of these representations. The ease with which that small hand might be overlooked calls attention more generally to the missing of the particular that inevitably accompanies mass violence and its representation. The war

Пензенские,

новгородские,

The people of Penza, of Novgorod,
and of Tver...

тверские...

65

66

Саксонские,

вюртембергские,

The people of Saxony,
of Wurtemburg, of Bavaria...

67

68

corpse tableaux use cinema's unique ability to evoke a world that extends beyond the edges of the frame—and beyond the horizon within the frame. Just as sound cinema made it possible to make audiences "hear" silence, as Fritz Lang's *M* so aptly demonstrates, cinema all along has had the power of using the visible to evoke the invisible.

This formal trait is crucial to the murder scene, which hinges on the invisible, occluded point of view of the victim. Pudovkin inserts a long shot featuring nothing but several pairs of dead legs draped over the walls of a trench (fig. 69); a high angle shot of a trench, the back of a head visible in the upper left corner of the frame, a leg jutting out over the trench in the upper right corner, the face and the rigid hand of a soldier emerging from the muddy water lining the hole, the lineaments of a coat in the foreground (fig. 70); an extreme long shot of bodies lying in front of, behind, and within the snarls of a barbed-wire fence (fig. 71). The markedly partial visibility of the corpses is a powerful representation, through negation, of their former, vital integrity. After a title saying that three years of war have passed, the shot of the single dead hand against the horizon reappears, joined now by a silhouette of a pair of dead feet. Just as shots of individuals stand for entire peoples, shots of pieces of corpses of a particular moment stand for the countless dead bodies that accumulate throughout the duration of the war. The very repetition of these shots of the hand across two distinct time frames reveals in them a symbolic rather than mimetic tendency. The film does not—indeed, cannot—show the mass warfare that belongs to its story world. It can only partially represent World War I through images; instead, it must work to imply, rather than show, the overwhelming loss of life. Through repetition, the symbolic aspect of the shots increases. The heightened symbolism calls attention to what necessarily escapes representation. The very use of the same dead hand to indicate two different periods of the war signals a reflexive resignation: all the lives destroyed cannot be shown in their specificity.

In the war corpse tableaux, Pudovkin's film draws attention to the promise of cinema to show reality and to its inability to grasp that reality, particularly the reality of mass slaughter, except through ultimately reductive processes of signification. No such irony tempers the incipient monumentalism that inheres in some of his images of gigantic, immobile workers and Bolsheviks (figs. 72–73). It is here—and not in the shots of corpses— that Pudovkin "kills" the "living man" as he "pick[s] out . . . the pieces he requires."

69

70

71

72

73

## Aural Montage and Pudovkin's *Deserter* (1933)

Eisenstein, Pudovkin, and Alexandrov wrote, in 1928, a manifesto welcoming sound as a powerful new dimension of montage, while at the same time warning against its use as mere accompaniment to the image.[40] If silent montage could channel visual attention and determine the meaning of the individual shot by creating chains of associations, then aural montage held the potential to bring even greater complexity and force to the process, allowing for what Eisenstein called "vertical montage" and also filmic "inner monologue." Notable Soviet sound montage films include Dziga Vertov's *Enthusiasim* (aka *The Donbass Symphony*, 1931), Pudovkin's *Deserter* (1933), and Eisenstein's *Alexander Nevsky* (1938). *Deserter*, Pudovkin's first sound film, with its scenes of class violence and massacre, has much in common with his work in the silent era, particularly in its evocation of workers' voices and their silencing.

The initial setting of the film is Germany. The hero, Karl Renn (Boris Livanov), loses his enthusiasm for proletarian action as a shipyard worker's strike stretches out, and he fails to show up at the pickets on the day the police gun down unarmed strikers. His mentor, the Communist Ludwig Zelle (Vasily Kovrigin), nevertheless elects to send the young and healthy Karl as an emissary to the Soviet Union, where Karl becomes a heroic worker who enables a factory to meet its five-year plan. Shortly after proving himself a Soviet worker-hero, he reads about the murder of Zelle in the paper and returns to Germany to lead the shipyard workers in a mass protest. He appears to get killed in the final conflict of the film, but the flag he was carrying marches on, apparently without human aid, optimistically signaling the future victory of the international proletariat.

One of the dominant audiovisual tropes of *Deserter* couples a sound track featuring ballet music with an image track featuring a traffic cop moving his arms to direct traffic, but in a pantomime of a ballet dancer's movements. The chauffeured wealthy sit, half asleep, in the back seats of luxury cars. The sounds of political agitation—the voice of a young woman selling a Communist paper reporting on the shipyard strike—occasionally cut into and disrupt the sardonically deployed ballet music, but the music always returns, silencing the proletarian voice. The sound symbolism—ballet music as a sign of the obtuseness of the bourgeoisie in the face of working-class reality—has much in common with the image symbolism of the nondiegetic insert (the shot of the mechanical peacock, for instance, to which Eisenstein compares Alexander Kerensky in *October*). The ballet music is the aural equivalent of shots like those of the porcelain statue of Napoleon that Eisenstein manipulates in *October* to signify Kerensky's vanity and downfall. The statue does not appear as an object simply present within the story world. Instead, it appears in a frame of its own for purely symbolic effect. Similarly, the ballet music is an extradiegetic signifier, reminiscent of René Clair's use of the ambient noise of a soccer match in *Le Million* (1931) in the classic scene where impoverished artists and a horde of gangsters interrupt a stage performance to engage in a slapstick struggle for a moth-eaten jacket whose pocket may hold a winning lottery ticket. In both cases the sound is not only nondiegetic: it explicitly implies one arena while the accompanying images belong to another—traffic jam versus ballet; theater stage versus sports arena. The sound functions not primarily as an index of its source, but as a sign of something outside itself.

A sign of the bourgeoisie's blithe refusal to acknowledge the social injustice upon which its wealth rests, *Deserter*'s ballet music quickly fills the void when a hungry, striking worker, caught in the act of stealing food from a sleepy bourgeois, breaks free and flees his pursuers only to be killed by a passing car. On the image track a rapid montage sequence of close-ups of bourgeois faces shouting shows that the attempted theft has roused them from their usual slumber. A series of brief shots show the worker extricating himself, pausing, and then throwing himself headlong. The next frame shows the passing car that, by Kuleshovian implication, crushes him. (The smooth flow of German traffic suggests the same capitalist juggernaut that first appears as a metaphor in the opening pages of Balzac's *Le Père Goriot*.) The film cuts to a close-up of the traffic cop's hand, then to a close-up of a bored-looking bourgeois having a smoke in his car as he waits for the human body to be cleared, then to the policeman, arms outstretched on his traffic pedestal. The ballet music begins again, the cars recommence their flow, and the suicide scene, which, the film implies, is really a species of murder, ends with a long shot of workers scrubbing blood off the street to the sounds of the traffic cop's ballet. Sound and visual montage thus associate the ballet music, the motif of bourgeois traffic, with the society's failure to be moved by or even, simply, to take note of the death of a starving man. The seemingly innocuous music does not literally cover up the murder in the diegetic world; it signifies such a cover-up. The character of the anonymous worker crushed beneath the car attains significance precisely as the site of an erasure (his blood is literally erased from the sidewalk). Outside of his own erasure, he has little significance within the discourse. This does not mean, however, that the discourse itself erases him; it portrays the erasure of his erasure, the aural drowning out of his "drowning out."

Like Fritz Lang's *M* (another early sound film centered around murder), Pudovkin's *Deserter* uses sound to emphasize silencing. The silences of the film differ from the ballet music. Pudovkin's pointed, skillful negation of sound within a sound film has its own eloquence. Silence accompanies images of German society's unremarked violence: from a drowsy bourgeois couple in a car, dressed for an evening's entertainment, the film cuts to the leap of a suicide into the harbor. From the harbor suicide the film, still with its empty sound track, cuts to a scene of policemen beating a poor man at night. Even images showing the daily lives of workers—getting to work via crowded streetcar, a political rally, and shipyard labor—are marked by silences. Rhetorically, they suggest that the voices and sounds of oppressed workers remain unheard.

Silence plays an important role in the film's pivotal scene of the massacre of shipyard strikers. The workers spot armored vehicles and recognize the threat to themselves. Someone cries, "Guard Zelle!" and this cry is followed by three seconds of silence. Then we hear six seconds of machine-gun fire matched with close-ups of workers. A brief, inarticulate cry interrupts the sound of automatic weaponry, which resumes and continues for another three seconds while the image track focuses on fallen men. A voice shouting "Shame!" breaks in on the gunshots, which recommence for another four seconds as the image track shows the striking workers fleeing in a panic. A worker cries, "We're not armed!" again interrupting the fire, which then continues for seven seconds, accompanying images of workers, their mouths open as if shouting—but unheard—in a realization of the way that violence silences. A pause in the firing lets us hear an inarticulate cry. Then gunfire returns for twelve seconds, while, on the image track, we watch more shots of workers falling. Another wordless cry followed by five more seconds of machine-gun fire is matched with the image of a heroic worker's charge straight at the gun.

Isolating the voice from the noise of the gun, Pudovkin composes from these two types of sounds an alternating aural montage rhythm in which the automatic-weapon fire endures longer than the voices that punctuate it.[41] This interplay between deafening violence and comparatively frail human voices reflects the mutually exclusive relation between violence and speech. Machine-gun fire and voice belong to separate spheres. In classical Soviet cinema, collective political speech is always the preferred means of the revolutionaries; violence the instrument of the ruling class.

At the end of the massacre we *hear* a full sixteen seconds of silence while on-screen we see images of people bearing off the dead and a long row of bodies covered by a tarpaulin. The extensive silence is then replaced by a full forty seconds of a solitary individual's soft cry of pain. This forty-second sustained sound is matched initially with a high-angle long shot of a single body curled in a fetal position on the cobblestones, but most of the forty seconds focus on titles and images that emphasize the defeat of the strike, so that the individual moan of pain is partially, but not fully, absorbed into the collective loss: as with the recorded image, recorded sound retains a degree of autonomy from surrounding discursive material.

Unfortunately, *Deserter's* sound montage turns into far more conventional dialogue by the end of the film. Stilted lines and hackneyed speeches obscure the particularity captured in that enduring whimper. And the narrative transforms first Zelle and, finally, Karl into martyrs. In "Re-viewing the Russian Movies," Robert Warshow (whose political inclinations tended toward social democracy rather than communism) writes: "The glare of triumphant righteousness is so blinding that one can't see any victims at all, only a few martyrs of the working class, their lives well expended, and a few bourgeois or monarchist anachronisms, swept properly into the dustbin of history. No death is without meaning; even that baby hurtling in its carriage down the Odessa steps in *Potemkin* is part of the great plan."[42] "No death is without meaning." Is the solution, then, to represent a meaningless death? Warshow is too subtle a thinker to claim this. In an essay on Roberto Rossellini he writes:

The "message" of *Paisan* . . . is that the whole meaning of war (indeed, the whole meaning of history) is suffering and death. Moral and political differences are obscured: the death of a Fascist equals the death of a partisan, and, as Siegfried Kracauer points out, the American liberators look much like the German conquerors; even the German officer of the Po River episode is presented sentimentally (and therefore with relative success; Rossellini's

complete failure with the sadistic German officer of *Open City* is evidence
of his inability to deal with real moral distinctions). This view of war is always valid: Falstaff is more nearly right than Prince Hal, and Thersites than
Ulysses. But it is also a view that has a special attraction for a defeated Fascist
nation, and Rossellini cannot restrain himself from taking a special advantage of it; there must always be one more push—and it always destroys his
position, for if death and suffering are not in themselves the greatest of mis-
fortunes, then we are back in the field of politics and morals, and it is Prince
Hal who is right.[43]

Falstaff and Hal, Thersites and Ulysses—their debates concerning meaning and meaninglessness take place precisely around the event of killing,
just as the act, and scene, of murder is so intricately a part of the theory and
the practice of cinematic signification. The photographic images and recorded sounds of twentieth-century cinema constitute a revolutionary new
means for confronting this old aesthetic problem emblematized by the os-
cillation between Falstaff and Hal, Thersites and Ulysses: how to represent
the world in such a way as to make it mean without destroying it.

## Anatomy as Alphabet and the Occlusion of Interiority

The impact of the murder scene rests on its implication of suffering and
loss; in other words, it rests precisely on the ground of interiority as it
is obliterated. And yet the dismissal of the *actor's* interiority in Soviet avant-
garde theories of film performance frequently extends to that of the character: individual psychology typically has little importance in the films of
Eisenstein, Kuleshov, and Pudovkin. Eliminating the distraction of inwardness facilitates the display of larger social forces that determine human behavior. Downplaying the inner experience of actor and character, the breakdown of the actor's body through biomechanics and montage amounts to
an embrace of silent cinema's tendency to render people and things equally
as on-screen signifiers. The Soviet avant-garde took full rhetorical advantage of the facility with which film objectifies the human.

The training of Kuleshov's Meyerhold-inspired "model" actor emerges
from the premise that acting does not proceed from the inside out, that inner feeling does not reliably register itself on the human body in performance; hence the necessity for training the actor to master a vocabulary of
legible muscular movements. But for Meyerhold's mentor Konstantin Stanislavsky, only by becoming, inwardly, the character he plays can the actor
manifest, outwardly, the imagined human being. The actor "channels" the

character. The resonances and divergences between Meyerhold and Stan-islavsky, as their theories of acting developed and changed, are complex and rich, but we can distinguish Meyerhold's biomechanics from the philoso-phy of actor preparation, which Stanislavsky sets forth in this passage of *My Life in Art* (1924): "The concentration of the actor reacts not only on his sight and hearing, but on all the rest of his senses. It embraces his mind, his will, his emotions, his body, his memory and his imagination. The entire physi-cal and spiritual nature of the actor must be concentrated on what is going on in the soul of the person he plays. I perceived that creativeness is first of all the complete concentration of the entire nature of the actor."[44] In theory, Stanislavsky's concept of an acting that proceeds from the inside out con-tradicts Meyerhold's biomechanics, which relieve actors of the need to "be," inwardly, the people they play, but actual acting practice often renders this disagreement less sharp.

Consider, for instance, that Griffith and his actors, in their collabo-rations, instinctively made use of both Stanislavsky-like (this is before the introduction of Stanislavsky to the United States)[45] and Delsartian approaches—they are not mutually exclusive. Griffith's directorial method and statements about performance suggest that he wanted his actors to en-ter the state of mind of the characters they were portraying. Roberta Pear-son writes, for instance, "When he tried out the Gish sisters for *An Unseen Enemy* (1912), he [quoting Lillian Gish] 'pulled a real gun from his pocket and began chasing us around the room, shooting it off.'[46] Desiring a fright-ened reaction from Mae Marsh, he would have a shotgun fired off a few feet away."[47] But in contrast, Pearson quotes Henry Walthall as saying: "I don't place much confidence in actors who rely on feeling and emotion for expres-sion. Inspiration is undependable. Our way, Lillian's and mine, is Griffith's method: to build systematically and tediously a structure *complete in ev-ery detail* that the mind can conceive and that tiresome repetition can per-fect. Thoughtful analysis of a character and concentration on minute ways of expressing it produce a more logical and sustained interpretation. . . . We don't depend on inspiration but we build. And the more carefully your foundation is laid, the more conscientious your attention to every *detail*, the more solid will be your edifice."[48]

Walthall's remarks suggest that the key issue is not how one arrives at a performance, but rather the amount of detail with which one por-trays a person. Pearson observes that in the Griffith Biograph films, the histrionic code, which requires less detail, tends to be used in melo-dramas where characters—villain, hero, heroine—are relatively un-ambiguous. Here there is little psychology. The villain does bad things simply because he is a villain. Describing such characters, Pearson quotes Daniel Gerould: "Characters in melodrama are devoid of individuality, either personal or everyday realistic; they are interesting to the spectator not . . . because of their . . . psychic substance, as are the characters in realistic, psychological drama, but only because of their role in interweaving plotline, their creation of dramatic situations."[49] Actors can create such characters by drawing on the appropriate set of gestures from the histrionic code. In contrast, Pearson associates the verisimilar performance style with nineteenth-century realism and psychological narratives, which make more of character motivation (i.e., a villain is no longer simply a villain—he becomes one). According to Pearson, it is with the rise of the verisimilar code that the face and eyes gain importance in the cinema—even prior to widespread use of the close-up. With this inclusion of a greater number of details comes greater ambiguity. Pearson quotes critics in the *Moving Picture World* and the *New York Dramatic Mirror* who worry that use of the verisimilar code might make the story insufficiently clear.[50] Walthall recalls: "I was everything good and bad together, brave and a coward, a dreamer and a bit of a cad, which is to say that I played my hero as a human being."[51] (That is, a villain is no longer simply a villain—he is a mixture of good and bad.)

While the Soviets learned from Griffith and his actors, their theoretical writing and film characterizations suggest certain resonances with the histrionic code that Griffith, in crafting his persona as innovator, publicly abandoned. According to Pearson, Griffith, in making the shift from histrionic to verisimilar (with the aid of talented and experienced actors like Lillian Gish and Henry Walthall), began to associate the histrionic with theater in order to promote the motion picture as a medium capable of greater realism. But a repertoire of readily legible gestures and relatively static characterizations typical of the histrionic code is well suited to narrating historical progress with its right side and wrong side. Performance in the films of Kuleshov and Eisenstein might not look the same as the histrionic style that Griffith came to reject—indeed, Kuleshov, Eisenstein, and Pudovkin learned from Griffith's actors in films made after Griffith distanced his work from the histrionic[52]—but there is a resonance between the histrionic method and the Soviet montageurs' (particularly Kuleshov's and Eisenstein's) *theories* of the film actor.

With the exception of persons in need of a political education, most great films of classical Soviet cinema do not dwell much on the psychological changes of characters. Great detail is not necessary. We need only know a character's social class or political stance. In contrast, Griffith, in order to express the intensity of certain inner experiences, would encourage incoherence, demanding of his actors inappropriate gestures. Joyce Jesionowski writes:

> Griffith introduced excessive performance in the Biograph period, cresting in Lillian Gish's post-partum meltdown in *The Mothering Heart* (1913). In *The Birth of a Nation* many characters experience emotions that are illicit or too deeply felt to easily express. In either case, the feelings that arise resist "natural" performance and break out of the continuity of character building with exceptional gestures. Sightless catatonia might erupt into a display of unrestrained violence. Passionate love or hatred may suddenly break the surface of simulated control. . . . Mae Marsh's Flora, the beloved and playful little sister . . . was given to demonstrations of feeling that did not just alternate shadows with sunlight but paralyzing gloom with flashes of lightning.[53]

Griffith, as demonstrated by Jesionowski, aims to evoke an inner life that exceeds representation by revealing the inadequacy of gesture to express certain states of inwardness. In contrast, the emphasis in Soviet montage theory is not on ineffable inwardness, but on explicit signification, even in films that focus on the evolving consciousness of their characters.

### Putting Stanislavsky Actors through the Montage Machine: Revolvers and Revolutionary Consciousness in *The Mother* (1926)

While Meyerhold may trump Stanislavsky in montage theory, the adoption of their different philosophies of acting are more variable in practice. Pudovkin's *The Mother*, made in the same year, 1926, as *By the Law*, casts Stanislavsky actors Vera Baranovskaya and Nikolai Batalov in the lead roles, and close-ups of their faces occupy a significant amount of screen time. Whereas Kuleshov, in *By the Law*, initially establishes character traits by exploiting the connotations of inanimate objects, Pudovkin relies on elaborate point-of-view shots to realize the interiority of his characters.[54] *The Mother*, his first feature-length film, realizes the intentionality of a budding revolutionary consciousness through the image of a stash of underground weapons. In a series of montage sequences featuring point-of-view shots of a bundle of guns (and, later, revolutionary pamphlets) hidden beneath a floorboard, the film figures the mother's evolving relationship to power and authority. Her consciousness materializes, for a significant amount of screen time, in and through the image of the cached gun.

The first part of the film focuses on a dysfunctional prerevolutionary family: Vlasov, an alcoholic, reactionary father (Alexander Chistiakov); a cowed mother (Baranovskaya); and a revolutionary son (Batalov). The son helps organize a strike at the local factory while his father enlists as a strikebreaker. In the ensuing skirmish, the father is shot dead, and the authorities arrest the son when his mother, hoping to win clemency for him, reveals the weapons he has hidden. After the revelation, the authorities beat and arrest the son, and the mother revolts. The second part of the film moves away from the intense focus on mother and son to feature collective revolutionary activity. During a large protest march, the son escapes from prison and reunites with his mother, who is among the marchers, and both are killed.

The bundle of underground weapons first appears on the eve of the failed strike. Pavel and his mother have gone to sleep after an unpleasant encounter with the drunken Vlasov. A young revolutionary (Anna Zemtsova) raps at Pavel's window. A close-up shows her face through the pane, framed by a ring of frost. This image prefigures the famous final images of the film, which align revolutionary forces with spring, thaw, and the flow of water in contrast to the seeming stasis of a tsarist power associated with ice (fig. 74). This initial framing of Zemtsova's face, through the chain of associations established by the film as a whole, channels, more complexly than in Kuleshov's basic experiment, the significance of her visage, metaphorically pitting youthful revolutionary activity against the hoarfrost of reaction. Pavel goes outside to meet the young woman, and in a medium shot she hands him the bundle, briefly unveiling the guns it contains.

Pavel returns inside to hide the guns. The sequence begins with a close-up of the mother, whose eyes open slightly, indicating a state of half sleep (fig. 75). The film cuts from a close-up of the partially awake mother to a point-of-view shot showing the son placing the wrapped guns beneath a loose floorboard. Pudovkin racks focus, so that as the shot begins, the plane in which the son appears is blurred and grows clearer. This racking focus signifies the mother's gradual registration of the scene despite her sleepiness (figs. 76–77). The sequence ends with a dissolve back to the close-up of the mother (fig. 78) and a fade. The soft focus of the point-of-view shot suggests the vagueness of the mother's consciousness as she first perceives her son's

74

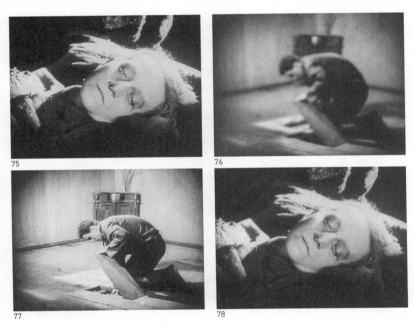

75    76

77    78

revolutionary activity. Just as Zemtsova's rap at the window awakens Pavel, Pavel's hiding of the guns interrupts the mother's sleep: with these images the film figures recognition of political responsibility as a more or less gradual awakening. The illegal weapons are seeds whose burial beneath the floorboard leads to the growth of the mother's revolutionary consciousness.

In the clash between the strikers and strikebreakers, the father dies by the same kind of underground weapon that ultimately gives birth to the revolutionary consciousness of his wife. Just before the body of her murdered husband is borne into her home, the mother kneels praying before her icon and notices the loose floorboard that hides the guns. To show the distance between the mother's political consciousness and her son's, the film cuts to this sequence from a medium close-up of Pavel shaking his fist after the failed strike to a medium close-up of the mother using her own fist to make the sign of the cross (figs. 79–80). An iris in and out on a flashback point-of-view shot shows how the mother, in her mind's eye, vaguely remembers seeing Pavel burying a bundle beneath the floor while she lay half asleep (fig. 81). The film thus returns to that previous sequence, now locating the burial of the revolvers not in the subconscious of halfsleep, but in the glimmerings of a hazy memory. Now fully conscious, she removes the floorboard and unwraps the guns. The rapid editing of the ensuing point-of-view sequence— the mother's face, the guns—expresses her shock. The final close-up of the

79    80

guns in this sequence appears, disjunctively, not from the mother's angle of vision, but from the side, dislodging us from her perspective (figs. 82–84). Her discovery of the guns coincides with her learning of the death of her reactionary husband. After the weapons, the next close-up from her point of view shows the soles of her dead husband's shoes as his corpse is carried into the room; we can see the cobbler's nails (fig. 85).

Mourners come to pay their respects to the dead Vlasov, and an old woman warns the mother that the father's death is the son's doing: "He'll be the ruin of others and of himself, too." The film shows that the old woman's words worry the mother by cutting from a close-up of the mother (fig. 86) to a complex dissolve that reveals the buried guns: the first dissolve removes the floorboard, revealing the bundle (fig. 87); the second dissolve removes the wrapping, revealing the guns (fig. 88); the third dissolve replaces the wrapping (fig. 89); the fourth dissolve replaces the floorboard (fig. 90); the fifth dissolve returns us to the mother (fig. 91). This series of shots, separated by dissolves, figures the mother's consciousness of the guns (which, since they remain under the floorboard, are not literally visible to her) as a process of unveiling and reveiling. This figuration of consciousness reveals its distance from the mother's implied subjectivity, which could never be so tidy and symmetrical. The dissolve signifies rather than shows conscious process.

Pavel returns to remove the guns to a safer place and encounters his mother, seated by the head of his father's body, facing the spot where the weapons lie hidden. The spatial relations of this scene are significant. The mother, alongside the dead father, looks at her son from across the divide of the floorboard that conceals the weapons. A nested point-of-view sequence shows Pavel's discovery that his mother knows the secret of the guns: a long shot of Pavel (fig. 92), a close-up of the mother (where she lowers her eyes from Pavel to the floorboard; fig. 93), a close-up of the floorboards (fig. 94), back to the close-up of the mother in which she raises her eyes to look at

Pavel (fig. 95), and ultimately back to the long shot of Pavel (fig. 96). If we use Edward Branigan's terminology, Pavel's point-glance shot (A) has as its point-object (B) the mother. The mother's point-glance shot (B1) has as its point-object (C) the floorboard. Pavel's point-of-view sequence, ABA, contains the mother's, B1CB1.[55] At the heart of this chiasm we see the spot where the guns lie buried. This wooden plank, which serves to realize, on-screen, the intentionality of the mother's consciousness, now serves to realize Pavel's self-reflection. He sees his mother look uneasily at the floorboard in a glance that enfolds him in its sweep, implying, as it does, a questioning of his relation to the illicit arms. The structure of the scene forcefully conveys Pavel's consciousness of how—implicated in his father's death and responsible for

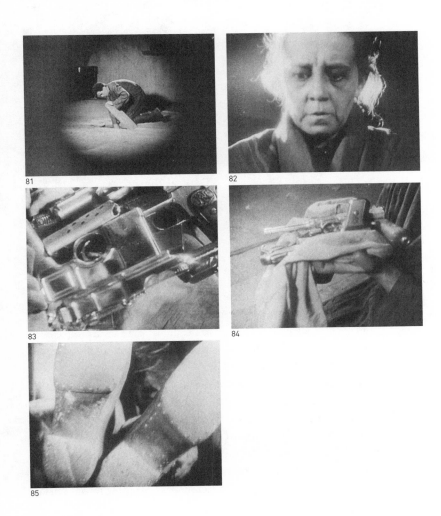

81

82

83

84

85

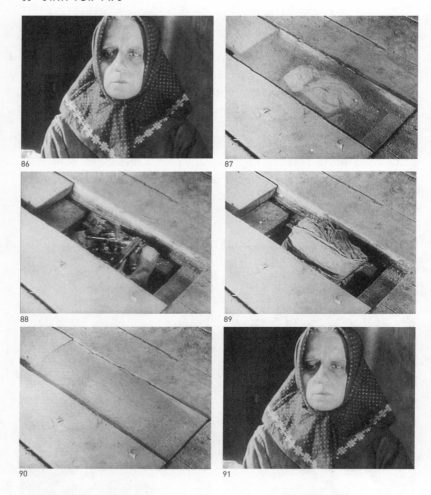

86

87

88

89

90

91

bringing illegal weapons into the home—he must appear in his mother's eyes. The scene locates the mother on the opposite side of the divide (the weapons) from her son because she still pays heed to the old woman's warning; cowed into respect for authority, she remains, with the dead father, on the side of reaction as the ensuing struggle between her and Pavel makes clear.

The chiasmic structure of this point-of-view sequence is worth considering. To move from the point-glance of the mother to the object of her consciousness and back to her point-glance is cinematically to realize not simply intentionality or the object of consciousness, through which consciousness itself can be contemplated: the chiasm suggests the surrendering of self that is part of this process. Five point-of-view sequences make the guns the center of the mother's consciousness: (1) their initial burial,

(2) the mother's memory of Pavel hiding something, (3) her discovery of the guns, (4) her mindfulness of the guns, and (5) her gaze at the spot where they lie buried as she confronts her son. In many of these sequences, Pudovkin uses dissolves to soften the line between the mother's face and the guns she contemplates. Neither image of the resulting, brief double exposures can claim dominance: whether the face contains, or takes precedence over, the guns, or vice versa, remains undecidable. In these sequences, the mother's consciousness and the guns she contemplates momentarily coverge. Just as the floorboard serves as part of the foundation of this workers' home, the objects it conceals—first the guns, and then the revolutionary literature—both realize and change the mother's subjectivity so that she, in turn, comes to serve as part of the foundation of the revolutionary society that is

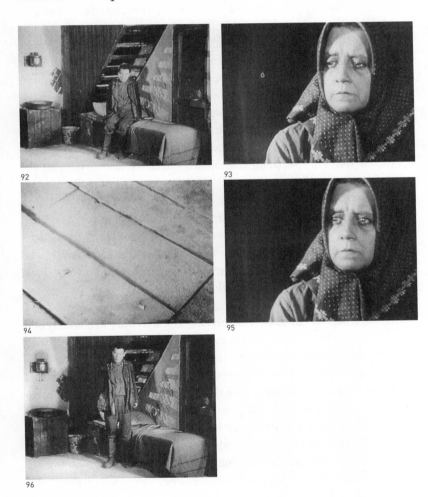

92

93

94

95

96

developing. In other words, through its elaborate point-of-view sequences, the film realizes the mother's consciousness as an evolving perspective on a hidden bundle of revolutionary weapons, and ultimately, in fine Hegelian fashion, makes the mother herself into a revolutionary weapon. Subject and object merge. Shortly after this sequence, the film narrative moves away from its grounding in the mother's consciousness; she ceases to be a dominant focalizer and instead joins the crowd of demonstrating workers, becoming part of a general force for social progress.

The explicit spatial relations of this nested point-of-view sequence contrast markedly with the looser structuring of space in the scene where the mother gives up the guns, betraying her son. That scene, which begins with the reentry of the military authorities after an initial failed search, has but a scant establishing shot, after which the scene is broken down into several close-ups and long shots that isolate single characters. The infrequency and brevity of shots that show the relative positions of only some characters make it difficult for the spectator to maintain orientation. But the overall choreography makes sense. The mother stands not only between her son and the colonel (played by an actual former tsarist officer), but between the choices each represents: oppressive authority on the one hand, revolutionary struggle on the other (fig. 97). A low-angle, extreme close-up (the frame cuts off the top of his head) shows the colonel in profile in an oversize image that signifies his menacing dominance within the scene even as it abstracts him, spatially, from it (fig. 98).[56] A title says, "Let him confess, and we'll forgive everything." The mother, still trusting in authority, gives in to these words, promising that Pavel will tell all. She runs toward the camera to get the buried guns, and the next several shots fragment the scene to focus on individual characters: the mother as she removes the guns; Pavel as he struggles with the men who hold him; the colonel in close-up; and, perhaps most spatially confusing, Pavel's fellow organizer (whose location is unclear, since he has been out of frame in all of the establishing shots; fig. 99). Spatial relations are partially reestablished as the mother hands the commanding officer the guns and backs away from him toward Pavel (fig. 100). The scene again dissolves, this time into a series of close-up reaction shots including shots of anonymous bystanders.

The breakdown of the space into disconnected and somewhat confusing pieces marks the crucial realignment of the mother's position vis-à-vis her son and the authorities: stunned by the mistreatment of Pavel and remorseful for the role she played in his arrest, she takes up his cause. The consequences of surrendering the guns have given birth to a revolutionary mind: the mother moves beyond the space of her home (whose threshold,

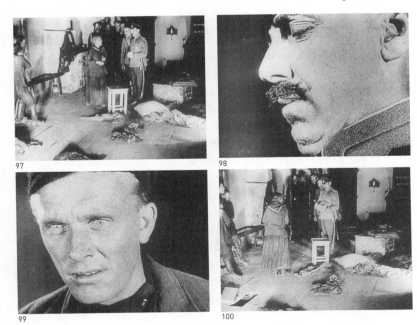

97

98

99

100

until this point, we have not seen her cross). She goes to court to witness her son's trial, visits him in prison, and joins the protesting masses. The hidden guns—the primary intentional object through which the mother's consciousness is realized—disappear from the film once she surrenders them. Revolutionary pamphlets take their place under the floor. The mother's inner life also "disappears." Indeed, the film changes qualitatively from this point. More people enter the frame, as domestic drama no longer dominates the scenes but gives way to the drama of the courtroom and the streets. The film ceases to be so grounded in the title character's point of view, adopting, instead, an increasingly external, historical perspective.

Struck down by tsarist forces while carrying a red flag, sign of her now revolutionary consciousness, the mother dies. In the scene of her violent death, the camera shows the Cossacks that trample her. Like the images of the cracking ice, these fragmentary shots of flitting riders suggest a dynamic of disintegration within the forces of autocracy (fig. 101). As with the dismantling of the statue in *October*, we see a concerted, but often thwarted, effort to overthrow an oppressive regime even as we see signs of that regime falling apart on its own. In order to divest the old order of its claim to natural historical and cultural continuation, Pudovkin, like Eisenstein, exploits the poetics of rupture, temporal and spatial, inherent in montage.

Ultimately, the film shows the triumph of the mother's cause: via the omniscient historical perspective of the film narrative, the red banner she carries at her death reappears, fluttering against the city skyline in a flash-forward to a postrevolutionary time. From beneath the floor of a worker's hovel, the sign of the revolutionary consciousness has, in its metamorphosis from weapons to flag, risen out of hiding to its victorious place above the domes of a public building. The tears in the flag suggest the losses sustained by martyrs like the mother, whom we last saw as a trampled corpse, the flag gripped in its dead fingers. The world in the concluding shot contains no human figures; it is figured as static, with a single symbol, the flag, at its center (fig. 102). The representation of the Revolution's triumph in both *The End of St. Petersburg* and *The Mother* reveals the difficulty of envisioning the postrevolutionary world in a narrative discourse where characters derive their significance based on where they fall in the class struggle. In both films, the triumph of the progressive cause marks the end of the story—and implies the end of history. The class warfare through which many of the human figures in early Soviet films derive their narrative significance gives the fight that constitutes the central action of the plot such narrative weight that when it ends, the story world appears voided of every possible arena for meaningful human action. Correspondingly, in *The End of St. Petersburg*, the revolutionaries strike static poses, transforming themselves into monuments; and the final shots of *The Mother* show a series of cityscapes empty of people. If we follow the rhetorical logic of *The Mother*, then the committed revolutionaries, parents and children, have given their lives for the cause and the city *is* empty.

Pudovkin makes Eisenstein's signature move and replaces the people with a thing, the flag. Despite Pudovkin's privileging of point-of-view sequences and Baranovskaya's performance, which allows for subtle facial close-ups for the point-glance shots, the film ultimately subsumes her char-

101

102

acter under its one-dimensional mapping onto history's "right side."[57] All those on the "right side" can be represented by that final image of the flag. They are dead. The discursive channeling of the human image into a single historical stance shows how montage can strip the photographic trace of a person of its just ambiguity. Even as the Revolution's triumph requires the blood of mother and son, its signification requires the martyrdom of its images.

And yet the practice of montage also resists reification of the human image. Films like *The Mother* and *The End of St. Petersburg* realize on-screen a political account of the way large-scale industrialism can treat workers as if they were mere things; they do this, paradoxically, by manipulating the radical equivalence between persons and things as they appear as instruments of signification on the film screen. The promise of montage lies in its power to draw attention to, or scrutinize, reifying signification, as when, in *The End of St. Petersburg*, Pudovkin underscores the utter pathos of any attempt to represent the bloodshed of World War I by placing all that weight on a twice-repeated shot of one tiny, dead hand. Scenes of deadly violence can powerfully index the inadequacy of the victim's representation, aesthetic and political. But when characters are put to death because of their irrevocable placement in an abstract social category, and the scene of their murder does little to shake the historical identity imposed upon them, montage threatens to squander its promise.

### Coda: Eisenstein, Inner Speech, and Murder

Pudovkin's use of Stanislavsky-trained actors and point-of-view structures is not the only example, in Soviet montage practice, of an effort to realize inner experience. Although Eisenstein, in the twenties, made a virtue out of refusing to devote attention to the psychology of individual characters, in the late twenties and into the thirties, an interest in a cinematic inner speech (of both character and spectator) emerges in his essays and projects. This interest has multiple sources of inspiration, including the work of psychologist Lev Vygotsky,[58] Russian Formalist Boris Eikhenbaum,[59] and novelists Fyodor Dostoevsky and James Joyce.[60] Since inner speech entails thinking in pictures as well as in words, Eisenstein believed cinema to be the privileged medium for its realization. Always aiming first to provoke an emotional, even physiological, response in his viewer, he believed a cinematic thinking in pictures could touch a more primitive layer of the psyche. Correspondingly, he saw fairy-tale logic, marked by magical substitutions, replacements, and doublings (forms of metaphor and metonymy), as a model for a powerful cinematic interior monologue. A key place where he located the vestigial traces of such thought was nineteenth-century prose fiction. Elaborating the concept of a folkloric form of thought, he develops a fascinating literary canon—Dostoevsky's *The Brothers Karamazov*, Honoré de Balzac's story "The Red Inn," Émile Zola's *Thérèse Racquin*, and Theodore Dreiser's *An American Tragedy*.[61] All of these texts revolve around a homicide. From a montage of attractions to cinematic inner speech, a key paradigm, for Eisenstein, is murder.

In "Chapter on Dostoevsky (Metaphor and Metonymy in Plot)" (1943) Eisenstein considers the way that in all of the above literary texts except *Thérèse Racquin*, the thought of murder uncannily—and against the thinker's wishes—becomes the act of murder, so that the thought is punished as if it were the deed. Eisenstein's attention to, and elaboration of, this remnant of a fairy-tale cognition that does not fully distinguish between thought and deed, accident and fate, guilt and innocence, presents a striking contrast to his drive to create types and caricatures. Ivan and Dmitri Karamazov, Balzac's ill-fated Prosper Magnan, and Dreiser's Clyde Griffiths confound judgment in ways that Vakulinchuk and his murderer Giliarovsky do not. The tension, in Eisenstein's thought and practice, between the creation of characters who clearly fall, and die, on the right or wrong side of history and the consideration of characters who cannot be reduced to simple guilt or innocence suggests not a contradiction, but a dialectic. This dialectic constitutes an aspect of that broader opposition between cinematic signification, which narrows the meaning of an image, and visual reference, which exceeds and eludes definitive meanings.

Eisenstein's murder scenes—the ones he creates and the ones he considers—underscore and elaborate the stakes of this conflict. In films like *Strike*, *The Battleship Potemkin*, and *October*, he devises, like Dickens and Griffith before him, characters who are exaggerated types. For his concept of typage, Eisenstein drew inspiration from the commedia dell'arte. He aimed to re-create a system of stock characters whom, like Columbine, Harlequin, and Pierrot, an audience would instantly recognize. According to Marie Seton, "when he wanted to create a character, a street cleaner, for example, he went out into the streets and there observed the characteristics of people who were engaged in cleaning the streets. From the general characteristics he observed, he formed a composite image of a typical street cleaner. Then he searched for the individual who possessed the greatest number of traits observed in the many street cleaners, though he might in fact not be a street cleaner."[62] The man who played the ship's surgeon in *Potemkin* Eisenstein found shoveling coal in a Sevastopol hotel; the man who played the priest was a gardener. These examples suggest the unreliability of outward appearance as a signifier of a particular social type, and of a consciousness assumed to correspond to that type. There are instances where Eisenstein finds his "type" already living the role he wants her to play, as when a real-life farmworker plays a farmworker, Marfa Lapkina, in *The General Line*.[63] Marfa, unlike *Potemkin*'s doctor and priest and the fat, kvas-drinking kulaks who deny her aid, is not a caricature.

In contrast to the more understated, detailed Marfa, Eisenstein's caricatures, to a greater degree, engage in, suffer, and are defined by violence. The *Potemkin*'s sailors knock the vindictive priest down the stairs and throw the heartless doctor overboard. The overfed kulaks of *The General Line* leave Marfa to starve. In one instance, the actor's image deceptively signifies that which the person is not: the coal shoveler is not a cruel doctor; the gardener is not a sadistic priest. In the other instance, the imaged person implies an illusory reference to an actual group of people, imposing on them a lethally reductive significance: the kulaks caricatured in *A General Line* historically succumbed to engineered starvation and the first wave of purges. Such complicity between a cinematic image of a people (e.g., kulaks) and the government's image of them (or at least the image the government wishes to promote) underscores the stakes of the murder scene at their most extreme, which lie in this potential synergy between a violent cinematic image and a mental one.

Although Eisenstein renders his types legible at a glance, the characters he discusses in "Chapter on Dostoevsky" display a more fully elaborated interiority precisely in order to reveal their complex relation to the murder around which their story pivots.[64] In suggesting depth as well as surface, the characters point up a potential discrepancy between an image and its allotted meaning. They exceed, or elude, the definitive significance that more successfully contains Eisenstein's proletarian martyrs and bourgeois villains. But such characters do not present the only, or even primary, occasion for cinematic inner speech. For Eisenstein, cinema need not *represent* inner speech; it can *be* it. As early as 1925, before he began to write specifically about cinematic possibilities for interior monologue, Eisenstein aspired to bequeath a form of consciousness to the spectator. Anne Nesbet writes: "Potemkin, too, would like to contain a self-realizing point of view that does not just inspire but actually *is* a new form of consciousness."[65] This early aspiration foreshadows Eisentstein's later conceptions of cinema as "sensual thought" and "inner speech." These concepts go beyond Metz's theory of the spectator's "primary" identification with the camera's gaze: Eisenstein wants the film to feed its spectator the "thought process as montage form."[66] In a sense, he recuperates, on the level of the cinematic enunciation, the complex consciousness he so often denied his characters.

To conceive of montage as a reconstruction of the thought process implies a coincidence between the cinematic image and the spectator's mental image. Soviet montage's progressive politics, coupled with its often violent reference, means that Eisenstein's enterprise is at once full of promise and fraught with risk. Most starkly, his concept of a cinematic inner speech implies that the murder scene's dual demonstration, in story and discourse, of a person's delimitation and disposability can proceed from montage form to spectatorial thought process: in watching a murder scene, we, together with the discourse, can find ourselves, to a greater or lesser degree, complicit with its murder. Such complicity is an extreme, a limit case. But murder itself is an extreme. As aesthetic object-event, it casts in relief the stakes of representational practice—the impact of formal choices, the exigencies of reference. Drawn to extremes, Eisenstein, throughout his career, turned to murder because it is the most powerful and efficient vehicle for getting to the crux of film aesthetics.

# 3 Murder Outside the Poetics of Montage: André Bazin and Jean Renoir

## André Bazin and the Preservation of Loss

The murder scene's power both to reduce the victim to a legible (and disposable) set of traits *and* to imply the irreducible particularity and inviolability of a life situates it at the heart of long-standing questions of signification and reference in film. This is why we see an intense focus on a cinematic grammar of murder both at a key moment in the development of cinematic *discourse* (Soviet montage theory and practice) and at a key moment in the philosophy of film *reference* (Bazin's theorization of cinematic realism). Many of Bazin's most influential case studies center around narratives of violence: Renoir's films of the thirties; Hitchcock; Bette Davis's murder of her husband in *The Little Foxes*; the war and its aftereffects in neorealist films such as *Paisan*, *Germany Year Zero*, and *Rome Open City*; Dreyer's *The Passion of Joan of Arc* and *Day of Wrath*. Bazin's realist theory takes shape, to a significant extent, around murder scenes.

*

Some parts of Bazin's sizable body of criticism have received more emphasis than others. Partly because of this, his reception since his death has been mixed. Film theorists of multiple stripes, from Lacanian and Marxist to neoformalist and historicist, have tagged him with various oversimplifications including championing cinematic illusionism, siding with the United States in the cold war, and essentializing such formal choices as shooting in depth and employing classical découpage. But the irrepressible subtlety of Bazin's writing (at once elliptical and dialectical), as well as a resurgence of interest in the complex question of film form and reference in the work of contemporary critics such as Miriam Hansen, Mary Ann Doane, Philip Rosen, and Garrett Stewart, has also created conditions for a reconsideration of Bazin's legacy.

Rosen's *Change Mummified* has already put to rest many familiar critiques of Bazin with his argument that "spatial likeness and deviance are finally not the crux of Bazinian realism" and that Bazin "disentangles" spatial likeness from indexicality.[1] At the heart of Bazin's realism Rosen locates the "mummy complex," or the desire to preserve. This preservation of a given reality through photographic registration necessarily entails "the inevitable abstraction from reality inherent in the effort to form representations."[2] Abstraction entails a gap between referent and signifier, which Bazin freely acknowledges. Rosen writes, "It is precisely this gap that is filled in variable manifestations of human imagination, which are, in effect subjective projections."[3] The gap thus powers stylistic changes and a plurality of evolving realisms; it permits Bazin to historicize film style. But his historiography is teleological: with each new stylistic and technological innovation, cinematic realism evolves. According to Rosen, this teleology depends on Bazin's claim that the desire to preserve is an ahistorical constant of human subjectivity. Rosen sees this assertion of a universal human desire to preserve as the problematic linchpin of Bazin's theory.

To Rosen's analysis I would add that the flip side of the desire to preserve is the power to efface, and this dialectical turn is equally crucial to Bazinian realism. Effacement in Bazin takes a variety of forms. In "Death Every Afternoon" (1958), for instance, a film's mechanical reproduction of the sight of a death can both efface the uniqueness that the moment holds for the dying subject and, at the same time, set that uniqueness in relief against its cinematic repetition. Of death on film in general, Bazin writes, "The representation of a real death is . . . an obscenity. . . . We do not die twice. . . . Thanks to film, nowadays we can desecrate and show at will the only one of our possessions that is temporally inalienable: dead without a requiem, the eternal dead-again of the cinema!"[4] Here Bazin suggests that the cinema obliterates that which has epiphanic or transcendent potential, transforming everything into, if not one thing after another, then the same thing over and over. But turning his attention specifically to Pierre Braunberger's *The Bullfight*, he writes:

> The representation on screen of a bull being put to death (which presupposes that the man has risked death) is in principle as moving as the spectacle of the real instant that it reproduces. In a certain sense, it is even more moving because it magnifies the quality of the original moment through the contrast of its repetition. It confers on it an additional solemnity. The cinema has given the death of Manolete a material eternity.
>
> On the screen, the toreador dies every afternoon.[5]

As with the dramatic, one-sentence final paragraph of "The Ontology of the Photographic Image" ("On the other hand, cinema is also a language"), Bazin, with the penultimate paragraph of "Death Every Afternoon," powerfully encapsulates the antithesis of a thesis he unfolds at greater leisure. The essential repetitiveness of cinematically reproduced reality extracts all particularity, even from the moment of an individual's death. But in these brief final paragraphs, cinematic repetition "every afternoon" also provides the backdrop against which the singularity of Manolete's death (he was killed by a bull in 1947) flashes in sharp relief. Bazin's argument here resonates with Walter Benjamin's concept of aura, a quality that accrues to objects that are singular and possessed of a certain distance, spatial and/or temporal. Benjamin conceived the concept of aura as it emerged in all its clarity on the verge of its disappearance in a sea of mechanically reproduced cultural artifacts, including cinema. Whereas Benjamin finds the death of aura in cinema taken as a whole, Bazin, in one brief cinematic moment, finds both aura and its loss as they emerge in their difference from one another in a scene of killing.

At the end of *Strike* Eisenstein intercuts the real death of a bull so that its shock effect might transfer to the obviously fake death of his strikers. Bazin begins this passage with the filmed death of the bull only to replace, in the final sentence, the bull's death with that of a man, the famed toreador Manolete; both deaths are real. With this startling insertion of the death of a man where we expect to find the death of a bull, Bazin suggests the easy slippage between bull and man revealed by Braunberger's film. In *The Bullfight*, the two face each other as antagonists, rather than as victims of anonymous butchers, as in Eisenstein's *Strike*. Following Bazin (and returning to the example from *Strike* with which this book opens), we might acknowledge that to personify the bull is indeed to taurify the man: both processes admit some denial of the very difference they rely on. Similarly, we see Bazin's recognition in "Death Every Afternoon" that the drive to archive or preserve the singular moment through cinematic means—to reveal it as different or unique—is, at the same time, the possible effacement of that singularity, the denial of its difference.

When everything is recorded or reproduced, nothing stands out. All is lost to serial anonymity. This particular form of effacement, an obverse of the desire to preserve, *can* be historicized. Indeed, Benjamin's concept of aura—and loss of aura—in the "age of mechanical reproducibility" constitutes one such attempt at historicization. Like Benjamin, Bazin expresses ambiguity toward the power of the movie camera, praising, as we saw in chapter 1, its "blinding" in Renoir's *The Rules of the Game* ("This invisible witness is inevitably made to wear blinders; its ideal ubiquity is restrained by framing, just as tyranny is often restrained by assassination").⁶ Throughout his career, Bazin praises moments when films obscure and elide precisely that which they make us desire to see, as if in the very act of showing and preserving the camera also threatens to destroy.

\*

Death, real and fictional, connects many instants where Bazin suggests that the camera, by showing, also threatens to diminish. In the tension between preservation and effacement, it would seem that life itself hangs in the balance. But life in what sense? In making a distinction between Erich von Stroheim's actors and the Hollywood star, Bazin writes, "Against the sociological myth of the star—an abstract hero, the ectoplasm of collective dreams—[Stroheim] will reaffirm the most peculiar embodiment of the actor, the monstrosity of the individual."⁷ "Monstrosity" can mean something "abnormal," or "excessively large." If individuality is "monstrous" and "peculiarly embodied," then it is vulnerable to the repetitions of mechanical reproduction, the systematicity of signification, the delimitation of framing, and the disembodiment inherent in representation. It is life in this sense of a monstrous individuality that is at stake.

Consider Bazin's criticism of the characters across the courtyard from James Stewart in Hitchcock's *Rear Window* (1954): "At the end of the film, we know everything about the past and future of these characters whom we have merely glimpsed. Nothing is kept in the dark, not even what might be ambiguous due to missing information. We aspire as if for a breath of fresh air to *not* knowing something about someone, to be left in doubt, which would allow these characters to have an existence beyond the scenario of the film."⁸ For Bazin, the trace of a human being on-screen has the potential to suggest a personhood that exceeds the dialogue and mise-en-scène. In an essay on Dreyer's *The Passion of Joan of Arc* (1928) he writes, "Seen from very close up, the actor's mask cracks. As the Hungarian critic Béla Balász wrote, '. . . In addition to the expression one wears, the camera reveals one's true face. Seen from so close up, the human face becomes the document.'"⁹ Bazin's dislike of the caricatural pantomime of *Rear Window*'s (mostly) silent characters contrasts with his praise for the apophatic reticence of Robert Bresson's *Diary of a Country Priest* (1951): here Bazin suggests that the "sheer epidermis" of the nonacting face and the "awkwardly drawn" cross advertise the film's inability directly to show spiritual life.¹⁰ Whether *Diary* portrays a short, sad life or a spiritual triumph remains undecidable.

\*

Like "Death Every Afternoon," "William Wyler, or the Jansenist of Directing" (1948) and "The Myth of Stalin in the Soviet Cinema" (1950) dwell on
cinematic representation, death, and effacement. The Wyler essay describes
a fictional murder, the scene in *The Little Foxes* (1941) where Bette Davis murders Herbert Marshall by refusing to fetch his heart medicine while he suffers an attack of angina. (Bazin uses the names of the actors, not the names
of the characters.) And "The Myth of Stalin" has as its implicit context the
Stalin regime's elimination of real people through the rewriting of history
and through actual murder. The reference to murder, fictional and historical, in these two essays is crucial. Murder is an allegory of representation:
if murder (legally, axiologically) hinges on the stark negation of an individual, cinema, which must represent the victim with discursive techniques
that can never fully comprehend a human being, courts complicity with the
murders it depicts. But at the same time, murder can paradoxically endow
the victim with a referential fullness: the transformation of a person into
a victim dramatically suggests the subjective plenitude and particularity
which have been lost. Murder scenes are thus poised between reducing and
registering the person implied by the storied victim.

The murder scene's dual potential for registration and reduction resonates with Bazin's meditations on photography-based cinema. In "Will Cinemascope Save the Film Industry?" he draws attention to a medium-specific
tension between revealing reality (through the photographic image) and
signifying from reality (in the arrangement of images). If this tension informs his theoretical and critical stance in crucial ways, it also resonates
with the dialectic between referential comprehension and discursive reduction, which structures the logic, or "grammar," of the murder scene.

Bazin describes the murder of Marshall's character in *The Little Foxes*
twice. First, he writes:

> Marshall is obliged to stand up and go get the medicine himself. This effort
> will kill him on the first steps of the staircase. . . . [Bette Davis's] frightening
> immobility takes its full impact only from Marshall's double exit from the
> frame, first in the foreground on the right, then on a third plane on the left.
> Instead of following him in this lateral movement, as any less intelligent eye
> would naturally have done, the camera remains imperturbably immobile.
> When Marshall finally enters the frame for the second time and climbs the
> stairs, the cinematographer Gregg Toland (acting at Wyler's request) is care-
> ful not to bring into focus the full depth of the image, so that Marshall's fall
> on the staircase and his death will not be perfectly visible to the viewer. . . .

We have to discern in the distance the outcome of a drama whose protagonist is nearly escaping us.[11]

Ten pages later, he again refers to Marshall's double exit from the frame and to the decision not to shoot, in focus, the background plane, where Marshall falls on the stairs. He associates the spectator's inability to see the dying character with anxiety, writing, in his second description of the scene, "[Wyler] elected to have Toland envelop the character of the dying Marshall in a certain haziness, to have his cinematographer, as it were, befog the back of the frame. This was done to create additional anxiety in the viewer, so much anxiety that he would almost want to push the immobile Bette Davis aside to have a better look."[12] For Bazin, Wyler's ability to produce anxiety by choosing *not* to show Marshall constitutes an aesthetic strength: even in this exemplary depth-of-field shot, the marked limitation of the camera's gaze (here it does not follow the convention of following the movement of the actor) replaces its "tyranny."

Twice Marshall leaves the frame, and twice Bazin brings this departure back into critical focus. Bazin's persistent attention to the murdered man's occlusion demonstrates the power of murder to make us care about a character precisely as he vanishes. The camera's "blinders" make us want to see. Indeed, Bazin imagines a temptation to "push aside" Davis to see Marshall—a surprising sentiment to be teased out by a critic known for delighting in shots that feature a plurality of figures occupying multiple planes. We might attribute Bazin's keen aesthetic pleasure in Davis's immobility to the peculiar correspondence it creates between story world and enunciation: in the story world, her immobility *is* the act of murder—she kills her husband by not moving to help him. Her motionless figure eliminates the murdered Marshall from the story and, together with the relative stasis of the camera (it moves slightly), from the discourse; she both kills Marshall and displaces him as the focus of the shot. The structure of the image signals the violence inherent in its own formal processes. Here too we see the erasure that is the flip side of the impulse to preserve, which Rosen finds at the heart of Bazin's ontology.

But Marshall's absence also functions to make him present. The sequence ending with his collapse on the stairs provokes a strong desire to see the sight denied us—the dying character. The denial of this desire has the effect of allowing him, in his absence from—and obscurity on—the screen, to exceed his discursive appearance. Central to the scene, and yet, in a sense, missing from it, he transcends his realization in sight and sound to persist as a manifestation of desire and imagination. This shift might hide him from our sight, but it also frees him from the potentially reductive power of the camera's "tyrannous witness."

Bazin's analysis of Marshall's movement recalls his argument in "Theater and Cinema—Part Two" (1951). Here Bazin observes of the theater stage "its absence from anything beyond, as the painting exists by virtue of its frame."[13] He contrasts theater and painting with the film screen, which "is not a frame like that of a picture but a mask which allows only a part of the action to be seen. When a character moves off screen, we accept the fact that he is out of sight, but he continues to exist in his own capacity at some other place in the décor which is hidden from us. There are no wings to the screen. . . . In contrast to the stage the space of the screen is centrifugal."[14] For Bazin, the distinction between masking and framing is ultimately a matter of aesthetic negotiation as well as medium specificity. Of Dreyer's *The Passion of Joan of Arc*, for instance, he claims that "the cinema may very well impose itself upon the theater."[15] Similarly, we might say that theater imposes itself on cinema when the dying Marshall moves off-screen in *The Little Foxes*. Here it becomes more difficult to make a clear distinction between masking and framing: when he steps out of sight beyond the edge of the frame, Marshall is in the process of ceasing to exist.[16] The very frustration with the immobility of the camera, posited by Bazin, implies an awareness of the scene as framed—and not simply masked. It is Marshall's absence from the frame—not his prominence within it—that makes him the center of our concern.

We might describe Toland's in-depth construction of this shot as an instance of Bazinian ambiguity. Bazin's valorization of ambiguous images is sometimes cited to distinguish his concept of realism from "realism" as it has come to connote narratives that conceal their forms in order to naturalize their ideologically suspect illusions. But Bazin's insistence on the ambiguity of the image is not merely his alibi: more than his championing of certain aesthetic choices such as depth of field, it lies at the crux of his theory of a realist poetics. This poetics is much closer to the modernism and formalism with which it is so often contrasted. Like other instances of modernist fragmentation and abrogation of meaning, this ambiguity can serve to remind us of the partiality of what we see and hear, and the uncertainty of the meanings we draw from it.

Bazin specifically valorizes *characterizations* that entail ambiguity. It is the ambiguity of the individual subject over time, and in relation to history, that occupies his interest in "The Myth of Stalin in the Soviet Cinema." Bazin writes, "From the perspective of Stalinist Soviet Communism, no one can 'become' a traitor, because this would mean that he hasn't been one all along . . .

that the man who has become detrimental to the party and to History had once been useful to both." The living Communist leader turned (alleged) traitor confronted Stalinism with what Bazin calls "the scandal of subjectivity, with the implicit acknowledgment of subjectivity as the driving force of History—a force that is nonetheless said to be purely objective."[17]

Constituting the implicit historical backdrop of this essay are the highly cinematic show trials and the purging, both from life and historiography, of individuals who were tried and found guilty. Here political representation and discursive representation crucially overlap: the "monstrous" individuality of Grigorii Zinoviev, Nikolai Bukharin, and László Rajk, all three of whom Bazin mentions, is erased from historical discourse even as the three men are physically annihilated. In response, Bazin declares with an exclamation point, "Where a human life is concerned, one can never be sure of anything!"[18]

The Stalin myth, as Bazin describes it, entails, in addition to an attempt to cement or monumentalize an abstractive historical projection, the aim to erase, or, in some cases, kill off certain obstacles to that abstraction (e.g., Zinoviev, Bukharin, and Rajk). Thus, the cinematic preservation of a myth is implicated in the obliteration of some inconvenient people. Here both the camera's gaze and its disregard prove tyrannous: on the one hand we have the abstractive show trials; on the other we have the erasure of the pasts of the old Bolsheviks purged by Stalin. To be caught and preserved within the frame is as fraught with danger as to be excluded from it.

"The Myth of Stalin" proves a key essay in Rosen's analysis of Bazin. According to Rosen, Bazin must confront the Stalin myth because it "suppresses the gap" between subjective "imaginative projection" and "actual, concrete objectivity." (Precisely in suppressing this gap, Stalinist cinema renders itself complicit with a murderous regime.) But Rosen locates a correspondence between the Stalin myth, which imposes "telos by politically motivated fiat," marking "a fatal imbalance, whereby the side of subjectivity that projects toward the objective concrete is overwhelmed by the abstractive side of subjectivity,"[19] and Bazin's own "myth of total cinema," noting that for Bazin

there are ... three coexisting levels at which the history of subjective investment in images manifests itself. We have noted those of the individual subject (artist, spectator) and the collective subject (social and/or cultural myth, with the Western and Stalinist cinema as relatively pure examples). Throughout Bazin's writings, these are subsumed by a third, which, in effect mandates the other two and functions as a universal, dating back to the origins of representation: the fundamental preservative impulsion of the subject to overcome time, with the consequent desire for "objective" representation. But if Bazin is driven by his project and his logic to posit a universal, the question arises whether his history of subjectivity has truly evaded the dilemma of Stalinist cinema with its abstractive hypertrophy of the atemporal. Has not the desire to control time taken over his own formulations, perhaps from the other side of subjectivity, which projects toward the concrete? . . .

. . . Ultimately, if Bazin's analysis has shown how the Stalin myth becomes a kind of "second nature" for Soviet filmmakers, then so does the myth of total cinema for Bazin as historian; and is the ultimate ideological consequence, the abstract transcendence of historical time, that dissimilar?[20]

Rosen exaggerates his polemic with Bazin in order to crystallize a key problem. But here it is important to recall the antithesis to the "preservation impulsion" provided by Bazin's crucial reflections on cinema's reductive essence: the various forms of exclusion, repression, and erasure entailed by film are not manifestations of any universalized desire; they are historically specific phenomena. For Bazin, "total cinema" is only a myth, a useful fiction rather than an objectively achievable outcome. But the loss of reality, for Bazin, is a cinematic fact: "Every form of aesthetic must necessarily choose between what is worth preserving and what should be discarded, and what should not even be considered. But when this aesthetic aims in essence at creating the illusion of reality, as does the cinema, this choice sets up a fundamental contradiction which is at once unacceptable and necessary: necessary because art can only exist when such a choice is made. Without it, supposing total cinema was here and now technically possible, we would go back purely to reality. Unacceptable because it would be done definitely at the expense of that reality which the cinema proposes to restore integrally."[21] If cinema answers to a desire to preserve, then, for Bazin, it does so through "unacceptable and necessary" exclusion and effacement. We have seen how so many scenes on which Bazin chooses to focus throughout his writing formally and thematically display loss; many of them are scenes of death. In addition to the "befogged" figure of the dying Herbert Marshall in Little Foxes, Bazin writes of the enshadowed Susan when she is discovered having tried to kill herself in Citizen Kane; of a killing represented as a random piece of news accidentally overheard by the victim's lover in the Florentine episode of Paisan; and, in the same film, of the narrative repression of most details surrounding the slaughter of a family.

For Bazin it would seem that cinema best responds to our need to record what is, or will be, lost, by showing us how that which we want to keep has already been missed. He quotes with approval Wyler's realization of

Hollywood's failure to show the world: "I know that George Stevens has not been the same since he saw the corpses at Dachau. We were forced to realize that Hollywood has rarely reflected the world and the time in which people live."[22] And yet a page and a half later he suggests that cinema cannot really show a corpse: "'Realism' consists not only of showing us a corpse, but also of showing it to us under conditions that re-create certain physiological or mental givens of natural perception, or, more accurately, under conditions that seek equivalents for these givens." With each phrase, Bazin's sentence puts greater distance between film and corpse. If a crucial "equivalent-seeking condition," for Bazin, is shooting in depth, it is not because it will bring the corpse to our attention, but because it allows for the risk that the corpse will be missed. It is through Bazin's dialectical insistence on the cinema's power to efface and need to "discard" that historical particularity comes to color the impulse to preserve. Cinema, for Bazin, is not only an instrument of preservation, but of loss.

## Bazinian Ambiguity and the Murder Scene

"A baby cries beside its dead parents. There is a fact. How did the Germans discover that the parents were guilty? How is it that the child is still alive? That is not the film's concern."[23] *Paisan*'s restricted narration, which Bazin privileges, stands in marked contrast to the classics of Soviet montage, which clearly show the wealthy classes harming peasants and proletarians. The clarity of the montage imbues the violence with political significance and facilitates the transformation of victims into martyrs. Whereas Bazin praises narratives and images that retain ambiguity, Soviet montage manipulates images to make their meaning unambiguous. The extent to which a narrative or an image is ambiguous acquires heightened importance in scenes of killing. This is because the very act of murder inherently refuses ambiguity: murder and killing rely on a decision about the victim—a decision that the victim can be made to, deserves to, or must die. To act on such a decision requires at least a momentary suppression of doubt.

In *Paisan*, partly because of its restricted narration, political significance, if any, attaches more loosely to the violence of the story world, prompting Robert Warshow to argue that it precludes political judgment.[24] Like Rossellini's film, Bazin has come under attack for not being political enough. Keith Reader articulates the general tendency of this criticism: "Peter Pappas alleges that Bazin and Truffaut between them attempted to depoliticise Renoir's work during the Cold War years, and while this may smack of conspiracy theory there is little doubt that Bazin's general critical approach, favouring as it did the 'visual democracy' of Wellesian or Wylerian deep-focus and denigrating the coerciveness of a Kuleshov or an Eisenstein, was well in tune with the Cold War climate."[25] But Bazin specifically expresses admiration for the achievements of the Soviet montageurs. To cite one such example: "Was it not from the outset their search for realism that characterized the Russian films of Eisenstein, Pudovkin, and Dovjenko as revolutionary both in art and politics, in contrast to the expressionist aestheticism of the German films and Hollywood's mawkish star worship?"[26] Rather than seeing Bazin as "in tune with the Cold War climate," it makes more sense to situate him on the democratic left and thus not "in tune with" totalitarianism.

Bazin does not propose eradicating montage, but maintaining it as one of many effective cinematic techniques: "In the silent days, montage evoked what the director wanted to say; in the editing of 1938, it described it. Today we can say that at last the director writes in film. The image—its plastic composition and the way it is set in time, because it is founded on a much higher degree of realism—has at its disposal more means of manipulating reality and of modifying it from within."[27] Although one "means of manipulating reality" may dominate at a particular place and time, the various means do not so much displace one another as accumulate. Paradoxically, the greater the means for manipulating reality, the greater the possibilities for realism. In the same essay, Bazin critiques montage, writing that it "presupposes of its very nature the unity of meaning of the dramatic event" and "by its very nature rules out ambiguity of expression."[28] (He is harder on découpage, writing that it "insidiously substituted an intellectual and abstract time" for "the real time of things, the duration of the event.")[29] But the essay concludes with a clear acknowledgment of Soviet montage as a powerful technique, one of many means for "inflecting" and "modifying" "reality."

While at one point Bazin asserts that montage merely "alludes" to reality, with another example he declares the uses of montage for revealing the real: "Take, for example, a documentary about conjuring! If its object is to show the extraordinary feats of a great master then the film must proceed in a series of individual shots, but if the film is required subsequently to explain one of these tricks, it becomes necessary to edit them. The case is clear, so let us move on!"[30] In this example, it is the long take that is illusive, and the editing, or montage, that shows the underlying reality—how the illusion is made. Indeed, in this particular example, we might detect a conceptual affinity with Vertov's ideal of a montage that "decodes" reality by revealing underlying systems. (We may also think, here, of Vertov's conjurer in *Man with a Movie Camera*. As Yuri Tsivian has noted, Vertov does not use montage to reveal the making of the conjurer's illusion; instead, he uses it to reveal the making of the cinematic illusion, with shots of the film's editor [Eliza-veta Svilova] at work.)

Bazin may privilege depth of field as a dialectical (and technological) ad-vance beyond montage, but he ultimately describes it as a formal choice *in addition to* montage and classical continuity editing. This becomes clear in the following remarks on Hitchcock: "So far from wiping out once and for all the conquests of montage, this reborn realism gives them a body of reference and a meaning. It is only an increased realism of the image that can support the abstraction of montage. The stylistic repertory of a director such as Hitchcock, for example, ranged from the power inherent in the ba-sic document as such, to superimpositions, to large close-ups. But the close-ups of Hitchcock are . . . just one type of figure, among others, of his style."[31] Of Hitchcock's deployment of classical continuity editing Bazin writes that while "the technique of analytical cutting tends to destroy the ambiguity inherent in reality," Hitchcock "excels in suggesting the ambiguity of an event while decomposing it into a series of close-ups."[32] Clearly, what re-mains consistently important for Bazin, regardless of the "figure of style" or technique used to achieve it, is an allowance for ambiguity. Such ambi-guity can complicate political judgment, but does not necessarily exclude it. Bazin is concerned with what is inevitably lost through representational practices, all of which work to narrow the significance of the imaged world rather than allowing its full intricacy. This concern suggests a self-critical mindfulness which does not easily fit within the rightward spectrum of cold war politics, and neither is it necessarily antithetical to Marxism.

For Bazin, cinema never can adequately contain or do justice to its refer-ents. His famous either/or, "faith in reality versus faith in the image,"[33] res-onates, far more than has been acknowledged, with thought considered to be at the opposite end of the spectrum from "realism" and "humanism." Ba-zin emphasizes the ambiguity of the film image because ambiguous images advertise their incompleteness as representations. How is this so very dif-ferent from, say, Heidegger, who "makes it clear that Being cannot be con-tained by, is always prior to, indeed transcends signification"?[34] For Bazin, the filmic image, at its best, shows a consciousness of itself as partial. It is time to reconsider Bazin in relation to powerful twentieth-century critiques of "realism" and "humanism," because Bazin has been associated too sim-plistically with these categories, and, perhaps, even the categories them-selves have been oversimplified.

Bazin's claim that realism entails an "unacceptable and necessary" choice between what to keep and what to get rid of underscores the impor-tance of the murder scene, which inscribes this choice in the story world:

which persons to keep, and which to get rid of. But his film criticism more broadly suggests that this ineluctable judgment also applies to the poetics through which that world appears. Bazin repeatedly turns to moments in which films discard established convention—framings that do not follow the movement of key characters, actors who do not act, mise-en-scène that aims to effect the artificiality of the theater stage rather than the illusion of a natural world. Breaking convention draws attention to convention and, more generally, to film as a series of formal choices. These choices are indissociable from the choice of what to "preserve" and what to "discard" from the story world. Bazin's elaboration of a fluid realist aesthetic is inflected by formalism—not opposed to it. If, in the above passage, Bazin emphasizes the unacceptable and necessary choices made in the construction of any filmic illusion, many of the films he writes about also draw attention to their own formal processes, reminding us that we are watching a film to which abridgement, reduction, and exclusion are intrinsic. We come upon such surprising formal decisions in Renoir's films of the thirties, a touchstone for Bazin's historiography of film style and his theorization of cinematic realism.

## Murder Scenes in Renoir's Films of the 1930s: An Overview

Renoir's films from this period present a far more subtle contrast than *Paisan* with the films of the Soviet montageurs. As in the films of the Soviets, murders resulting from class tensions abound. Of these films, Christopher Faulkner observes, "Again and again a murder is the decisive (central) act in Renoir's films of this period: *La Chienne, Toni, Le Crime de Monsieur Lange, Les Bas-Fonds, La Grande Illusion, La Bête humaine,* and *La Règle du jeu.* And whether it is committed wittingly or not, the murder in all of these films can be considered a class action, and in most of them it is a crime of passion as well."[35] Expanding Faulkner's list to include films containing any scenes of deliberate killing, we might also add *La Nuit du carrefour* (1932) and *La Marseillaise* (1937; released 1938), bringing to a total of nine (out of fifteen) films Renoir made through the 1930s that have murder or killing at their crux. We might particularly emphasize *La Marseillaise*, which received a better reception in the Soviet Union than it did in France.[36] *La Marseillaise* features the character Bomier (Edmond Ardisson), sacrificed in the cause of the French Revolution just as Eisenstein's Vakulinchuk and Pudovkin's (and Gorky's) Pelageya Nilovna (*The Mother*) helped to pave the way to October 1917.

Renoir's stylistic realism of the thirties displays a surprising affinity for murder. And some of his films also manage to intertwine a revolutionary politics with a certain ambiguity of cinematic signification. Arguably, Renoir's most unambiguous portrayal of revolutionary violence occurs not in *La Marseillaise*, but in *The Crime of Monsieur Lange*, specifically the scene in which Batala (Jules Berry) is murdered. One formal decision that structures the scene, a pan just before the murder, has spawned decades of debate. This pan functions as a crux; it, and the critical dialogues to which it has given rise, illuminate the stakes of the intertwining of murder and realism, revolution and ambiguity.

### Case Study: Jean Renoir's *The Crime of Monsieur Lange* (1936)

In *The Crime of Monsieur Lange*, Batala, the owner of a commercial publishing house, takes advantage of a train wreck to fake his own death and thus evade his creditors. In his absence, the workers form a cooperative, jointly running the press and sharing in its profits. With this new structure of ownership and labor, the oppression that marked Batala's tenure comes to an end. Thus, Batala's return prompts one of the workers, Amédée Lange (René Lefèvre), creator of the press's most successful serial, *Arizona Jim*, to kill him. The plot begins and ends in the setting of a border tavern to which Lange and his lover Valentine (Florelle) have fled. At the beginning of the film, the tavern patrons commence listening to Lange's story (as told by Valentine while Lange rests in an adjoining room). The film then shows this story in flashback, and, in the end, returns to the tavern and its patrons, who proceed to pass judgment on Lange's action. They decide to help him safely cross the border, rather than turn him over to the police. Daniel Serceau articulates the parallels between the tavern patrons who hear Valentine's story and the film audience that experiences the flashback:

> Valentine's story becomes a cinematic image for us, the spectators, as it is a mental image for the customers in the café. Through a fictional spectacle, we become part of an exegetical story of which we are the no less fictional judges. Through the purely imaginary impression of reality, we are placed at once behind and beyond our equivalents in the café. Behind them, for we do not enjoy their (fictional) right to set free or to imprison. Beyond them, for we substitute for their mental images the real images of a (cinematic) fiction which, projected in our imagination (in the cinema, the spectator is so to speak the second projector of the film), are then experienced as real. . . . If the popular court, in the film, reviews a case, it also draws a conclusion in the form of a decision. That is its function. By freeing Lange, unknowingly a prisoner in his room, it justifies his crime and thereby the use (even if only defensive) of a violence that can politically be described as revolutionary.[37]

It takes a tavern "jury" to hear the story of, discuss, and pass judgment on the killer and his victim. The judgment is not pregiven. As we shall see, a similar moment occurs in *La Marseillaise*, when Bomier's friends discuss his death and conclude that he has not died in vain. They confer meaning on the death well after it has occurred. In both instances, there is the story, a delay, and then a judgment about the meaning of the story; the film specifically shows the process of arriving at this judgment through discussion and consensus. We can see the resonance of this pattern with Bazin's ideal of a cinema that shows before it means: first the films show us the stories of Lange and Bomier as these stories unfold, and then they show the formulation of the meaning of these stories (which takes place in the story world as well as in the discourse). This process of making meaning reflects the spectator even as it encourages the spectator to reflect. Explicit signification does not instantaneously arise from the image. The structure of the story substantiates the structure of the image, which is to show before it means.

In the scene in which Lange murders Batala, there are few cuts; the camera moves to direct our attention to persons and their movements. Batala, for instance, enters the setting, the circular courtyard where he is shortly to be murdered, in the middle of a pan that has been following the drunken concierge of the building that houses the cooperative (Marcel Lévesque). The concierge's arcing trajectory intersects with Batala's exit from the building, in long shot, into the courtyard. Shortly after, Valentine enters the courtyard and the camera moves to frame her and Batala in a medium shot. Batala pulls her off to the side, and the camera moves in even closer and cuts to a medium close-up of the two, directing our attention to Batala's attempt to seduce an unwilling Valentine (now romantically involved with Lange). From this medium close-up, the camera cranes up to the first-floor window and then pans left to follow Lange as he moves through the building and down the stairs. The film cuts to a medium close-up of Lange as he enters the courtyard, punctuating the start of the murder scene (fig. 103). At this point, rather than frame any character, the camera leaves Lange to pan counterclockwise around the empty side of the courtyard (fig. 104). This unusual pan ends in a reverse shot of the initial medium close-up of Lange: a medium close-up of Valentine and Batala looking at Lange as he, unlike the camera, walks straight toward them (and eventually into the frame; fig. 105). We hear, rather than see, Lange firing his pistol, and Batala falls out of the frame, leaving Lange and Valentine. They, too, leave the frame.

Bazin writes of the pan around the empty part of the courtyard: "This surprising camera movement, seemingly contrary to all logic, may have secondary justifications, psychological or dramatic (it gives an impression of

103

104

105

giddiness and insanity, it creates suspense), but its real reason is more fundamental: it is the pure spatial expression of the whole *mise-en-scène*."[38] Bazin draws attention to the formal importance of this pan, which displaces more conventional options, such as a shot-reverse-shot confrontation between killer and victim, or a wider framing that simultaneously features both men in long shot. Prior to Bazin, this pan was taken for "bungling." Bazin, for instance, sets his own shrewd analysis in contrast with Roger Leenhardt's criticism of the film: "The directing, along with some flashes of genius, includes some typical Renoir bungling. Oh, those zigzag tracking-shots! Are they a mistake or due to shortage of money?"[39] Leenhardt's complaint suggests that the pan deviates sufficiently from filmic convention to draw attention to itself. Moreover, in the very negative way in which he views such a "zigzagging" shot, Leenhardt points to something central to this particular representation of a murder, and to the representation of murder more generally, which Bazin misses in his eagerness to wed form to meaning. Except in the case of switchbacks leading up and down the side of a mountain, the nature of a zigzag is inefficiency, redundancy. Rather than taking the shortest distance between two points—say, the point where the killer stands and the point where the victim faces him—the zigzag, or here, the arcing pan, covers "unnecessary" ground. After all, the space of the courtyard has already been established.

Bazin brushes past his initial observation that the pan is "seemingly contrary to all logic." He justifies it as "the pure spatial expression of the whole *mise-en-scène*," which is structured within and around the circular courtyard of the cooperative, with its concentric paving stones. Building on Bazin's observation of the pan's formal or aesthetic rhyme with the set, Keith Reader also finds a rhyme with the circular structure of the narrative, which begins and ends at the border tavern. In tracing the history of the film's criticism, Reader emphasizes the importance of Serceau's post–May 1968 interpretation of the pan as a rhetorical justification of Lange's violence. Serceau writes: "Lange's trajectory, the camera's movement of 360°, the concentric paving of the courtyard, the whole *mise-en-scène* participates in a circular movement. Renoir thereby gathers the entire cooperative in the field of his camera, the volume of his shot, and the trajectory of his character. The meaning is obvious. Lange acts to save the cooperative, in its name and for it, to preserve its existence and its continuity. In this the film is endowed with a construction perfectly internally consistent."[40] But the history of the criticism shows that the meaning was not always so obvious. Indeed, at least three major film critics—Leenhardt, Raymond Durgnat, and Bazin—interpret the pan differently. Leenhardt criticized the pan as distracting and pointless. And while Bazin saw in the pan a formal significance, he did not explicitly make Serceau's interpretive leap.[41] Finally, what Bazin saw as secondary motivations for the pan, Raymond Durgnat understood as primary: "As so often I would offer an alternative perspective to Bazin's, whereby the 'secondary justifications' are primary and the three-fold repetition of the effect constitutes a climactic progression from routine through love to revolt. It also evokes an inner reality, a flowing, capsizing, giddy world—Lange catching for a moment at the ultra-reality of instability, of freedom."[42] In Durgnat's interpretation—which, unlike most other criticism of the scene, emphasizes Lange as an individual rather than as an agent of a collective—the pan functions not, primarily, to justify the murder, but to express Lange's subjectivity.

Despite the many alternative interpretations that appear in the critical literature, Serceau's close analysis of the pan is compelling; its attraction lies in the way it connects the film's form (on multiple levels: plot, camera movement, and mise-en-scène), with the role of the spectator and the political context in which the film was made. Reader writes:

> Serceau's formulation (like the subtitle of his chapter, "The collectivization of murder") returns to the fundamental political question posed in the title of *The Crime of Monsieur Lange* and answered in its form and its narrative

alike. The all-embracing circularity of community evoked by the 360 degree pan, as by the circular narrative structure, can be preserved only by its partial destruction—by the annihilation of the menacing intruder and the resultant extrusion of Lange and Valentine. *Lange's "crime" is then not a crime at all, but—until the improvised solidarity of the bar-room court becomes universal—he will have to live in the knowledge that that is how it is likely to be treated.* Going beyond Bazin's ontological formalism, Serceau reminds us that Lange not only poses ethical and political questions, but gives unequivocally committed answers to them.[43]

Reader's remark that "Lange's 'crime' is then not a crime at all, but—until the improvised solidarity of the bar-room court becomes universal—he will have to live in the knowledge that that is how it is likely to be treated" resonates with the depiction of class violence we see in Soviet films. In these films, killing is impersonal and political. The individual killed stands for a group; the filmic discourse aims to discard particularities. But it is precisely this tendency that can also transform "the collectivization of murder" into the murder of a collective. Reader gives a one-sided interpretation of the film's title. As he indicates, the title is ironic; it suggests that Lange's crime is also not a crime even though it retains a taint of criminality. To interpret this persistent tinge of criminality solely as a symptom of a lack of social solidarity is reductive. It fails to account, as we shall see, for Batala's intricate characterization. And it fails to account for the full complexity of the unusual pan, which raises the question of its own reliability as discourse, precisely as it signals that Lange is killing for the good of the community.

Serceau and Reader, like Bazin, interpret the "zigzagging" of Renoir's camera; they do not, like Leenhardt, dismiss it as "bungling." But rather than write off Leenhardt's analysis as paying insufficient attention to the signifying power of this formal choice, let us ask what we can learn from the feeling the shot produced in him. We do not need that circling pan to explain and justify Lange's killing of Batala. The plot cues us to sympathize with Lange's motives by killing Batala twice, first, only apparently, by train wreck, and then, for real, by murder. Even before his faked death, we see how Batala nearly ruins the lives of two young lovers, the laundress Estelle (Nadia Sibirskaia) and the concierge's son Charles (Maurice Baquet). He rapes and impregnates Estelle and boards up Charles's window when Charles is bedridden, effectively preventing the two from seeing one another. After the train wreck, we see how Batala's "death" benefits an entire community. Those impoverished by Batala's greed enjoy, in his absence, the fruits of their labor.

The first time Batala is "killed," there is a pan that rhymes with the pan in the scene of his second, real death at the hands of Lange. From a shot of train tracks, a wipe shaped like a star exploding from the center of the screen opens onto a man and a radio. The camera reframes on man and radio in a signature Renoir shot, which places us outside a window at night, looking in on a well-lighted room. We see this in Renoir's earlier film *La Chienne*, in the scene in which Maurice Legrand (Michel Simon) discovers his mistress, Lucienne Pelletier (Janie Marèse), in bed with her pimp, André Govain (Georges Flamant). Gilberto Perez writes of this framing in *La Chienne*: "No mere stylistic flourish, this camera technique serves to refer the inside to the outside—the drama coming to a head inside that bedroom to the material circumstances that have governed it, the emotions stirring inside the characters to the social existence that has shaped their consciousness. The personal in a Renoir film of the thirties is always seen to be a function of the social. Whatever takes place inside—inside a room, inside a person's mind, inside the frame of a film image—takes place in relation to the world outside."[44] Following Perez, we might say that in the *Lange* scene, the pan ties together Batala's (seeming) death and the larger community: once outside the window, the camera pans left (or counterclockwise, as it does in the murder scene) along the face of the co-op building. It pauses on another lighted window through which we see Valentine and Lange together in bed as they hear the radio announcement of Batala's demise. Lange, still ignorant of Batala's duplicities in running the press, reacts with surprise and dismay at the news, but Valentine's more knowing response is muted. They turn out the light and the camera leaves their window to pan right, returning, after a cut, to a close-up of the radio. The next day, the community evoked by this pan begins to realize the extent to which Batala cheated them.

Batala's faked death demonstrates that the community is better off without him. Even Batala sees how the cooperative has thrived in his absence and tells Lange, just before the murder, that Lange should kill him. Viewing the scene of his second death, the real one, we might conclude that while the zigzagging of the camera may indeed have its motivations, it remains a somewhat redundant gesture if its main point is to demonstrate, rhetorically, that the good of the community justifies the murder. We can describe what happens in the murder scene as a shifting of the dominant from one register, that of the story with its characters and sequence of actions, to another—camera movement or the inscription of space, which draws attention from the story world to the circumscribing discourse. In this crucial scene, the camera does not follow the character; it opposes the convention that character movement dictate camera movement. The pan thus draws attention to itself as a pure and, for some viewers, unmotivated movement of the frame.

In addition to making Batala die twice in the plot so that we can see the desirability of his absence, the film prolongs the scene of his real death. The famed pan culminating in Lange's gunshot is soon followed by another pan, which begins with the drunken concierge, who has stumbled upon the dying man. Batala, dressed, ironically, as a priest (the disguise that enabled him to fake his death), asks the concierge to call for a real priest, prompting the concierge to circle the courtyard, interrupting a kiss between Charles and Estelle, with his cries of "Un prêtre!" This interruption of a kiss serves as yet another reminder of the way Batala kept these lovers miserable and apart. From the interrupted kiss, the camera circles back to Batala, who has now become a corpse. This corpse is then superimposed on the road (along which, presumably, Valentine and Lange flee) and only gradually fades. We might interpret this superimposition of Batala's corpse as another, redundant, rhetorical justification for the murder. The image of the corpse blends with the image of the road, making it a metaphorical paving stone on the way toward progressive social justice.

Might the murder scene's rhetorical flourish, the pan, betray concern about shoring up the film's justification of this killing? Instead of the shortest distance between two points—the 180-degree line that structures a reverse shot, for instance—Renoir's camera traces a zigzag, as if arriving at a proper understanding of Lange's violence involves such a steep learning curve that we need a switchback to take us there. Christopher Faulkner claims that the pan is not redundant, but necessary in order to "locate the 'subject' of the film elsewhere than with the consciousness (or psychology) of the character." He values it as "a formal breach of the text's predominant illusionist practice."[45] Where Durgnat sees in the pan an expression of Lange's "giddiness," Faulkner sees the opposite: a downplaying of Lange's subjective experience. For Faulkner, the pan is what makes the scene a political proposition rather than a psychological drama.

But Faulkner's characterization of the film as otherwise "illusionist" and lacking in desubjectivized shots is erroneous. As Serceau suggests with his observation that the tavern crowd mirrors the spectator, the film is reflexive rather than illusionist. The film's reflexivity has many facets. The publishing house, like a film studio, produces narratives for mass consumption (and profit). Indeed, the courtyard of the storied publishing house *is* the courtyard of the Billancourt studios where the film was made. According to Bazin, even the atmosphere on the set mirrored the atmosphere of the storied cooperative: "What is striking about the way the film is acted is the fact that to a certain extent it was made for the pleasure of those who were working on it as much as for the appreciation of the public. . . . *The Crime of Monsieur Lange* was made for the pleasure of all, from the director to the stagehands, and particularly for the actors."[46] Jean Castanier, who wrote the story on which the film is based, supports Bazin's claim: "On the team which we formed with Renoir, no one had an idea solely to himself. We worked with a community spirit. The essential thing was to make a film that interested us, to make it together; it mattered little who signed it. And if ever a film was the collective effort of a team it was that one."[47]

In addition to the film's profound reflexivity, there are many desubjectivized shots. Indeed, the film features relatively few point-of-view shots, including shot-reverse-shot sequences. Most conversations take place with both interlocutors in the frame.[48] A few notable exceptions to this tendency include the introductory sequence at the border tavern and the conversation between Batala and Lange when Batala returns from "the dead." Also, in its character-system, the film works to emphasize a collective rather than individual protagonist.[49] One strategy by which it does this is through its focus on couples—Lange *and* Valentine, Estelle *and* Charles. The title character shares his centrality. Faulkner himself observes how the film associates women with labor and hence with the collective: "Batala's abuses against women are consonant with his abuses of capital and labour."[50] His observation implies that characters such as Estelle and Batala's secretary Edith (Sylvie Bataille) stand for a collective that suffers injustice. Thus, while Faulkner claims that the pan is necessary for de-emphasizing Lange's individual subjectivity in the murder scene, the entire film tends, often impersonally, to stress the social whole. And other techniques could serve as well to de-emphasize character subjectivity in the murder scene. The murder could be shown, for instance, in long shot from the side, with both men in the frame. The discourse does not *need* the pan.

*

The actors' performances signal the complexity of the murder: after shooting Batala, Lange remarks that killing him was easy, but his posture—he grasps a post as if to hold himself up—suggests otherwise. The characterization of Batala makes his murder at once justified *and* regrettable. Jules Berry's more stylized gestures and movement stand out from the other, relatively understated performances. Bazin points this out when he describes Berry as "the super-actor whose very incongruity with the rest of the group served both Renoir's desires and the sense of the movie."[51] Of Berry's performance, he writes: "Berry's is a sublime creation of villainy, which for all its brilliance does not move us to hate him, so removed is that violent emotion from Renoir's work."[52] Berry is certainly not the fat stereotypical capitalist of Eisenstein's *Strike* or the deceitful bespectacled doctor or cruel priest of *The Battleship Potemkin*. Faulkner's description of Berry's acting corresponds to Bazin's claim that the performance does not give rise to "violent emotion": "The film is very funny (Jules Berry's stuttering, gestural performance not least of all)."[53] And Goffredo Fofi writes, "Jules Berry's incomparable Batala . . . is so brilliant that he provokes a certain sympathy for the 'baddies' which was typical of the revolutionary literature in that period and which plays quite an important role in creating Renoir's carousel atmosphere. In the end it is a shame that he has to be eliminated."[54] Similarly, Alexander Sesonske writes, "if his heart is black, Batala's exterior designedly conceals it. He moves with grace, seems single-mindedly attentive to each person he approaches, talking with a vivacity and charm that both flatter and disarm his hearers. Yet, not always insincerely, for he is his own most appreciative and convinced audience."[55]

Bazin's assessment of Berry's performance—it "does not move us to hate"—raises an interesting point: how can a film simultaneously provide narrative and rhetorical justification for a homicide and at the same time be devoid of violent emotion? The film does not, like so many Hollywood Westerns, lead us to desire, unquestioningly, the death of the bad guy at the hands of the heroic gunslinger. Indeed, Lange's identification with his fictional creation Arizona Jim reflexively raises the question of such movie murder scenes. Killing represented naively as the simple justice of a Western gunfighter appears, as in a palimpsest, with killing represented as a problematic political solution. The circling pan encompasses these very different nuances of the represented killing. But what encompasses the encompasser? The pan, as it exceeds the discursive labor necessary for expressing the story of a justified murder, draws attention to itself and, in doing so, implies an outside that lies beyond its circle and the story world it encloses.

The famed pan is overdetermined. My own "pan" of interpretations of the camera movement shows that for many critics, the device rhetorically justifies the murder. But it also casts into question the very grounds of this justification by calling attention to its own discursive delimiting. Just as the pan encircles the circular mise-en-scène, it is in turn encircled. The world represented within its circumference—indeed, the circumference itself— reveals itself as arbitrarily demarcated or cut out from a space perhaps less tidily circular. The discourse thus becomes excessive in its justification of Batala's murder precisely as it reveals its own partiality and consequent unreliability. Revolutionary violence is justified as staged within this circle, but justified provisionally. To say that the rhetoric of the film justifies Batala's murder purely and simply is to miss the film's complexity—and the complexity of the history of the film's criticism. But to argue that *Lange* does *not* provide compelling justification for the murder of Batala, or even, more broadly, for revolutionary violence, would be sheer nonsense.

The *Crime of Monsieur Lange* presents its justification of the murder self-consciously—as a staging, and without the illusion of direct reference. It weds a formal excess (ruled, above all, by the process of circling) to a particular content—a murder, on the threshold of being justified. The dialectics of this represented encircling, which fails to contain its own most striking encirclement, emerge such that the moment of rhetorical excess—the arcing pan—equals the moment of rhetorical collapse. But collapse occurs not only from the pressure of an outside on the encircling form, but from an emptiness within as pertains to "content." The murder of Batala is an allegory for revolutionary violence, and allegory "means precisely the nonexistence of what it (re)presents."⁵⁶ While Eisenstein and Pudovkin make fictional films about a revolution that *has*, historically, occurred, *Lange* allegorizes a revolution to which the French Popular Front never gave rise. These very different historical and social conditions are, perhaps, not unrelated to the way that Renoir's films are more tentative than Eisenstein's, allowing for less political Manichaeism in their characterizations.

Formal choices like the pan in *Lange* receive much attention in Bazin's writing. In his theoretical historiography, such choices as moving the camera and focusing in depth take the cinema to a new level of aesthetic realism. While more recent historical research and formal analysis have pointed to weaknesses in this historiography, it is the larger ground of realism, so central to Bazin's thought, that gives us a context to encompass Renoir's own most extravagantly represented—and representing—act of encompassing. Collapsing the overall interpretation of *Lange* to focus on this one murder scene with its discursive overload allows for a concentrated reconsideration of the very concept of realism, bringing it much closer to twentieth-century modernism and its tentative significations. The pan, in pointing toward an unknown outside that is beyond its circling sweep, undermines the implication of the camera eye's centrality. The camera draws an arbitrary circle; it not only inscribes, but also circumscribes revolution.

## The Rules of the Game (1939)

In *The Rules of the Game*, French aviator André Jurieux (Roland Toutain) publicly announces his infatuation with a married marquise (Nora Grégor). This social misstep produces the disequilibrium that propels the plot until it is forcibly resolved through Jurieux's death. A mutual friend of the marquise and Jurieux, Octave (Jean Renoir), brings the opposed parties together for a reconciliation; instead, he unwittingly engineers a murder. The murder is also an accident. It is not the marquis, Robert de la Cheyniest (Dalio), who shoots his rival, but the marquis's game warden, Shumacher (Gaston Modot), who mistakes the marquise for his flirtatious wife, Lisette (Paulette Dubost), and the aviator for the genially lecherous Octave.

The Crime of Monsieur Lange and The Rules of the Game frame Renoir's Popular Front years: we begin with the murder of Batala, consciously undertaken for the political and economic good of the community; we end with the murder of André Jurieux, conveniently dismissed as accident and misfortune, thus obscuring the fact that it reinforces the privilege of the *haute bourgeoisie*. The murder of Batala liberates the women he treats as property; the murder of Jurieux cements a wife's status as the property of her husband. Lange self-consciously kills for a more just economic and social order; the marquis unselfconsciously reaps personal benefits from a murder committed by one of his servants (who confuses the class identity of his victim). The sweeping pan of the collective's courtyard, preceding Batala's murder, has its negative counterpart in a short pan of de la Cheyniest's property (hothouse, woods) preceding the shooting of Jurieux. Each murder has its reasons.

With Renoir's decision to play Octave, the scenario seems to accent the presence of the historical author in the story world of the film. When Octave asks the marquis to invite Jurieux to his estate La Colinière, thus assembling the fatal cast of characters, the marquis calls him "a dangerous poet." And it is Renoir/Octave, an amalgam of author and character, bridging discourse and story, who is arguably most responsible for Jurieux's death. In the story world this death allows the marquis to keep his wife while maintaining the spectacle of propriety. On the level of the discourse, it creates the spectacle of resolution and narrative unity: Jurieux creates disequilibrium with his injudicious public remarks; his death resolves it. But the problems repressed in order to produce the spectacle—the unacceptable criminality of Jurieux's death and the impossibility of a satisfactory resolution—persist. In the story world, we see the marquise and her niece Jackie (Anne Mayen) hide their feelings as they return to the chateau after the shooting. The discourse undercuts its resolution with irony.

Through this irony, The Rules of the Game questions the very convention of narrative resolution. On the level of the story we may well ask, as Robin Wood does, "Why must Christine choose?"[57] And when she hesitates to choose, why is choice forcibly taken from her? Why does narrative form demand a return to an equilibrium that is really the continuation of an unjust social status quo? And why is the killing of a character so often the cost of this return?

The Rules of the Game disappeared from screens soon after its release and did not resurface until after the war. Watching the film through the prism of this subsequent war, many critics have interpreted the hunting scene as a sign of the latent, or not so latent, violence of Europe between the wars.[58] This entails seeing the animals as potentially interchangeable with people, just as Eisenstein's slaughtered bull functioned as a metaphor for the massacred strikers. But Renoir's shots of the animals, and their arrangement within this film, do not necessarily encourage us to make that bridge. In contrast to the sequence shots and ensemble acting of the other scenes, the hunted animals appear isolated in shots by themselves, innocent, terrified, and doomed. With the possible exceptions of Christine and Jackie, no such innocence belongs to the human animals in the film. They are creatures who have adapted well to a social system that Renoir called "rotten to the core."[59] Even in Georges Franju's The Blood of Beasts (1950; ostensibly a documentary on Parisian slaughterhouses, but difficult not to watch without thinking of the camps that had so recently preceded it), the butchers and the animals at least share a common bodily vulnerability and both face inescapable, albeit different, fates. In The Rules of the Game, it is impossible to see any connection between the film's hunted animals and its human ones. Only Christine and Octave expose any serious vulnerability. The real shooting of a rabbit appears far more disturbing than the staged, almost perfunctory murder of Jurieux. With all due regard for Bazin's claim that sequence shots and depth of field represent, against montage, an advance in realist aesthetics, here it is the formally incongruous *montage* of animals that bears a startling realism in contrast to the surrounding scenes. Eisenstein was right: footage of the actual killing of a bull has referential power unmatched by the fictional death of a person. But unlike Eisenstein, Renoir does not harness this power for his characters; he lets it stand in stark contrast to them. Next to the terrified animals, the people, in story as in discourse, appear strangely trivial.

By preceding the murder of Jurieux with the much more compelling hunting scene; leaving Jurieux's charcterization sketchy, even shallow;[60] and making it clear that his death resolves nothing—even though the general (Pierre Magnier) accepts the pretence that it does: "La Cheyniest has a touch of class"—Renoir deflates the "climactic" murder scene. It is not an instance of what McKinney would call "strong violence," and Jurieux, as a character, gains little or nothing by being killed. Instead, Renoir's treatment of this

murder places in relief the conventionality—and suspect convenience—
of so many narrative resolutions that rely on the killing of a troublesome
character to restore a temporary peace and forestall meaningful systemic
change. If, for Bazin, creating a believable story world entails unacceptable and necessary exclusions, the murder scenes in films like *Lange* and *The
Rules of the Game* make such exclusion visible.

## A Montage of Distractions: *La Chienne* (1931), *Toni* (1935), *La Bête humaine* (1938), and *La Marseillaise* (1938)

The formal distinctions Bazin makes between the cinemas of directors like
Renoir, who "put their faith in reality," and German Expressionism or Soviet montage, where directorial faith resides "in the image," are not so tidy.
The murder scenes in early films such as *La Chienne* and *Toni* make use of
the same kinds of shots given as examples in Soviet montage theory: *La Chienne's* murder scene features two close-ups of the weapon, a paper knife
with which the victim cuts open the pages of a novel (fig. 106). When Josefa
(Cecilia Montalvan) kills her husband Albert (Max Dalban) in *Toni*, a high-
angle medium shot momentarily excludes the action to focus on the murder weapon, center frame (fig. 107). Once Josefa has the weapon in hand, the
film cuts from a close-up of Albert, his face registering alarm, to a medium
shot, which tracks into a close-up of Josefa, enraged (figs. 108–9). This shot
breakdown is not dissimilar to Eisenstein's description of a murder scene in
his 1924 essay "The Montage of Film Attractions": "a throat is gripped, eyes
bulge, a knife is brandished, the victim closes his eyes, blood is spattered
on a wall, the victim falls to the floor, a hand wipes off the knife—each fragment is chosen to 'provoke' associations."[61] Renoir's fragmentation of the
mise-en-scène continues in the aftermath of the murder. The title character Toni (Charles Blavette) and Josefa's lover Gabi (Andrex) hear the shot and
enter the house. The camera cuts from them looking through the doorway
to a medium shot of Josefa; it pans down her body to the pistol held at her
side and further, to Albert at her feet (fig. 110). Although Renoir uses camera movement rather than cutting, the camera's movements work to break
down the mise-en-scène into its signifying elements: the glance of the murderer, then the weapon, then the corpse. A few shots later, this pan is repeated in the reverse direction: from a high-angle medium shot of Albert's
body, the camera pans up to the gun held at the side, and then to a medium
shot of the person holding the gun—now Toni (figs. 111–12). This tight framing results in very explicit signification: although Josefa killed Albert, Toni
will be the one caught holding the gun.

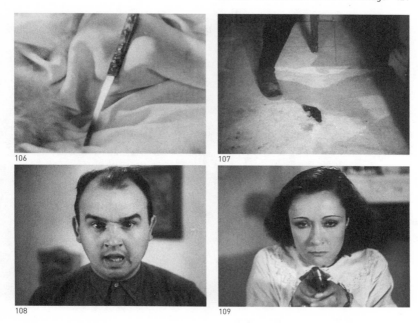

106

107

108

109

Even in *La Grande Illusion*, we find a symbolic close-up after a medium shot of the gloved hand of Captain Von Rauffenstein (Erich von Stroheim) shutting the dead eyes of Captain de Boeldieu (Pierre Fresnay), whom he has killed (fig. 113). The film cuts to a medium long shot of a window in the same room, Von Rauffenstein enters the frame, and the camera tracks in to a close-up of his hand snipping the flower off of a geranium (fig. 114). We arrive at this close-up via a tracking shot rather than scissors, but the breakdown of the scene into one small signifying element is the same. In these films of Renoir, then, we have close-ups of the face, the murder weapon, and the symbol, which correspond to numerous descriptions of the functioning of montage. Likewise, the images of Eisenstein, Pudovkin, and Kuleshov often feature depth of field. The scene of Vakulinchuk's funeral, for instance, includes plenty of long shots and extreme long shots.

Let us compare the scene showing the mourning of Vakulinchuk with the scene of Toni's death. *Toni* begins with a group of persons arriving by train in a town near a quarry where they hope to find work. A series of group scenes works to situate the protagonist, Toni, as one of *many* migrant laborers who sought work in post–World War I France from the early 1920s until the rise of fascism. The plot is complex and leisurely, interweaving the stories of several characters. Toni boards with a woman named Marie (Jenny Hélia),

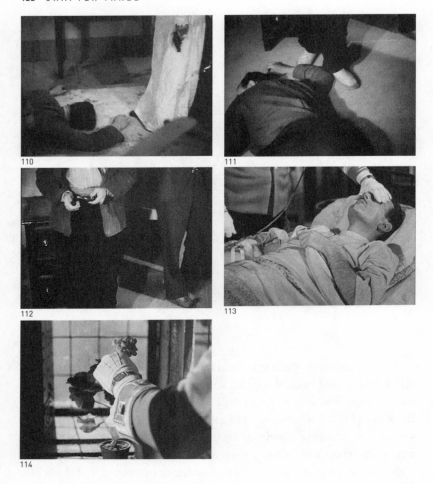

the two begin an affair, and Toni gets work in the quarry. Despite Marie, Toni falls in love with a local farmer's daughter, Josefa. He wants to break up with Marie, but the manager at the quarry where he works, Albert, rapes Josefa and marries her, not because he loves her, but because he wants to acquire her father's property. Albert is not a southern European immigrant like Toni and his friends; he is Belgian. Sesonske writes that he "seems less simple than the rest; at least he believes this and treats the others with condescension."[62] Albert abuses Josefa and Josefa takes a lover, Gabi (Andrex). Toni, who still loves Josefa, learns from Gabi that Josefa plans to steal Albert's money and flee. He chastises Gabi for permitting Josefa to take such a risk, and the two hasten to Josefa's farm only to find that she has killed Albert. Toni offers to make it look as though Albert committed suicide, but, in the process, he is caught, and, rather than accuse Josefa (who turns herself in to save him), he tries to run and is shot dead.

Toni's death is shown mostly in long shot and extreme long shot. The shifting frame captures people engaged in other affairs and oblivious to Toni's demise. Renoir sets the scene, appropriately, at a point of departures and arrivals, the rail bridge Toni first crossed to make his home in the town three years before (fig. 115). A medium shot shows the killer fire, and in long shot we see Toni fall (fig. 116). Rather than immediately cut in to the wounded protagonist, the film cuts back to an extreme long shot of him clutching at his abdomen while his friend Fernand (Édouard Delmont) rushes into the foreground of the frame and runs to him (fig. 117). From this extreme long shot of Toni, we cut to a medium close-up of him and Fernand together (fig. 118). This is the only shot that closely frames the dying hero. The film cuts to a low-angle shot of the two men, who appear almost in silhouette against the sky. Then, from the opposite side of the tracks, we see Fernand in a long shot as he supports Toni's dying body. A train passes, obstructing our view of them (fig. 119). Through its flitting wheels, we glimpse Fernand laying Toni's corpse on the ground. Once the train has passed, we leave Toni behind and cut to the train as it pulls into the station (fig. 120). New migrant workers and their families disembark (fig. 121). From this scene of disembarking workers, one of whom, we may surmise, will replace Toni at the quarry, we cut back to a long shot of men standing around, and partially blocking our view of, the fallen protagonist (fig. 122). The film cuts back to a low-angle, extreme long shot of this crowd of men at the top of the rail bridge (fig. 123). Below, at camera level, the newcomers who have disembarked from the train file through the frame, and the camera turns away from the death of Toni to follow them (fig. 124). One last time the camera returns, not to Toni, but to his grieving friend: a low-angle medium shot shows Fernand looking down at the corpse (fig. 125). But immediately we cut back to a straight-on shot of the new workers (fig. 126), while, on the sound track, we hear one of them sing the same song Toni sang when he arrived in town, looking for work.

What distinguishes Toni's death from that of Eisenstein's Vakulinchuk is not shot scale, but, rather, the *distraction* Renoir includes in the frame— the arrival of still more migrant workers who have nothing to do with the drama that has just taken place. These new arrivals effectively render Toni's death meaningless from any progressive standpoint within the story world. Toni's death does not make a difference to this society. Indeed, the immediate cause of his death appears to arise out of his personal relationships. These relationships may be structured by tensions between northern European "management" (Albert) and southern European migrant labor, but

115

116

117

118

119

120

121

122

123

124

125

126

Toni's death changes none of this. In the larger social world, he is a wage laborer replaced by other wage laborers. There is no sign of visible progress, nothing to give his death general significance. Toni's death causes only private grief for Fernand, Marie, and Josefa. Just as the panning camera in *Lange* points to an outside beyond the film's particular staged circle, the crowding of the frame with action unrelated to Toni's death implies the absence of a central point of reference.

Toni's violent death, the result of a mistake, starkly contrasts with Vakulinchuk's martyrdom, represented as historically necessary and significant. In *The Battleship Potemkin*, the crowd converges on the dead; in *Toni*, they blindly rush past the dying. Perez writes that Eisenstein's innovations differ from Renoir's in that Eisenstein makes cinematic space "rhetorical," whereas Renoir makes it "social."[63] But if Eisenstein develops a cinematic rhetoric, it is with an aim similar to that which Perez attributes to Renoir: to get people to see the operation of larger social forces. Is Renoir less successful than Eisenstein in achieving this aim? After all, it is hard to miss the point of an Eisenstein film, whereas the political "content" of Renoir's films historically has been a matter of contention. Renoir's ambiguity does not have to do with framing in itself, but instead resides in the way he maintains, often through framing, a separation between character as particular individual (e.g., Toni as hero of his own private tragedy) and character as social type (Toni as generalized migrant worker). Let us examine more closely how Renoir maintains this separation.

At *Toni*'s end, the migrant workers, of which the hero once formed a part, obscure him. In literally blocking our view of his death, these newly arrived workers and their families demonstrate that many other lives, and deaths, could be shown, again underscoring the absence of a central point of reference. At the same time, the distraction might be said to heighten our attention to Toni through frustrating it. Obscured by the workers who will take his place, Toni appears *irreplaceable*, as Fernand's reaction shots suggest. Formally, the killing of Toni compares to the murder of Lucienne in *La Chienne*, the death of Bomier in *La Marseillaise*, and the murder of Severine (Simone Simon) by Jacques Lantier (Jean Gabin) in *La Bête humaine*. In *Toni*, the wide, inclusive framings, the cut to the arriving train, and the way the camera moves to follow the disembarking crowd serve to distract attention from the protagonist's death. In *La Chienne*, the camera moves out of the room and pans down to the crowd in the street rather than show Maurice Legrand in the act of murdering his mistress Lucienne Pelletier. In *La Marseillaise*, the camera repeatedly pans away from the revolutionary soldier Bomier, dying of a bullet wound, to look through an archway at the revolutionary struggle taking place in the street. And in *La Bête humaine*, the film leaves the scene of Lantier's murder of Severine to return to the dance hall. When it finally returns to the scene of the murder, the dance hall music remains just as loud on the sound track, creating an auditory-visual collage or "collision" of dance hall and murder scene.

Perez's observation that Renoir's moving camera serves to connect the inside and the outside, or the individual and the social, has importance precisely because such connections have not always received sufficient critical recognition. Indeed, the history of Renoir criticism suggests that Renoir's expressions of these connections between the individual and the social are not as rhetorically explicit as they might be. Renoir's films express not merely the connections between particular and general, but their agonistic collisions, the way that the one threatens to obscure the many, and the many the one. Perez makes a strong case that the political meaning *is* there to be read, but the real originality of his analysis of Renoir lies in the way he reclaims the filmmaker as a modernist, freeing him from simplistic notions of humanism and realism that have tenaciously clung to Renoir, as they have to Bazin. Perez compares Renoir to Brecht:

Brecht has been much discussed in connection with films but seldom in connection with Renoir. Yet the playwright famous for his alienation effect and the filmmaker celebrated for his humane sympathy (aside from the fact that they were friends) shared important artistic concerns. In their work they both endeavored, each in his own medium and with his own outlook, toward what Brecht called "complex seeing": not a single focus but a multiplicity of perspectives that invites from the audience active reflection rather than mere acquiescence. Mixing modes, shifting representational gears, bringing together what isn't supposed to go together, served both Brecht and Renoir as a principal means to complex seeing.[64]

Note that the phrases "multiplicity of perspectives," "mixing modes," and "bringing together what isn't supposed to go together" could also describe Soviet montage. But Brecht's concept of a "complex seeing," which Perez extends to Renoir, acquires a specificity in Renoir's films of the thirties, precisely around scenes of killing. In these scenes, Renoir always makes us aware that much remains out of frame, offstage, or unseen by people in the story world, by the camera, and by the film viewer. Complex seeing entails seeing that one does not see.

*

Critics have long pointed to different ways in which Eisenstein's montage undoes signification in the very process of producing it. Here we might include Roland Barthes's essay "The Third Meaning: Research Notes on Some Eisenstein Stills," Kristin Thompson's identification of sites of "excess" in *Ivan the Terrible, Parts I and II*, and Anne Nesbet's demonstration of how Eisenstein perpetually delinks image from concept even as he aims to channel images into concepts. Perhaps criticism dialectically, or defensively, seeks the undoing of signification in Eisenstein's films precisely because it would otherwise suffocate under the weight of such heavily laded political meaning. *Potemkin's* petite doctor with his fussy, "effete" mannerisms lacks the honest, "virile" brawn of the working-class sailors; he can only get away with telling them a bald-faced, bullying lie about the rotten meat they must eat because he has the power of the state to back him up. Likewise, the ship's hypocritical and cowardly priest beats his crucifix into his palm as if it were a hatchet; he wants to see good men hang. Of Renoir's characterizations, Perez writes, "Renoir doesn't moralize, doesn't put the blame on individuals—not because he loves them too much, but because he sees the social picture that blaming them would obscure, because he tells the social story that determines their stories."[65]

In contrast to Eisenstein's characters, Renoir's tend to chafe under the constraints of the social categories in which they find themselves. In *La Chienne*, these constraints prove fatal. *La Chienne* tells the story of Maurice Legrand, a middle-aged petit bourgeois who steals money from his wife and employer to support his mistress. He works as an office clerk but fancies himself a Bohemian artist and a munificent lover. His fantasies collapse when he realizes that his mistress, Lucienne, despises him and loves her pimp boyfriend, André (Dédé) Govain, from whom Legrand thought he had rescued Lucienne. (He first discovered her in a street, where André was beating her.) The film's structure pointedly compares Legrand to the petty criminal André. This comparison emphasizes their shared exploitation of Lucienne as a commodity rather than a person: Legrand buys; André sells. More subtly, it demonstrates how their respective social positions determine how each is judged: the petit bourgeois thief and murderer goes free while the pimp and petty thief, although no murderer, is condemned to death. A clerk, a prostitute, and a minor criminal, these characters bear the connotations of the social roles they inhabit, but they also suffer from the limitations their roles impose. In suffering the constraint of the category, they transcend it. André, for instance, gains in complexity and ambiguity as it becomes clear that the state will execute him for a crime he did not commit.

After Legrand murders Lucienne, the camera remains in the street to show the discovery of the murder. Legrand leaves the building unnoticed just as André, showing off his new car (purchased through Legrand's gifts to Lucienne), self-importantly disrupts the crowd that has gathered around a violinist, pulling right into their midst. He orders them to get out of his way, parks, and goes inside. Lucienne's concierge (Jane Pierson) criticizes him. Soon after, André exits the building, visibly shaken, gets in his car, and drives off as the violinist finishes one song and begins another. The camera remains in the street while the concierge goes upstairs and screams from Lucienne's window. The film thus shows us how the unseen guilty lover will be exonerated, and the flamboyant but "innocent" pimp accused. Through the camera's relative immobility in the street, we see how André is subject to bad timing.

From being subject to bad timing, he goes to being subject to time, as he awaits interrogation, then the jury verdict, and finally execution. From a close-up of André awaiting interrogation at the police station, the camera moves in a U-shaped trajectory, tracking back around a wall and forward again to end in a close-up of Legrand, who also waits. In the course of this shot, Lucienne's landlady exits the interrogation room and reacts unfavorably to André, whereas Legrand receives from her the greatest respect. This moving shot is not a parallel edit, in the montage style, where shots are juxtaposed for the sake of comparison or contrast, but it works toward a similar rhetorical end. Renoir maintains a greater degree of temporal and spatial continuity through longer takes and through camera movement, so that the ironic comparison of the relative positions of the two men appears blended into the narrative unfolding of the scene. To make its social critique, the scene could simply cut from a shot of André's bravado and unfriendly reception by the concierge to a shot of the withdrawn Legrand, receiving the concierge's effusive greeting. The cut would leave the two shots to emphasize André's social position against Legrand's and the way these different positions elicit opposite judgments by the concierge and, ultimately, by the authorities. But the use of a track rather than a cut here adds another factor to the scene: the diegetic experience of time. The track reveals men nervously awaiting interrogation in a police station corridor. They do not appear solely as representatives of a particular class. The longer take afforded by moving the camera rather than cutting shows them as persons subject to time.

A close-up of André awakening in a prison cell the morning he is to die shows a subjection to time reminiscent of great nineteenth-century portrayers of executions such as Victor Hugo and Fyodor Dostoevsky. Hugo's "Le Dernier Jour d'un homme condamné" and Dostoevsky's execution narratives in *The Idiot* both imply that the man facing death by execution is more than a criminal. Indeed, that designation or definition of him falls away at such a moment. Characters represented as a persons subject to time and death starkly contrast with characters represented as markers of a social or legal position.[66] Renoir's depiction of André in relation to time in these scenes thus introduces to his character ambiguity, complexity, and irony: André facing interrogation and execution for a crime he did not commit transcends André the pimp and petty thief.

Renoir's characters inhabit their social roles and class categories more uneasily than Eisenstein's. Even his slain revolutionary, Bomier, is transformed into a martyr only with uncertainty and hesitation. Unlike Vakulinchuk, who, as he is shot, collapses into a pietàlike pose that can prompt an instantaneous association with Christ as a martyr, Bomier spends his dying moments talking about things that, because they are personal, seem relatively trivial: his mother, his girlfriend, his debts. It takes a *belated* act of consensus to give his death a more general meaning. This explicit transformation occurs a few scenes later through dialogue. One of Bomier's friends worries that, if the Revolution fails, Bomier will have died in vain. Another assures him that France, having tasted liberty, cannot go back, and that thanks to men like Bomier, the Revolution will succeed. First there is simply the misfortune of death, then its potential meaning. The moves are separate. Universal meaning comes belatedly. Historical significance does not completely subsume the contingent, particular death—even in a highly political, Popular Front historical drama like *La Marseillaise*.[67]

A key difference between 1938, the year *La Marseillaise* was released, and 1928, the year *October* was released, is sound. Writing of the shift in characterization from the silent to the sound era in American film, Otis Ferguson notes, "The old stock roles of City Slicker, Cranky Spinster, Deacon, and Uncle Tom were being chased off the set simply because they had become cartoons and cartoons don't talk."[68] We might say that, in his silent films, Eisenstein also deals in cartoons—Kerensky, the women's brigade, the bourgeoisie who put the brakes on the Revolution. But sound, while undeniably a powerful tool, does not determine characterization. Characters in Eisenstein's sound films remain "cartoons." (Nesbet, for instance, demonstrates the extent to which Eisenstein's Ivan was influenced by Walt Disney.)[69] Eisenstein celebrates the exaggerations permitted by the caricature, reveling in their expressive power; in contrast, Renoir's characters remind us that people are often "hard to read."

Central to each of Renoir's scenes of killing is not sound technology, or even such devices as depth of field or a moving camera, but the way technology and formal choices serve, pointedly, to obscure or elide the dying. These scenes brilliantly embed the long-standing convention of reticence (going all the way back to Greek tragedy) within the logic of realist poetics. All of these murder scenes emphasize the presence of a larger social world that is unaware of, and seemingly indifferent to, the killing that has taken place. More than this, like the pan in *The Crime of Monsieur Lange*, they direct attention back to the arbitrariness of the discourse itself. Renoir's striking decisions to obscure and elide key elements of his scenes emblematize the role of choice in narrative form. Bazin, ever mindful of such "unacceptable and necessary" choice, gravitated toward Renoir's films, not because they hide abridgment, but because they bare it. Obscurations, elisions, and distractions appear starkly—and not by accident—in murder scenes. Murder, an act that is so often partially elided in film form, and an act that instantiates, within the refracted story world, the starkest forms of elision, is a paradigm for realist narrative.

# PART TWO

# Murder and Genre

# 4  Individual and Series

## Montage and Genre

Film criticism has historically placed Soviet montage in opposition to continuity editing, but like the shot breakdowns and arrangements, hypothetical and actual, of Eisenstein, Pudovkin, and Kuleshov, the narrative syntax and stylization of paradigmatic Hollywood genres revolve around the murder scene. Westerns, crime films, combat films, horror—these key Hollywood genres rarely appear without at least one scene of killing. In part 1 we saw the repeated, varied and profound connections between montage and murder. Part 2 establishes the formative effects of the murder scene, as a site, in two foundational genres, the Western and the crime film. The murder scene, a keystone of these crucial forms, starkly reflects the predicament that the genre film shares with the mass culture out of which it emerges: any claim to a precarious singularity and indispensability must be made within a system based on disposability and sameness.

If large-scale industrialism demonstrates the replaceability of the individual worker, twentieth-century warfare demonstrates (as the title of John Ford's 1945 film *They Were Expendable* declares) the disposability of the individual. In *Wartime*, Paul Fussell amasses ample evidence—war recollections, literature, journalism, criticism—of this devaluation. He writes: "Uniform and anonymous, undifferentiated in essentials whether Marine replacements or aerial gunners, these boys turned by training into quasi-mechanical interchangeable parts reflect the success of human mass-production between the two world wars, a process fueled by dramatic increases in population and assisted by the rapid rise of 'media culture,' with its power to impose national uniformities. A result was that servicemen in the Second World War seemed even more anonymous and bereft of significant individual personality than their counterparts in the Great War."[1] For

Fussell, "media culture," which includes cinema, helps to impose the monotony that renders people killable on a mass scale. Genre films can work to
establish uniformity because they partake of it, and depend upon it for their
marketability. Within genre films, the murder scene's blunt display of the
expendability of persons can crystallize the individual's sense of his or her
own expendability within a mass society. At the same time, it can function
as a classic negation of a negation, potentially inspiring at least a momentary revolt against a social system that presumes, in so many ways, to fix the
finite, even monetary, value of a life. Just as the individual genre film can resist being classed, undifferentiated and forgotten, with others of its kind,
the generic murder victim—the grunt, the gunslinger's peaceable friend,
the good girl gone bad—can exceed, and thus call attention to, the lineaments of the type, making the limitations of representation palpable. At its
best, the generic murder scene renders its victim indispensable precisely at
the moment it dispenses with her.

The major postwar critics of Hollywood cinema strain against what
Greg Taylor calls "an expanding culture of sameness" that is evident within,
and attributable in part to, Hollywood movies.[2] Bazinian realism, defined
by openness to ambiguity, refuses the disturbingly facile legibility, reliant
on conventionality and sameness, that Bazin identified as a pernicious tendency of découpage. Similarly, Robert Warshow attacks Hollywood's un-
subtle signifying practices in such essays as "The Anatomy of Falsehood"
(1947), "Father and Son—and the FBI" (1952), and "The Movie Camera and
the American" (1952); James Agee rejects the generalizing tendency evident
in movie characters; and Manny Farber's reviews challenge audiences to sa-
vor the well-crafted details of B movies—the slightest gesture of an actor,
a bit part—which are as likely to be obscured as cast in relief by the predictable story lines that house them. (Farber's touchstone genres are violent
ones. But murder as such will not feature prominently in my analysis of Farber's writing; at issue, instead, is his keen critical awareness in his 1957 essay
"Underground Films" of the problem of achieving singularity within a culture industry that encourages serial monotony. Farber's concern for imper-
iled singularity emerges against a representational regime that recognizes
and privileges certain forms of sameness and, ultimately, against the backdrop of mass society's demonstration of the dispensability of persons.) All
of these critics, in their own way, oppose what Fussell calls serial anonymity.
Although they may have serious differences of opinion (Bazin, for instance,
praised Welles as one of the harbingers of a new realist aesthetic while Farber blamed *Citizen Kane* for what he claimed was a pseudointellectual preci-
osity that overtook Hollywood cinema in the fifties), these midcentury crit-

ics sense a complex intertwining between the movie industry, the war, and the overwhelming of the particular by generalities.

## Manny Farber and the Logic of Genre

In *Negative Space*, a selection of film criticism by Manny Farber written between 1950 and 1970, we can derive one intricate answer to the question of how a genre film might stake a claim to singularity. Many of the essays collected in this volume are written in the mode of crisis.[3] Farber registers a change in Hollywood that has to do with the death of a certain kind of genre film, often a B picture, often a Warners film, which uses background detail—particularly minor characters—to achieve, within the framework of a "junky" plot, effects that remain, at least in Farber's mind, long after the picture has come and gone. According to Farber, these films, while well crafted, avoid stylization that calls attention to itself. Farber's own prose style, alternately seeming carefully wrought and exceedingly casual, is well suited to the films he discusses ("Through the station door—which bangs back and forth, back and forth, until, at last, exactly as anticipated, it bangs some poor cop in the behind—swarm riffraff, the mulcted, mouthpieces, and minions of the law, each a walking caricature in physiognomy and mannerism of certain familiar Manhattan types").[4] His writing brims with uniquely remarked and appreciated details from countless films. This surprising and painterly close attention to detail—Farber was a painter and he often places the motion pictures in dialogue with, simply, pictures—coalesces into a complex account of the paradoxes of Hollywood's "male" genres.

Farber's classic essay "Underground Films" (1957)[5] contends that the best American films are not the A pictures that (falsely) lay claim to artistic or moral seriousness superior to that of lower-budget genre films: for Farber, the great films, A or B, are the most blatantly generic. The genres he means are the male, even puerile, ones: "soldier-cowboy-gangster" (he readily acknowledges "their twelve-year-old's adventure-story plot" [12, 14]). His essay offers a complex description of the dialectic between individual and series that powers genre.

Farber writes of the makers of these films—including directors "Raoul Walsh, Howard Hawks, William Wellman, William Keighley, the early, pre-*Stagecoach* John Ford, Anthony Mann" and actors "the Barton MacLanes and Frankie Darros"—"The fascinating thing about these veiled operators is that they are able to spring the leanest, shrewdest, sprightliest notes from material that looks like junk, and from a creative position that, on the surface, seems totally uncommitted and disinterested" (12, 20, 14). Here he begins to locate a series of paradoxes: well-crafted cinema ("the leanest, shrewdest, sprightliest notes") emerges out of cliché ("material that looks like junk"). The makers of this art, ostensibly little more than factory workers who repeatedly use the same molds to fashion their products, emerge as Hollywood's most creative artisans precisely because they must work within the restrictions of popular genre: "When the material is like drab concrete, these directors, become great on-the-spot inventors" (17).

How, according to Farber, do these restrictions lead to greater creativity? And how does the creativity manifest itself? Farber seems to suggest congruence between subject matter and style: violent action realized through a harsh aesthetic. He writes of Hawks's *The Big Sleep*, "Its gangster action is engineered with a suave cutting efficacy"; of Walsh's "worst" efforts, "All that saves the films are the little flurries of bulletlike acting that give the men an inner look of credible orneriness and somewhat stupid mulishness"; and of Mann, that he "likes to stretch his victims in crucifix poses against the wall or ground and then to peer intently at their demise with an icy surgeon's eye" (16). In sum, "the best action films are slicing journeys into the lower depths of American life: dregs, outcasts, lonely hard wanderers caught in a buzzsaw of niggardly, intricate, devious movement" (16). Farber prefers shots filled with movement to shots that seem static or staged, freighted with meaning in the stagnant arrangement of the mise-en-scène. He prefers the sequence shot to a montage of still images. He speaks dismissively of Eisenstein.

But his originality hardly lies in these preferences, or in his suggestion that a violent style best expresses a violent action. His originality lies in his assertion that, by delving deeply into the generic, the makers of underground films achieve a fleeting, precarious singularity. This achievement emerges in the details set within the framework of the clichéd story: "In the films of these hard-edged directors can be found the unheralded ripple of physical experience, the tiny, morbidly life-worn detail which the visitor to a strange city finds springing out at every step" (17). Note that even the detail is "life-worn," not new, and ubiquitous ("springing out at every step"); in other words, it, too, is a cliché. And yet, in its very staleness and commonness, it reflects experience. In reflecting experience itself as clichéd, Farber's "underground films" achieve their "leanest, shrewdest, sprightliest notes."

For Farber, the detail in these films has greater importance than the hero: "Though the action film is filled with heroism or its absence, *the real hero is the small detail which has arisen from a stormy competition between lively color and credibility. The hardness of these films arises from the esthetic give-and-go with banality.* Thus, the philosophical idea in underground films seems to be that nothing is easy in life or in the making of films" (19). Farber places "banality" and "credibility" in opposition to "lively color," suggesting that they implicate one another. But we cannot simply align "banality" with credibility, verisimilitude, or mimesis, since, in the next paragraph, Farber suggests that banality has to do with the stylized clichés of genre: "The small buried attempt to pierce the *banal pulp* of underground stories with fanciful grace notes is one of the important feats of the underground director" (19; my emphasis). Instead of "piercing" the "banal" by moving away from cliché, Farber writes, "usually, the piercing consists in renovating a cheap rusty trick that has been slumbering in the 'thriller' director's handbook—pushing a 'color' effect against the most resistant type of unshowy, hard-bitten direction" (19–20). Farber paradoxically associates "lively color" with "a cheap rusty trick" so that "lively color" itself does not escape the tinge of banality. By dwelling with the cliché, we arrive at the particular. Here are some of Farber's examples of "rusty tricks": "A mean butterball flicks a gunman's ear with a cigarette lighter. A night-frozen cowboy shudders over a swig of whisky. A gorilla gang leader makes a cannonaded exit from a barber chair" (20). He calls them "bits of congestion," meaning the congestion of generic convention and cliché.

Farber describes these "bits of congestion" as "the tracings of difficulty that make the films seem uniquely hard and formful," and writes, "In each case, the director is taking a great chance with clichés and forcing them into a hard natural shape" (20). What creates the hardness is the impacting of cliché. Clichés are worn conventions, stylizations, and yet Farber suggests that precisely by pushing them, underground films paradoxically achieve their particular "beauty" and "naturalness": "The beauty of the job is the way the cliché business is kneaded, strained against without breaking the naturalistic surface" (19). The "naturalistic" resides not in showing the world, but in an "unshowy" way of showing Hollywood's clichéd reflection of the world.

Farber's essay is built on paradox. The true "art" film is an unassuming factory product that follows the contours of a generic mold. The terms of the paradoxes rely on their difference from one another, and yet one term continually metamorphoses into the other. Stylization turns into mimesis, and mimesis into stylization. Stars do their best work when they perform as character actors: "A Cagney performance under the hands of a Keighley is ingrained in a tight, malignant story. One remembers it as a sinewy, life-marred exactness that is as quietly laid down as the smaller jobs played by the Barton MacLanes and Frankie Darros" (20). "Life-worn detail," "life-marred exactness"—these terms suggest mimesis, even particularity. But the "life-marred exactness" belongs to "jobs played by the Barton MacLanes and

Frankie Darros." Farber cites the actors as if they were household names, famously singular, and yet puts them in the plural, as if they were not individuals, but a series. It is fitting that "Underground Films" echoes Dostoevsky's *Notes from the Underground*: Dostoevsky achieves his own "sprightly notes" by creating a character frustrated by his utter incapacity for authentic, unmediated experience. He sees all of his roles, all of his encounters, through romantic clichés which he angrily tries to discard, only to take up others.

Farber describes the venues of underground films as if they were extensions of the hard-boiled settings of American crime fiction: "The hard-bitten action film finds its natural home in caves: the murky, congested theaters, looking like glorified tattoo parlors on the outside and located near bus terminals in big cities. These theaters roll action films in what, at first, seems like a nightmarish atmosphere of shabby transience, prints that seem overgrown with jungle moss, sound tracks infected with hiccups. The spectator watches two or three action films go by and leaves feeling as though he were a pirate discharged from a giant sponge" (15). Farber sees a mimetic relation between the venues of the films and their settings: "The cutthroat atmosphere in the itch house is reproduced in the movies shown there" (15–16). This mimesis is reversible: the film atmosphere mirrors the atmosphere of the theater in which it plays while the theater takes on the clichéd look of a film setting. Thus, the theaters look "like glorified tattoo parlors"—they appear as other than themselves. And the "nightmarish atmosphere of shabby transience," a phrase Farber uses to describe actual theaters, succeeds in transforming ordinary, urban, contemporary surroundings into the stuff of genre.

Farber stylizes the run-down movie theater which obscures the film by showing "mossy" prints with "hiccupping" sound tracks. The material conditions of the movie theater intrude upon, or partially occlude, the experience of the film—or perhaps, more precisely, they blur into it, so that theater venue and story world become somewhat indistinguishable. Just as the mossy print and the hiccupping sound track filter our view of the film, the film, with its clichés, inserts a stylized lens between the spectators and the reality they experience. Reality becomes part of the genre, actual experience becomes stylized, clichéd. Farber is imprecise about how many films the spectator sees: two or three go by. When they come from the same mold, the precise number does not matter. The films blur into one another. In this blurring resides the pathos of genre: low-budget genre films risk obscurity within the larger cycle of films whose clichés they share. At the same time, Farber's prose is riddled with his memories of small details from countless films. He does not specify film titles; he specifies details. These details transcend specific films; they are composites. We recognize them even if we cannot locate them solely within a particular film.

In Farber's account, the spectator, too, loses his particularity, leaving the theater "feeling as though he were a pirate discharged from a giant sponge." In other words, the spectator leaves, feeling like another stylized type, the swashbuckler, but a swashbuckler rendered ironic by being set within a hard-boiled frame, discharged, in mass fashion, from a giant sponge, the movie industry, which sucks people in for the space of a feature or two, or three, and then discharges them back into the streets. The generic penetrates not just the venue, but the filmgoers, who partly recognize themselves in the movie clichés. Who are we when we are absorbed in the concerns of the often violent men in these films? Farber's essay discovers a recognition moment born out of habitual filmgoing: the mimesis of genre lies in capturing our own clichéd, mass-mediated experience. This is why genre can be most "naturalistic," even mimetic, when it delves most deeply into stylized cliché. Consider Farber's examples of "rusty tricks" again—the mean butterball flicking the gunman's ear with the cigarette lighter, the shivering cowboy, the gang leader making a "cannonaded exit" from the barber chair. The mimesis resides not so much in our ability to find these characters credible as in the way each character must find his singularity within the cliché. This predicament, Farber suggests, is the same one that challenges the viewer.

For Farber, it is precisely by delving into cliché that the individual can lay claim to singularity. His stance is reactionary insofar as privileging cliché is reactionary. He looks back, with nostalgia, to the films of the thirties and the criticism of Otis Ferguson:

> The Hawks-Wellman tradition, which is basically a subterranean delight that looks like a cheap penny candy on the outside, hasn't a chance of reviving when intellectuals enthuse in equal amounts over Westerns by Ford, Nunnally Johnson, J. Sturges, Stevens, Delmer Daves. In Ferguson's day, the intellectual could differentiate between a stolid genre painter (Ford), a long-winded cuteness expert with a rotogravure movie scene (Johnson), a scene-painter with a notions-counter eye and a primly naïve manner with sun-hardened bruisers (John Sturges), and a *Boys Life* nature lover who intelligently half-prettifies adolescents and backwoods primitives (Daves). (24)

Farber renders his straw men effeminate with such phrases as "cuteness expert," "notions-counter eye," "primly naïve manner," and "half-prettifies." Each of the "rusty tricks" he singles out for praise features a tough, but bodily vulnerable man. He writes "The underground directors have been saving the American male on screen for three decades" (18). An image of masculinity—there is probably nothing more clichéd than American movie masculinities—is the focal point for his nostalgia. But Farber's writing is too intricate to be dismissed as a reactionary homage to an old-fashioned machismo. To declare something a cliché in need of saving amounts, at best, to only a crooked tribute. "Credible orneriness and somewhat stupid mulishness" hardly describes an appealing man. "The lower depths of American life: dregs, outcasts, lonely hard wanderers" are remote from "noble outlaws." Farber's "American male" possesses no unique sensibility. He is a type, prone, and vulnerable, to violence—expendable. But caught in, and thus exposing, a system of institutionalized expendability, he becomes, for Farber, indispensable.

*

Farber does not review Jules Dassin's *The Naked City* (1948)—Robert Hatch reviews it in the March 8, 1948, issue of the *New Republic*, and Agee reviews it for the *Nation* (two magazines for which Farber also served as film critic). Agee, with whom Farber sometimes agreed, panned the film. But *The Naked City* makes an illuminating juxtaposition with "Underground Films": the film adopts a blasé attitude toward a sensationalized news account of a murder, effectively declaring that the story amounts to what Farber might call "drab concrete" ("This too is routine," says the voice-over when we see a second murder committed). But the film, which tells the story of the same murder as the newspaper, also risks seeming "routine," or, like the newspaper story, a brief sensation, forgettable within a week. (In the *New Republic*, Hatch, in prose much less colorful than Farber's, refers to *The Naked City's* content as "old and safe.") At the same time, the film works to make its "telling" of a clichéd story stand out—often, as I will show, through small details. *The Naked City* thus self-consciously dramatizes a process similar to that detailed by Farber, delving into cliché in order to break through it. In doing so, it emphasizes the way that mass society, like murder, demonstrates the individual's disposability.

## Case Study: Jules Dassin's *The Naked City* (1948)

*The Naked City* has as a theme the withering of murder as a moral transgression and its rise as public entertainment and an object of labor for a variety of police specialists. Typical of formulaic murder mysteries, the victims— a model and a drunkard—serve primarily as traces of withheld information. But *The Naked City* adds another theme—the rapidity with which the

127

public forgets the victim, no matter how big a splash her murder makes in the papers. The film thematizes the public's consumption of the murder story. Producer Mark Hellinger's voice-over narrative gives the murder victim Jean Dexter a monetary value, the price of a newspaper: "Her name, her face, her history were worth five cents a day for six days." Hellinger compares her to food: "This time yesterday, Jean Dexter was just another pretty girl, but now she's the marmelade on ten thousand pieces of toast." (The notable quantity of toast suggests that the public appetite will always exceed its satiety.) The film figures the victim's final fade from the public imagination with the image of her face and name on yesterday's paper swept up from the streets (fig. 127).

But the disposability of the newspaper murder narrative *in* the story world implicates the disposability of the film narrative that tells the same story.[6] To stand out from the series of murder mysteries to which it belongs—and thus resist its own disappearance within the genre—*The Naked City* must lay claim to originality, or difference from others of its kind.[7] It does this by boasting a documentary realism (although it was not the first film to do so).[8] At the beginning of the film, Hellinger, who provides voice-over commentary throughout, guarantees: "I may as well tell you frankly that it's a bit different from other films you've seen. . . . This is a story of a number of people and a story of the city itself. It was not photographed in a studio. Quite the contrary: our star Barry Fitzgerald [and other members of the cast] played out their roles on the streets, in the apartments, and in the skyscrapers of New York itself. Along with them a great many thousands of New Yorkers played out their roles also. This is the city as it is—hot summer pavements, children at play, the buildings in their naked stone, the people without make-up." The film has two objectives: to tell the story of a murder and to show a city, as Walter Rutttmann once showed Berlin, or as Vertov, in *Man with a Movie Camera*, showed a day in the life of a conglomerate of Soviet cities.[9] While the film tries to weld together these two objectives, contemporary reviewers tended to criticize the murder story—Agee, for instance, called it "mawkish and naïve"—but praised the on-location shooting of New York. (Cinematographer William Daniels won an Academy Award.) The division of the film into these particular strengths and weaknesses—the murder narrative seen as a weakness, the photography of the city rewarded as a strength—suggests a tension between two genres, the murder mystery and the city symphony. How do these genres influence one another? *The Naked City* sets the individual quality of murder against the mass anonymity of the city, reprising the dialectic between the valorization and simultaneous devaluation of life, which lies at the heart of the murder scene.

The film is what Rick Altman might call a genre cocktail. The two genres, murder mystery and city symphony, while distinct, do not remain separate from one another. The film shows the process by which detectives Dan Muldoon (Barry Fitzgerald) and Jimmy Halloran (Don Taylor) solve the murder of Jean Dexter (uncredited), a New York model with ties to a burglary ring, one of whose members, Garzah (Ted de Corsia), kills her and the drunkard who helps him to anaesthetize her. Writer Malvin Wald spent months observing New York City homicide detectives at work, and he constructed this story by drawing from several actual case files.[10] In addition to relying on these files for his characterizations and for the details of the murder story, Wald took care to show actual police procedures and workers, including switchboard operators, the medical examiner, the lab men, and, primarily, the homicide detectives.[11]

We can disentangle the "city symphony" elements of the film from elements conventional for the crime genre. Initially the film appears to be a documentary about New York City, not a fictional police procedural. The discourse does not immediately specify its protagonists and chief conundrum. As in Vertov's *Man with a Movie Camera*, shots appear to be arranged according to categories: one-o'clock-a.m. New York scenes, five-o'clock-a.m. New York scenes, six-o'clock-a.m. New York scenes, and so on. Hellinger's voice-over specifies the time frame to which each shot belongs, thus styling itself as documentary commentary. After the credits, delivered in voice-over accompanied by aerial shots of Manhattan, the film commences, again like *Man with a Movie Camera*, with most of the city asleep. We see, as part of a series of nighttime scenes, a shot of Wall Street, an empty bank, an empty theater, a quiet textile factory (figs. 128–129; theater and factory both possible allusions to *Man with a Movie Camera*), a silent ship at dock, a sleeping man, a moving elevated train, an airplane in flight, and various people at work on the night shift—a factory worker, a cleaning woman, a typesetter,

128

129

130

131

132

133

a disc jockey—whose thoughts, excluding the factory worker's, we hear spoken in voice-over (figs. 130–33). Although each dominates the frame in which he or she appears (and sometimes the sound track), we never see any of them again. The frames are still; the takes last from three to nine seconds apiece, leaving ample time for Hellinger's leisurely commentary. But the penultimate group of shots of this series of one-a.m. New York scenes begins to provide narrative information. The first-time spectator, however, does not yet have the knowledge necessary to recognize these shots as significant. From shots of nighttime workers we cut to two shots of people "rounding off an evening of relaxation." Each shot contains a character who later turns out to be a murder suspect—Dr. Stoneman (House Jameson) and Frank Niles (Howard Duff; figs. 134–135). The film thus sets us up to see

134

135

136

137

narrative information—these characters have alibis—and to miss it. The
voice-over directs us to see these characters as part of three nested series:
"people rounding off an evening of relaxation," people in New York City at
one a.m., and people who are, quite simply, inhabitants of New York City.[12]
Nothing, at this point, differentiates them from the other characters, whom
we never see again. After these two shots, the camera tracks toward a window, whose blinds partially bar the view of what goes on inside. In silhouette, two people struggle with a third. Hellinger's voice-over announces
that, in relation to all the other New Yorkers at night that we've seen, "another is at the close of her life." "Another" implies that she, too, is part of a
series of people awake into the early morning (but about to be put to sleep
forever!), who in turn are part of a series of eight million. But this scene
stands out from the others that precede it because of its violence and its
form. In addition to featuring a moving rather than a still frame, it also includes diegetic voices, not voice-overs meant to express the pictured person's unspoken thoughts. Finally, this scene of a person at the close of her
life, which comes at the end of a series of night scenes, gets three shots,
whereas the others get only one each. After the camera tracks in toward the
blinds, the film cuts to a shot from inside the room, and then to a close-
up of hands in black leather gloves, which turn on the faucets of a bathtub

(fig. 136). (The film implies, but does not show, that the victim, on whom two men have forced an anaesthetic, is left to drown.)

Even though this murder scene stands apart from the other scenes because of its violent content and its form, it still belongs to a series of New York nighttime scenes. The following sequence of five-a.m. shots, which show bits of the city at dawn, toys with the suggestion that the murder scene will be forgotten. The film dissolves, in a graphic match, from the water shooting out of the faucets of the bathtub to the water squirted from a street-cleaning truck (fig. 137), connecting the washing away of a life with the washing of yesterday's dirt from the city streets. And it rhymes with the shot, at film's end, of the street cleaner sweeping from the gutter yesterday's paper, bearing the now old news of the murder. These visual metaphors thus draw parallels between the victim's life and the dirt and trash regularly cleared from the city.

Three shots, the first of a rail yard accompanied by Hellinger announcing a shipment of Texas beef (fig. 138), the second of a mail truck and a quip about "Uncle Harry's letter" (fig. 139), and the third of a man delivering milk by horse-drawn cart as Hellinger asserts "everything as usual" (fig. 140), have no apparent connection with the murder. They seem there for no other purpose than to provide information about a typical day in the life of New

138

139

140

141

York City. But, as in the first sequence, the final scene of this sequence again features a murder (fig. 141), contains diegetic voices in addition to the voice-over, and comprises more than one shot. Hellinger asserts, "And even this, too, can be called routine in a city of eight million." A drunk in his cups on a dock is, like the first victim, knocked unconscious and drowned. Without having seen the film, we cannot easily recognize murderer and victim as the two men from the previous murder scene. The low lighting of the one-a.m. scene partially obscures their faces and, in this five-a.m. scene, we see the murderer only from behind, and his victim only in long shot. Again, we see narrative information but do not necessarily recognize it as such. With this second murder, following so quickly on the heels of the first, the film begins to suggest that we might have more, here, than a New York version of *Man with a Movie Camera* and that we are watching a film that is about to take on the lineaments of a murder mystery.

And yet the following shots continue to appear organized according to category: six-a.m. scenes of awakening New Yorkers. The categories follow chronological sequence, but they are not predominantly narrative sequences, because they do not yet fully appear to coalesce around a protagonist or a particular story. From a shot of the sun hitting a skyscraper we cut to a close-up of an anonymous baby awakening with a cry, and then an establishing shot of the bedroom, where its mother rises to attend to it while the father lies with his head under a pillow. Next we cut to a shot of a grey-haired Irish man, singing as he prepares breakfast. We do not yet know that this is Dan Muldoon (although we may recognize Barry Fitzgerald), who will be the lead detective on the murder case. From shots of people awakening, we cut to shots of people getting to work: a long shot of an elevated train, a shot of people hastily grabbing a bite to eat at a crowded diner, Jimmy Halloran (not yet recognizable as a protagonist), kissing his wife (Anne Sargent) and son (uncredited) goodbye and heading off down the sidewalk, a crowd of people heading toward and into a subway entrance, people inside the subway station, people pushing to board a train. This organization of shots according to categories—New York City at night, New York City at dawn, New York City as people awaken, New York City as people head to work—ends only with the next scene, which shows the discovery of Jean Dexter's corpse.

The film's documentary stylization lies in the voice-over and the opening arrangement of shots by category rather than narrative sequence. But ultimately, Hellinger's voice-over does not provide documentary commentary so much as it embellishes a crime story. Voice-over narration is typical of film noir, as it is of documentary, but the voice-over of this film is *atypical* of noir:[13] Hellinger is the film's producer, not a character who appears in the film. He announces the film's opening credits, definitively establishing his externality to the story world.[14] Reading the credits, specifying the categories to which the shots belong, and glossing certain images, he has a role deceptively like that of a nonfiction commentator. But as the murder story takes shape, he begins to comment on its fictional events. He occasionally addresses the characters we see in the frame (who do not hear him). He taunts the detectives, for instance, with the difficulty of their task. As Halloran does the legwork, stopping to see the victim's pharmacist in order to find her doctor, Hellinger tells him how far he must walk from the pharmacy to the doctor's office: "The Chaffee Building, Halloran. Eighteen blocks south, four blocks west." When the police begin searching for a potential suspect, of whom they have only a partial and uncertain description, Hellinger quips, "He's a 'big man'—only half a million big men in New York." We might see these comments as informative about the often tedious nature of police work—and not simply as Hellinger's vicarious participation in the fictional story—but by the end, Hellinger is giving voice to the commonplace spectatorial desire to enter the story world and help out the characters. He appears to root for the fleeing murderer: "You've got to get out of this neighborhood, Garzah. That's it! A crowded bus is safer for you than a taxi." This strange mixture of commentary and apostrophe emerges out of the tension between the documentary and dramatic elements of the film.

If we return to the question concerning what the city symphony stylization adds to the murder mystery, we might say that the markedly gradual emergence of the mystery and of the chief protagonists emphasizes one of the main themes of the film: the ease with which the individual gets lost when placed in an urban crowd (and the ease with which a shot gets lost when placed in a sequence that features numerous city scenes arranged by category). Thus, as we noted, because the first shots we see of Dr. Stoneman and Frank Niles situate them as part of a series of other anonymous New Yorkers, we do not give them special attention and easily miss the fact that we are witnessing their alibis. But even without the opening arrangement of shots by category, the setting alone expresses this theme of the individual lost in the series. Interior shots almost always contain windows. Shot in deep focus, these windows look out on other windows. Since the murder scene itself begins with a tracking shot to a window, we may surmise that behind every window lies a potential story. We might make a similar point about the many crowded street scenes, which often do not frame one of the central characters right away. Thus, even as the film comes to focus on the story of the police investigation of Dexter's murder, the very setting and mise-en-scène repeatedly imply the existence of countless other stories on which the film could focus, lending an element of arbitrariness to the centrality of the Dexter murder.

The documentary stylization also adds to the hackneyed murder plot a connotation of realism, thus enabling it to stand out from other murder mysteries and police procedurals that follow many of the same conventions.[15] The flaunting of a documentary style betrays concern that the formulaic plot hopelessly lacks credibility. This concern with the verisimilitude of the generic murder mystery arises from difficulties posed by the murder scene. Popular murder mysteries, which follow the contours of a basic mold in their plots and characterizations, necessarily attribute, like murder itself, a delimited significance to the victim: the victim reduces to a corpse that acts like a cipher, standing in for missing information. This information typically concerns only the facts of the case. Aspects of the victim not immediately related to the story of his or her demise receive little or no attention. In *The Naked City*, all we see of Dexter are a silhouette, a photograph printed on a crumpled newspaper, and a police photograph of part of the corpse. The fragment of Dexter's body we see in the police photograph looks beautiful, not dead. The film avoids disturbing shots of a drowned body.[16] Unlike Devin McKinney's description of "strong violence," whose realism makes the killing of a person distressing for the film spectator, the murder mystery's cheerful reduction of the victim to a puzzle evinces the predominance of stylization over mimesis. The murder mystery must work against its very form in order to achieve "strong violence." But *Naked City* complicates the concept of strong violence and its association with realism by demonstrating that one story can have nothing but delimited significance against a backdrop of eight million other stories. How can we see Jean Dexter as singular when she makes up but one tiny part of such a large mass? *The Naked City* asserts that Dexter's life and death count for little in the larger scheme of things. Depicted primarily as a procedural rather than a moral problem, devoid of all epiphany, the murder of Jean Dexter, if it approaches "strong violence" at all, does so negatively, through its stated triviality.

Recall the opening voice-over—"the buildings in their naked stone, the people without make-up." With these words the film seems to promise revelation. But how can stone be naked?[17] (Indeed, how can a city be naked?) "Naked stone" and no makeup suggest that the city has depths that the film can penetrate. At the heart of the film, and thus at the heart of these "depths," lies Jean Dexter's murder. But the asserted penetration reveals only surface: indeed, the voice-over and editing suggest that murder itself is another "routine," or surface, fact about New York City, and that the film can show us this fact as easily as it shows us the delivery of milk. Murder is never exactly routine. But this very mode of understatement is highly stylized and thus routine: it is a classic hard-boiled move to adopt a jaded tone that implies the ordinariness of murder.

The opening commentary and editing thus frame murder as another piece of information about New York: both of the film's murders appear as part of a series; the voice-over declares the second murder "routine." By placing both murders at the end of the series—one-a.m. scenes, five-a.m. scenes—to which they belong, the film coyly suggests, of course, that they are not at all like the other elements in the series. This marking of the murders as events more notable than the other scenes, even while describing them as "routine," points to the complexity of murder. Murder is not one event like any other event in a series: it puts an end to an individual. From that individual perspective, murder cannot be routine. But from the perspective of statistics, a large homicide department, and newspaper salespersons aware of short-lived public interest, murder can appear commonplace. As a statistic, murder partakes of systematicity: we can correlate certain social conditions with a higher or lower murder rate. And yet the individual murder, because it always happens too fast to be stopped, or even witnessed, is the very opposite of systematic; it is chaotic.

The fictional narrative, like the film's early city symphony stylization, also treats the murders as "facts" or "routine" events. How does this narrative influence the film's award-winning photography of New York City? Why not simply make a New York City symphony, as D. A. Pennebaker did five years later with *Daybreak Express* (1953)? The filmmakers intended from the start to produce a police procedural. Wald and fellow screenwriter Albert Maltz were not torn between making a city symphony *or* a police procedural: cities and murder have gone together since Cain, and half a century of cinema had, by 1948, proven them to be film objects par excellence.

The earliest models of the popular murder mystery—the tales of Poe's Dupin and of Sherlock Holmes—are set in cities. Writing of the murder mystery, Geoffrey Hartman observes, "Mystery means that something is happening too fast to be spotted."[18] Early theorists of the modern city such as Georg Simmel and Walter Benjamin make similar claims about the fleeting movements of a city street. *The Naked City* nicely illustrates the conditioned missing of rapidly passing urban phenomena when we see shots of Dr. Stoneman and Frank Niles enjoying an evening out before we are able to recognize who they are and what these shots mean in relation to the murder. By framing these shots in relation to a city instead of cuing us to see them as part of a murder mystery, the film imposes on them a connotation of serial monotony, almost inviting us to miss their details. The murder mystery thus begins to suggest the bewilderment occasioned by the city, whose overwhelming details are too many, and sometimes too repetitive, to grasp, even though some of them are crucial.

In a murder mystery, what happens too fast to be spotted is the murder, which gives significance to everything around it. (Murder, for instance, is what transforms the first shots of Stoneman and Niles from city sights into alibi scenes.) The camera and the voice-over of *The Naked City* do spot the murders; they work against the structure of belatedness that typically characterizes the crime. They know more than the police and the spectator. Hellinger's voice partially corresponds to Pascal Bonitzer's description of disembodied voice-over narration: disembodiment privileges it, so that it comes to be associated with knowledge and thus with power and the universal.[19] I say "partially corresponds" because Sarah Kozloff convincingly takes issue with with the assumption that the disembodied nature of Hellinger's voice automatically implies truth claims or "voice-of-God" narration. Kozloff writes: "Far from keeping an elitist distance from us, the narrator does everything possible to accentuate his connection with the viewers and to place himself on our level. He starts *The Naked City* by introducing himself. . . . By the film's end, we have a very clear sense of the narrator's personality—his self-aggrandizement, his cynicism, his sentimentality, his devotion to The City and its inhabitants. This narrator combines both authority and warmth: he is powerful yet fallible, the voice of New York and the voice of one man, part lecturer, part tour-guide, part barside raconteur. In short, he is a very human storyteller."[20] As Kozloff points out, Hellinger does not entirely dissociate himself from the real setting or fictional world made to revolve around Dexter's murder. His commentary occasionally suggests an emotional investment in the outcomes of the action—as when Garzah flees. Hellinger was born in New York City, and his voice bears a trace of its regional accent; we might consider him one of the series of New Yorkers which the film partially shows. Nevertheless, despite Kozloff's apt choice of *The Naked City* as an example that complicates certain assumptions made by critics of disembodied (usually male) voices, Bonitzer's general insight still pertains, in a qualified way, to this film. An omniscient, disembodied, male voice guides our view of the film's object—the police investigation into the sensationalized murder of a beautiful young woman. This murder serves as the focal point around which the film organizes the "knowledge" of New York City it proposes to convey to the spectator. The narrating subject constitutes himself in relation to the murder of a woman. Outside the film, and a maker of it, Hellinger (as Elisabeth Bronfen says more generally of representations, by men, of the deaths of beautiful young women) establishes a distance between himself and the murdered woman, asserting "his signature, his gaze, his masculinity, and his survival."[21] The male voice—though humanly fallible as Kozloff points out—retains its privileged position over a woman who, as a corpse, is pure embodiment, without subjectivity.

*

The final sentences of the film—"There are eight million stories in the naked city. This has been one of them"—transforms the eight million people of New York (who already, with that very number, appear as an abstract statistic), equating each person with a single story. But to what one person does the murder story of the film belong? To the victim Jean Dexter? To the detectives assigned to the case, Dan Muldoon and Jimmy Halloran? To the murderer, the former wrestler Garzah, whose death scene entails one of the most spectacular shots of the film? (Just before the police fire at Garzah, who falls to his death from the Williamsburg Bridge, there is a moment that recalls Brueghel's *Fall of Icarus* [c. 1558] as well as Auden's "Musée des beaux arts" [1938]. A high-angle shot made with a wide-angle lens shows the fleeing Garzah, ascending a pylon along a metal staircase built into the bridge's lattice girder, while people far below play tennis, giving the life-and-death drama played out above them no attention [fig. 142].[22] The scene, which shows some New Yorkers missing another's final moments, corresponds to the voice-over's assertion that Jean Dexter's murder was little more than a week's entertainment for the New York City public. Treating murder as throwaway entertainment is another way of not noticing it.)

By beginning with the violent end to Dexter's life, the film suggests that it is her story that will be told, but the plot only indirectly and partially tells that story, focusing mainly on the police work. All of the stories—Dexter's, Muldoon's, Halloran's, Garzah's, and so on—are so intricately connected

142

that we cannot associate ownership of one story with one person. Consider, as well, that in the scripting, more than one story of actual documented murder feeds into the construction of the film's "one" of "eight million." Jean Dexter is the film's distillation of more than one real-life female murder victim. How do we judge where a story begins and ends? Depending on how we answer, we might find more than eight million stories in the naked city—or we might find only one big one. The answer partly depends on whether we view the city through a universalizing frame or through the prism of the individual—but neither frame can be separated from the other.

*The Naked City's* juxtapostion of a murder mystery with a city symphony suggests the reversibility of foreground and background. We can see the city of New York in relief against the conventional tale of a murder, or we can see the murder in relief against the photographic registration of the city.[23] The photographic images of New York, which bear a deliberate degree of arbitrariness, add variety to a tired genre. (Daniels often used a hidden camera.) And the film's "routine" murders give to this indexed time and place, and its people, the backdrop of murder, against which they appear as if in relief. The murder scene situates the individual between two poles, disposability and irreplaceability. The popular murder mystery and its characters are eminently replaceable. Against this planned obsolescence, the film juxtaposes the surreptitious registration of the life of a city. Like the bit parts and slight gestures that Farber notices and remembers, the New Yorkers who haphazardly walk into Daniels's frame are set against Dexter's, the drunk's, and Garzah's ostentatiously announced disposability; and in their brief screen moments, they assert their difference.

### "Cosmetics on a Cadaver": James Agee on War Films

What happens when cinema represents warfare? James Agee, who reviewed films for the *Nation* from 1942 to 1948, and for *Time* from 1941 to 1948, repeatedly returns to this question. While Farber's essay "Underground Films" concerns itself with realizations of memorable particularity in film characters—"soldier-cowboy-gangster"—who are little more than throwaway clichés, James Agee's body of war film criticism concerns itself with the gap between persons literally rendered expendable, through war, and their representation on film.[24] Agee views newsreels along with narrative fictions, frequently writing about them in the same column. Hollywood filmmakers often inserted strips of newsreel into their combat dramas, and Agee reflects on this juxtaposition of documentary with staged drama. He reviews international as well as domestic war films. His criticism displays a constant uneasy probing of the ethics and aesthetics of translating the reality of the war, as experienced by those immediately involved, into cinematic images for the home front. In Agee's reviews, we can find a loose but complex critical meditation on why representing men killing and being killed implicates film characterization more generally. And this meditation resonates with the work of other film critics writing in the wake of the war, especially Farber, Warshow, and Bazin.

Considered together rather than as separate columns, Agee's critical standpoint on war films (which I define broadly, including not just World War II combat films as described by Jeanine Bassinger, but also, following Agee's reviews, Disney films and documentary) undergoes a reversal between 1943 and 1945. In his October 30, 1943, column, titled "So Proudly We Fail," in the *Nation*, Agee associates direct experience of the war with an understanding of its horror and worries that, because of "geography," most Americans "will emerge from the war almost as if it had never taken place" "while every other considerable population on earth comes of age." He writes that motion pictures can address the "liabilities" this discrepancy poses: "I believe nevertheless that much could be done to combat and reduce those liabilities, and that second-hand knowledge is at least less dangerous than no knowledge at all. And I think it is obvious that in imparting it, moving pictures could be matchlessly useful. How we might use them, and how gruesomely we have failed to, I lack room to say."[25] Agee's correlation of geographic experience of the war with knowledge, and his hope—despite misgivings about war films to date—that movies could show things that would diminish home front complacency all but disappear by the spring of 1945. In his March 25, 1945, column for the *Nation*, in which he reviews two documentaries about Iwo Jima, he concludes, "Very uneasily, I am beginning to believe that, for all that may be said in favor of our seeing these terrible records of war, we have no business seeing this sort of experience except through our presence and participation."[26] In the one and a half years between these two columns, the act of viewing a war film, for Agee, assumes an entirely different status. Initially, he almost proclaims the watching of war movies a duty of informed citizens. But from duty, the viewing of war movies metamorphoses into degradation: "If at an incurable distance from participation, hopelessly incapable of reactions adequate to the event, we watch men killing each other, we may be quite as profoundly degrading ourselves and, in the process, betraying and separating ourselves the farther from those we are trying to identify ourselves with; none the less because we tell ourselves sincerely that we sit in comfort and watch carnage in order to nurture our patriotism, our conscience, our understanding, and our sympathies."[27] Agee's acquired distaste for the war film, however, does not prevent him from writing six months later, in September 1945, a rave review of William Wellman's combat film *The Story of G.I. Joe*. The analysis that follows explores the thinking behind this sinuous critical trajectory. Agee's disillusionment with cinema's power to provide "second-hand knowledge" of the war emerges through the process of repeatedly questioning the honesty and ethics of war films.[28]

Agee's early hope that war films would give home front audiences a sense of the experience they were missing suggests a belief in cinema's mimetic force: it would take a powerful realism to provide the "second-hand knowledge" that potentially exploded complacency. His disillusionment with Hollywood's representations of the war suggests not so much a loss of faith in the possibility of cinematic realism as a recognition that the uniquely cinematic absence of a recorded presence separates the home front audience from the screened battlefield even more irrevocably.

In Agee's criticism of war films, "honest" and "dishonest" are key terms. For Agee, "honesty" connotes an idiosyncratic concept of realism. His examples of dishonesty tend to focus on plots and commentary tracks. Of *Victory through Air Power* (1943), a Disney animated film adapted from Major Alexander P. De Seversky's book of the same title, Agee writes, "It was necessary here either (1) to show bombed civilians in such a manner as to enhance the argument, (2) to omit them entirely, or (3) to show them honestly, which might have complicated an otherwise happy sales talk."[29] The review demonstrates that for Agee, honesty in filmic portrayals of the war has little to do with the photographic recording or indexing of phenomena. Agee calls the Disney cartoon dishonest not because it does not use photography to show actual bombing; but because it does not show, via its cartoon drawings, how aerial bombing causes civilian death and suffering.[30] Honesty in representing the war entails showing the killing done by both sides; it demands a critical self-consciousness even of the Allies. Thus, Agee criticizes *The City That Stopped Hitler—Heroic Stalingrad* (1943) for its "strange suggestion that it is better for Russians to use flame-throwers on living Germans than for Germans to use them on dead Russians [and] . . . its managing, several times, to make the audience laugh and applaud at the sight of dead, dying, suffering, or humiliated Germans."[31] Agee fully supported Allied soldiers; he more than once calls them heroic. But he censures any lapse of intellectual or artistic honesty that in any way trivializes war death on both sides.[32]

While *Victory through Air Power* fails to acknowledge the suffering of civilians and *The City That Stopped Hitler* wrongfully approves of some atrocities more than others, John Stahl's *The Eve of St. Mark* (1944), according to Agee, gives its characters an improbable easy out. Based on a Maxwell Anderson play, the film concerns two lovers, Janet Feller (Anne Baxter) and Pvt. Quizz West (William Eythe), separated by a prewar draft. West goes to the Phillipines, where he is stranded after Pearl Harbor. Janet's letters help him maintain his morale. Agee objects to the way the film allows West and the men with whom he is stranded to preserve their appearance of courage while giving their story a happy ending: "When one of them insists that the purpose of this war is to guarantee an end of poverty everywhere, they all choose to stay and die—only to have that necessity removed by the demolition of their gun. This sort of half-honesty, which so comfortably spikes every possible charge of dishonesty, can be very deceitful; I'm not sure but what it is worse than none at all."[33] Even films that do not contrive a happy ending come under Agee's attack for "romanticized men and talk."[34] Indeed, Agee seldom, if ever, speaks with complete satisfaction of a filmic representation of the war. For him, the adequate war film does not exist. But while no war film is ever perfectly adequate, some are honest.

An honest film's claims match its achievements. *Bataan*, for instance, works precisely because it makes no claims to great realism: "its image of war is not only naïve, coarse-grained, primitive; it is also honest, accomplished in terms of its aesthetic, and true."[35] Agee locates *Bataan*'s "honesty" in its "minor claims on nature" and frank stylization; obvious studio artifice does not necessarily preclude truthfulness. In columns devoted to various war films, Agee praises the use of stylistic devices such as the freeze-frame, elliptical editing, and manipulations of the sound track, including the use of uncomfortably loud noises (munitions exploding) and the marked use of silence.

In contrast to *Bataan*, *Air Force* (Howard Hawks, 1943) has pretensions to realism that are simultaneously demonstrated and belied by the insertion of actual combat footage: the staged drama does not prove adequate to the documentary images. Agee writes: "The well-paid shamming of forms of violence and death which millions a day are meeting in fact seems of an order more dubious than the shamming of all other forms of human activity; so I cannot be sure how I feel about *Air Force*. . . . A few all but annihilating cut-ins of actual combat adequately measure the best of the fiction, and my own uneasiness about it."[36] The final sentence identifies a particular problem faced by the fictional combat film. The World War II combat film, like any other genre, relies, for its form, on previous filmic conventions for representing war. The emergence—simultaneous with the war it represents—of the World War II combat genre permits the critical comparison of documentary footage of the actual fighting with cinematic fictions that stage and dramatize the combat. Agee repeatedly makes such comparisons. Recalling his unflattering comparison of *Air Force*'s fictional drama to its inserted newsreel footage, we might ask whether dramatization can ever prove adequate to the filming of real fighting. Of William Wellman's *The Story of G.I. Joe* (1945) Agee writes, "It is also the first great triumph in the effort to combine 'fiction' and 'documentary' film. That is, it not only makes most of its fiction look and sound like fact . . . it also, without ever inflating or even disturbing the factual quality . . . gives fact the constant power and meaning beyond its own."[37] The film's ability to give to its documentary footage a meaning beyond that of the narrative discourse entails a negation: the filmic enunciation is "taciturn" around the inserted footage—it lets the sights, recorded for purposes other than the story, "speak" for themselves. Even so, this film, to which Agee gives high praise, also fails: "Though I am aware of my limited right to an opinion, it seems to me that the movie does fail in one important thing: to give adequate direct impressions—indirectly, it gives any number—of the individual's experience of combat."[38] Indirection works, but direct representation of mass mechanized killing, as experienced by an individual, fails.

Agee's juxtapositions of narrative fictions with war documentaries do not cause him to claim that documentary is necessarily more honest. Instead, his observation of a difference between the relatively accidental objects of a documentary and the staged objects of a fiction film continually point to the more crucial difference between being present in the theater of war and seeing images of the absent war in a movie theater. His review of *The City That Stopped Hitler* in the *Nation* debunks the idea that documentaries of the war are necessarily more honest than narrative fictions: "It may be harder to use *honest* cinematic images dishonestly—the truth insists on pushing through—than to use words dishonestly; but nearly every war film proves how actually easy it is, and suggests how hard it would be to use those images honestly, to say nothing of adequately. *Stalingrad* is sensibly and often sensitively edited. But there is hardly a moment in it where the editing—rather than a single shot—even begins to lift a series of images above prose coherence and towards the plain-featured, heroic poetry which might possibly be deserving of the subject."[39] Some of the documentary images of *The City That Stopped Hitler* fail to achieve honesty when, as noted earlier, they appear in conjunction with a commentary that encourages the audience to approve the torturing of Germans.[40] But they also fall short of honesty when they fail to achieve "poetry." Agee's review of *The Story of G.I. Joe* provides an example of what he means by poetry. Of the closing scene of *G.I. Joe*, "the scene which focuses on [Robert Mitchum's] dead body," Agee writes that it "seems . . . a war poem as great and as beautiful as any of Whitman's." Here the film focuses, much longer than most Hollywood films, on a corpse. A soldier squats by this corpse and holds its hand, in silence, for a long time. Agee writes of the end of the scene: "The sudden close-up, for instance, of a soldier's loaded back, coldly intricate with the life-and-death implements of his trade, as he marches away from his dead captain, is as complete, moving, satisfying, and enduring as the finest lines of poetry I know."[41] Agee's attention to this particular detail—a close-up of a back instead of a face that bears a readable expression of grief—is consistent with his praise of devices that resist easy comprehension. His description of this scene constitutes an example of his more general observation that "many of the scenes end abruptly; some are deliberately deflated or interrupted or made to end flat or tonelessly. All these devices are artful or, if you like, artificial, but on one seeing, anyhow, not one seemed dishonest either aesthetically or morally. It is about as taciturn a picture as I have seen."[42] Drawing on this review, and many others which make similar points, we might trace what I will call Agee's aesthetic of taciturnity.[43] This aesthetic uses devices such as "deflation" or "interruption" which prevent scenes from resolving into tidy meanings. Its essence lies in the refusal to explain every image, or to give every scene a clear moral or meaning: "You can show a wave of action, even very complex and cryptic action, more excitingly and instructively rather than less if you don't pause continually to explain it to the audience, and if you don't delete the inexplicable."[44] As examples, Agee cites "'meaningless' bits—such as a shot in which Ernie Pyle (Burgess Meredith) sits by the road while some soldiers straggle past." Insofar as such shots do not provide narrative information about a cause-and-effect sequence of actions, Agee's examples of film poetry resonate with the Russian formalist description of poetic cinema even though they remain within a larger narrative context.

Agee points to quiet details which the audience must discover on its own since the film does not emphasize them: "With a slight shift of time and scene, men whose faces have become familiar simply aren't around any more. The fact is not commented on or in any way pointed; their absence merely creates its gradual vacuum and realization in the pit of the stomach" (161). The ease with which we might miss this detail—the way the film "lets" us miss it—realizes, on a formal level, the sheer impossibility of *not* missing the countless faces that disappear in war. We might compare this to Paul Fussell's documentation of actual soldiers' inability to keep track of other soldiers' faces. In *Wartime* Fussell quotes a U.S. marine as saying, "It was common . . . throughout the [Okinawa] campaign for replacements to get hit before we even knew their names. . . . They were forlorn figures coming up to the meat grinder and going right back out of it like homeless waifs, unknown and faceless to us, like unread books on a shelf."[45] Agee points to other such quiet details, which contrast with Hollywood cinema's tendency to give redundant narrative information for latecomers and the inattentive. From the missing of the faces of the many he passes to the transformation in the face of one: "the silent uninsistent notice of the change in the face of the youngest of the soldiers, after his first battle, from that of a lonely, brave, frightened boy to something shriveled and poisoned beyond suggesting by words" (162). For Agee's aesthetic of taciturnity, poetry requires the editing out of explanation.

Agee wrote his rave review of *G.I. Joe* in September 1945, half a year *after* declaring his unease that showing war combat proves degrading. In it he seems to return to his 1943 position that war films can provide valuable "second-hand knowledge" to stateside audiences. But he does not endorse the film's ability to give "adequate direct impressions" of combat.

Agee's reviews of films *not* about the war also express distaste for easy legibility and overexplanation. Of Val Lewton's *Youth Runs Wild* (1944) he writes: "When the picture is good . . . you are seeing pretty nearly the only writing and acting and directing and photography in Hollywood which is at all concerned with what happens inside real and particular people among real and particular objects—not with how a generalized face can suggest a generalized emotion in a generalized light."[46] Of *A Tree Grows in Brooklyn* (Elia Kazan, 1945) he says: "The characters themselves bother me most, but here I have an even harder time defining my mistrust of them. It is, roughly, that the imagination has been used a little too glibly to blow up and trim off the presumptive originals of these characters into very comfortably readable, actable, easily understandable creatures, whose faults and virtues are all tagged or neatly braided."[47] Between these two reviews, one positive and one negative, Agee associates the real with the particular and the inauthentic with the "generalizable," "readable," and "easily understandable." We might attribute his sensibility, here, to a critical tradition that associates realism with the accumulation of particular details. But if we consider this critical valorization of particularity in the context of the serial anonymity being imposed at once by mass culture and modern warfare, we must admit that the stakes for Agee go beyond realist aesthetics. In his May 6, 1944, criticism of several newly released war films, "Death Takes a Powder," Agee attacks, explicitly in relation to contemporaneous combat deaths, Hollywood's "sugartit treatments of death and its consequences": "Whether we know it or not—I believe most soldiers and many civilians know it—we are beyond and above the cruel, fetid, criminal little myths about death which are the best, so far, that Hollywood has furnished out of its own immediate day: They are as evil as cosmetics on a cadaver."[48] For Agee, violent death presents a limit for film representation: it cannot be "shammed." To put cosmetics on a cadaver is "evil," not because it dishonestly tries to disguise the corpse that remains as the person who was, but because it implies that the lifelike, or life, is a matter of paint. If a film like Air Force shams death, cosmetics on a cadaver sham life, and Agee's criticism suggests that the two shams implicate one another. G.I.Joe garners Agee's praise because it shows the ease with which we miss the missing of the anonymous G.I. Dishonesty lies in pretending that the film, its characters, or the film audience can give a life adequate attention, particularly in the face of its violent loss. Together, the reviews of G.I.Joe, Youth Runs Wild, and A Tree Grows in Brooklyn tell us not simply that generalization kills off the original, or that the representation of particular people makes for a good film—but that at the time of Agee's writing, attention to, and representation of, the singularity of persons—against their implication in larger systems—has become rare, perhaps impossible.

*

While Agee favorably reviews Bataan, Warshow critiques the representation of the G.I. it inaugurates by contrasting Rossellini's Paisan with American films of the war: "In an American film, these men would be 'G.I.'s'—the rough and serviceable vessels of democracy; their personal qualities would be expressed through contrived and carefully differentiated patterns of symbols and ideas (one of the group might be a little comical, and another 'spiritual' or 'cultured'; one might be named Rosenbloom, and—at the very best—one might be a Negro); and their presence on the coast of Sicily would be given some specifically 'universal' relevance (probably the episode would begin with shots indicating the scale of the invasion, and then move in to pick up this 'representative' group)."[49] Warshow's scare quotes indicate the strained nature of Hollywood combat film values. His rejection of "the elaborate political, moral, and military framework that an American director would use to give [the situation of the men] 'meaning'"[50] recalls Agee's 1945 pessimism about Hollywood's right to present morally uplifting war stories to complacent people far removed from the violence.

A decade before Agee and Warshow, and in a way that speaks to their concerns about the way cinema seems to reduce war's bewildering horror, Walter Benjamin theorized the impact of twentieth-century mechanized warfare on mimetic desire. He began, "The Storyteller" (1936) with reference to the First World War, declaring that it made apparent the loss of our ability to share experience through storytelling:

> Wasn't it noticeable at the end of the war that men who returned from the battlefield had grown silent—not richer but poorer in communicable experience? What poured out in the flood of war books ten years later was anything but experience that can be shared orally. . . . Never has experience been more thoroughly belied than strategic experience was belied by tactical warfare . . . bodily experience by mechanical warfare, moral experience by those in power. A generation that had gone to school on horsedrawn streetcars now stood under the open sky in a landscape where nothing remained unchanged but the clouds and, beneath those clouds, in a force field of destructive torrents and explosions, the tiny, fragile human body.[51]

Benjamin's claim that twentieth-century warfare diminishes communicable experience provides a compelling explanation for why, in Agee's words, *The Story of G.I. Joe* fails "in one important thing: to give adequate direct impressions . . . of the individual's experience of combat." He writes that as "experience has fallen in value,"[52] information replaces experience. "The prime requirement" of information "is that it appear 'understandable in itself.'"[53] An event takes the form of information when it is "already . . . shot through with explanations." In contrast, "it is half the art of storytelling to keep a story free from explanation as one recounts it." Benjamin's critique of narrative "information" pinpoints the central objection that Farber, Agee, and Warshow raise in regard to many films.[54]

Benjamin charts the changing character of narrative knowledge (from experience to information) as it unfolds throughout the age of large-scale industrialization, and he locates cinema at a great distance from the art of the storyteller. A technologically reproducible medium born in the information age, the cinema, for Benjamin, might only anachronistically and anomalously achieve the storyteller's artisanal, "mouth-to-mouth" communication of experience—if at all. But the cinema does tell stories, and Agee, Farber, and Warshow, along with André Bazin, all value cinematic stories kept "free from explanation" over those "shot through with explanations." For them, such narrative "information" is, consistently, misinformation. For Agee, "information" in the combat film might take the form of "primer smatterings of technical realism" mismatched with "studio combat" and "romanticized men and talk which chemically guaranteed the defeat of all possible reality." Farber's contrast between "the gimp" and "the unworked-over immediacy of life" in the B movie also expresses distaste for films overloaded with explanatory information. Farber defines "the gimp" as "the technique . . . of enhancing the ordinary with a different dimension, sensational and yet seemingly credible. Camera set-ups, bits of business, lines . . . are contrived into saying too much."[55] "The gimp" leads to "the complete disappearance of reality in the fog of interpretation: the underground 'meaning' of every shot displaces the actual content and the moviegoer is confronted with a whole crowd of undefined symbolic 'meanings' floating entirely free."[56] In contrast, the "unworked-over immediacy of life" in the B movie lies most often in background details—bit parts played by character actors, minute physical adjustments of an actor's body to a set or a scene, the celebration of a cliché that announces itself as nothing more than a cliché. Farber's disdain for "saying too much" loosely corresponds to the "antiexplanatory" sentiment that characterizes Agee's aesthetics of taciturnity, Bazin's preference for a cinema that shows before it means, and Warshow's critique of figures who "say too much," ranging from the G.I. to the commentator. Warshow writes of the newsreel commentator, "Even in its most solemn and pessimistic statements, this voice is still a form of 'affirmation.' . . . At bottom, it is always saying the same thing: . . . that for every experience there is some adequate response; at the very least, there is always—there must be—something to say." That there is nothing to say—that the images of war which silently accompany the commentator's words attest to an experience that cannot be communicated—is Benjamin's point.

Of these three midcentury American critics—Agee, Farber, and Warshow—Warshow is closest to Benjamin in his concern with experience: "The most important effect of the intellectual life of the 30's and the culture that grew out of it has been to distort and eventually to destroy the emotional and moral content of experience, putting in its place a system of conventionalized 'responses.'"[57] The very title of Warshow's posthumous book,

*The Immediate Experience*, typical for its time, alludes to the unreflective immediacy that replaces what Benjamin might call "aura." In "The Legacy of the 30's" (1947), Warshow writes:

> The chief function of mass culture is to relieve one of the necessity of experiencing one's life directly. Serious art, too, is separated from reality, for it permits one to contemplate experience without being personally involved; but it is not an evasion: by its very detachment, it opens up new possibilities of understanding and pleasure derivable from reality, and it thus becomes an enrichment of experience.
>
> Mass culture, on the other hand, seeks only to make things easier. It can do this either by moving away from reality and thus offering an "escape," or by moving so close to reality as to destroy the detachment of art and make it possible for one to see one's own life as a form of art.[58]

Just as, for Warshow, the "separation" and "detachment" of art "opens up new possibilities of understanding," the "distance" intrinsic to Benjamin's concept of aura opens up space for reflection. Benjamin's work provides a theoretical underpinning for the responses to film aesthetics we find in these midcentury American critics—not in the sense that they read Benjamin, but in the sense that Benjamin conceptualizes a historical shift in the character of narrative knowledge that is resonant with Agee, Farber, and Warshow's writing on film. At the same time, Agee and Warshow's critical concern for a cinematic mimesis that does justice to war experience reflects the mimetic aesthetics in Benjamin. Benjamin states his mimetic theory in crisis terms—loss of communicable experience, loss of aura—but these concepts would make no sense without the underpinning of mimetic desire. The desire for, along with wariness of, mimesis, or realism, might still give us pause. Aesthetic judgment, assessing forms of representation, serves, for these critics, an important social function: it does not abandon the field of representation to those in power, allowing them to make their own reality.

Warshow, like Agee, expresses pessimism about the ability of the American combat film to show slaughter: "American culture demands victory; every situation must somehow be made an occasion for constructive activity. The characters and events in serious American films are given a specifically 'universal' or 'representative' meaning in order to conceal the fact that there are situations in which victory is not possible. The idea survives—that is a victory; the man dies—that is a defeat; the 'GI' is created to conceal the man's death."[59] Note the similarity between the G.I. and the figure of the martyr in early Soviet cinema. Both stand for something outside themselves. The Soviet film martyr is always a representative of the working class—the sailor Vakulinchuk, the mother Pelageya Vlasova, the peon Sebastian. Similarly, the G.I. is a representative "individual"—the Wasp, the Jew, the Pole, the African American, and so on. The types who stand in for a whole series of proletarians (shipyard workers, munitions plant workers, etc.) become a series of martyrs; the types who stand in for whole ethnicities and races become a series of G.I.'s. The larger aims for which they die conceal the irrevocable deaths of particular men who have already been rendered serially anonymous by their categorization as workers, naive Midwestern boys, or Brooklyn-born Italian Americans. "To conceal the man's death" is to conceal the man. We have seen how the martyr—by definition a person, the image of whose violently abridged life has been commandeered to signify something outside itself—is an emblematic figure of Soviet montage, which "martyrs" objects by photographing and arranging them to make them signify. Just as the figure of the martyr suggests the potential fate of all photographed reality under a montage aesthetic, the figure of the G.I., torn between serial anonymity and difficult individuality, encapsulates the logic of Hollywood genre.

For Agee and Warshow, war films such as *The Story of G.I. Joe* and *Paisan* stand out from the Hollywood World War II combat genre not because they carefully delineate the character of each G.I. in a central group, but because they show the impossibility of seeing the G. I. as an individual. By showing the institutionalization of expendability, which refuses to recognize the singular subject, these filmic representations of the war achieve a distinctive mimetic "honesty" (to borrow a term from Agee). More conventional combat films commonly stage the impersonal slaughter of warfare as a series of murders. They deny the war's nonnegotiable assertion of the soldier's structural expendability by emphasizing his individuality: he is a murder victim, not part of a statistic. By transforming combat scenes into a series of murders that decimate a small, and thus comprehensible, group of men, Hollywood combat films sustain the illusion that the individual counts in a situation where he does not. Paradoxically, by propping up this illusion of the individual G.I., the combat film only more irrevocably erases him. In contrast, certain postwar films and film criticism opt for a negative approach: if they assert particularity, they do so by insisting on the impossibility of showing the individual; indeed, they cease to take for granted the very possibility of individuality.

# **5**  Stylization and Mimesis

### Murder as Stylization

In popular, formulaic crime stories, murder typically has less importance as an event in itself than as a stylizing structural pivot. Murderer and victim function as agents who engineer the problem that the investigation, and narrative, must solve. By the end, the narrative satisfies the desire for information: there is one right answer to the questions Who? What? When? Where? Why? And how? For Parker Tyler, this eschewal of lingering ambiguity distinguishes the Hollywood murder mystery from tragedy; for Geoffrey Hartman, it marks the difference between "literature high and low." For our purposes, it neutralizes the murder scene's potentially rich referentiality. By revealing the abyss between representation and referenced life, murder scenes in film can be powerful sites for reflection. But when the murder scene's structural function dominates its referential meaning, as in conventional mysteries that lavish narrative attention on the investigation rather than the crime, the potential demand for reflection cedes place to the seductions of instrumental thought.[1] This is certainly the case with *Mildred Pierce* (Michael Curtiz, 1945). Its screenplay adds a murder to the James M. Cain novel from which it is adapted for structural reasons (and to capitalize on the popularity of Cain's crime stories). The tacked-on murder stylizes and genrifies, transforming a nonviolent melodrama into a murder mystery that reduces its victim to a cipher.

### *Mildred Pierce* (1945)

No murder occurs in the novel *Mildred Pierce* (James M. Cain, 1941), but its film adaptation begins with a man in evening dress shot point-blank. The setting for the novel is the middle-class suburb of Glendale, California; the base setting for the film, told in flashback, is a police station. The novel tells the story of a determined woman who breaks up with her philandering husband. Without financial resources and with two daughters, Ray (renamed Kay in the film) and Veda, to support, she seeks work. After much anxiety, she lands a job as a waitress, learns the restaurant business, and successfully builds her own restaurants. Cain claims that he initially intended to write about a "grass widow's" struggle to raise two children without the help of a husband, but as Roy Hoopes, Cain's biographer, points out, no contemporary reviewers saw this struggle as the book's primary theme.[2] Another plot line supersedes Mildred's rise to success and fortune: Veda gains recognition as a world-class singer. She takes everything she can get from her foolishly self-sacrificing mother, including her mother's second husband, Monte Beragon, before spurning her parent for the life of a diva. (The youngest daughter Ray dies in childhood.)

While Monte runs off with Veda at the end of the novel, the film version begins with the scene of the murder of Monte (Zachary Scott). We see Mildred (Joan Crawford) wandering the streets, desperate and suicidal after this opening scene. She tries to frame Wally Fay (Jack Carson), who, in both novel and film, buys her out of the restaurant business she worked so hard to build. Finally she arrives at the police station, where she recounts her story, which we see in flashback, ending with the revelation of the murderer's identity and motives. The murderer turns out to be her daughter Veda (Ann Blyth), who, unlike her novelistic counterpart, has no artistic talent but is, rather, a conglomeration of purely negative characteristics. Greedy, manipulative, and ungrateful, she disappears, like a bad dream, within the Los Angeles Hall of Justice at the end of the film, leaving her mother to exit into the dawn with renewed innocence. In the novel, the situations are reversed: Mildred loses her youth, her business, and her children; meanwhile, Veda heads east for a life of glamour.

How did a novel about the travails—financial and parental—of a suburban, middle-class woman come to be a murder mystery in its screen adaptation? From the start, Warners producer Jerry Wald wanted to add a murder to the story, even though he did not know, at first, who would be the killer and who would be the victim. In an early treatment, Mildred murders Veda after discovering her in a compromising position with Monte.[3] This early arbitrariness about the identities of murderer and victim attests to the purely formal purpose of the murder scene: there must be a murder to structure the plot, but who does it, who suffers it, when it occurs, and how it is done—that is, the possible permutations of the scene with all their semantic ramifications—Wald and the screenwriters treat as secondary concerns. Why insist on adding a murder scene to the novel's murderless plot? Cain believed that Mark Hellinger suggested this idea to Wald.[4] Assistant story editor Tom Chapman speculated in a February 1950 letter to Warner's general counsel, Roy Obringer, that Wald got the idea from the structure of the film adaptation of another Cain novel, *Double Indemnity*.[5] Roy Hoopes writes, "When Hollywood got around to making *Mildred Pierce*, it had to add a murder so the movie would not disappoint the real James M. Cain fans."[6] Both *Double Indemnity* and *Mildred Pierce*, unlike the novels from which they are adapted, feature similar flashback structures. According to Chapman, Warners added the murder scene to *Mildred Pierce* to motivate the flashback structure and provide what was perceived as a missing dramatic climax. The star Joan Crawford said in an interview, "You want to know about that? All I can say is, they tried it without the murder, and the thing seemed flat. The murder pulled it together somehow."[7]

We have been examining various ways in which murder scenes disrupt narrative processes of signification, but in this case, as Crawford reports, the filmmakers felt the murder "pulled it together." We can productively linger on the implicitly formal dimensions of this offhand comment. Crawford's remark suggests that the non-murder-mystery elements resist aggregation. According to Pam Cook, the murder never seamlessly brings these melodramatic, but nonviolent, elements under its domain: "To write about *Mildred Pierce* . . . as an example of film noir poses more problems than are immediately apparent. In spite of the fact that several articles about the film place it as typical of the 1940's genre . . . *Mildred Pierce* does not fit easily into the self-contained, homogeneous world created by those formal strategies now accepted as characteristic of film noir. . . . I would claim instead that that film deals explicitly with questions of genre as part of its project, that the ideological work of the film is to articulate the necessity for the drawing of boundaries."[8] Cook supports this claim by drawing on Joyce Nelson's observation that the flashbacks motivated by Mildred's police testimony do not share the noir qualities of the present-tense scenes.[9] She suggests that the discourse of truth (whose genre *is* the noir murder mystery with its ultimate revelation of fact) works to contain the complexity of the melodrama.

Cook's and Nelson's narrative of the struggle of one genre to corral the recalcitrant elements of another describes a crucial aspect of *Mildred Pierce's* form. The tensions observed by them play out most intensively on the level of characterization. Melodrama is a key genre for expressing the subject of suffering. The suffering portrayed in *Mildred Pierce* the melodrama emerges out of rigid categories and hierarchies of class, race, and gender that reduce the individual. In Cain's novel and, to a lesser extent, in the film, Mildred suffers slights from the wealthy, from her social-climbing daughter, and from her husbands. *Mildred Pierce* the noirish police procedural relegates this suffering to the background, displacing social injustice with a solvable and punishable crime. The subject that exceeds, and suffers from, the imposition of social categories, cedes place to the subject defined by her relation to murder. A generic palimpsest, *Mildred Pierce* allows us to see the organizational force of the murder scene at work.

The blatant force with which the murder mystery contains the potentially wayward narrative, organizing and subsuming diverse material, motivates Parker Tyler's decision to use *Mildred Pierce* to elaborate a theory of the detective genre. In *Magic and Myth of the Movies* (1947), he writes, "For the irrational or symbolic mystery of *the human soul* the murder mystery substitutes the rational or mechanical mystery of *incompletely available facts*."[10] The chief investigator of Monte Beragon's murder, Inspector Peterson (Moroni Olsen) illustrates Tyler's claim; he emphasizes the "rational and mechanical" work of detection. When Mildred asks him to tell her who killed Monte, he responds, "We start out with nothing—just a corpse. We look at the corpse and say, 'Why?' 'What was the reason?' We find the man who made the corpse." Like Inspector Peterson, the film, too, starts out with a corpse—the opening scene shows the victim drop dead of gunshot wounds. For Peterson, the process of detection is mechanical and reversible: the murderer makes the corpse and the corpse makes the murderer. The inspector suggests the latter when he tells Mildred that in detective work you "take all the pieces and put them together one by one and first thing you know you've got an automobile—or a murderer." Even as it plays on our resistance to finding automobiles commensurate with murderers, Peterson's jaded view of his work creates the illusion that murder, like an automobile assembly line—or a film—can, if necessary, run backward as well as forward. And as Peterson reconstructs the story of the murder, the filmic discourse returns us to it through flashbacks.

Thematizing, through Peterson's words, its reconstruction of the murder story, *Mildred Pierce* illuminates the syntax of many film narratives within and beyond the murder mystery genre. Numerous critics have noted the imprint of the murder mystery on Hollywood stories that have no murder. David Bordwell observes that in adopting psychoanalytic concepts as a new form of realism, "Hollywood films stressed the cathartic method of psychoanalysis . . . because of its analogy to conventions of the mystery film. The doctor's questioning recalls police interrogations. . . . Like the detective, the doctor must reveal the secret (the trauma) and extract the confession."[11] Bordwell locates yet another parallel structure in the murderless

*Citizen Kane* (Orson Welles, 1941), where a reporter replaces doctor and detective. Conversely, we can find homages to *Citizen Kane*, according to Albert J. LaValley, in screenwriter Ranald MacDougall's first draft of his version of the screenplay for *Mildred Pierce*. The detective, for instance, shows Mildred photographs that appear as live action later in the film. In his introduction to the screenplay, LaValley writes that even in its final form, "in its circular movement and structure, its beginning with a death and its fatalistic movement forward until the missing shot has been supplied at the end (here no Rosebud, but Ann Blyth firing the gun) *MP* resembles *Kane*."[12] Before Bordwell, Tyler made a similar comparison between the structure of the murder mystery, psychoanalysis, and Hollywood film, writing, "The psychological method known as the reconstruction of the crime is esthetically akin not only to my method of interpretation but to the artistic composition of the film product itself."[13] Even Eisenstein, in 1941, located the secrets to composing an effective scenario in the detective novel, which always had a crime, usually a murder, at its center.[14]

But while the murder mystery may serve as a template for a broader array of narrative structures, its intersection with the classical découpage of the Hollywood continuity system results in a form of narration alien to Eisenstein. Inspector Peterson's method of "taking all the pieces and putting them together one by one" suggests a metaphor for film editing that Eisenstein ridicules. "Part by part, brick by brick: the Hollywood cinema often evokes metaphors from architecture and masonry"—with these words, David Bordwell begins his description of the Hollywood practice of découpage, or the breakdown of the story line into scenes, each providing a key piece of narrative information, which are then assembled to make the film.[15] Bordwell is paraphrasing Eisenstein's quotation of a popular Russian song in "Beyond the Shot" (1929). Eisenstein, in turn, is mocking such metaphors, specifically in the writing of Kuleshov: "If you have an idea-phrase, a particle of the story, a link in the whole dramaturgical chain, then that idea is expressed and built up from shot-signs, just like bricks."[16] The brick metaphor suggests a repetitive monotony inappropriate to Eisenstein's conception of montage. We may recall, for instance, how Eisenstein criticizes Griffith's parallel montage for never moving beyond repetitive alternation.

It is precisely in Griffith's "principle of alternation" that Raymond Bellour locates the origins of classical Hollywood form, declaring that we find the "mise en abyme" and "mise en volume" of Griffith's alternating repetitions "in films by Hitchcock or Lang, Mann or Curtiz, Wyler or Thorpe." In addition to pointing out repetitive framings, Bellour famously writes of repetition as constituting the classical Hollywood couple (especially in

Hitchcock). Unlike films where stylistic patterns exist independently of, or take precedence over, narrative, and thus call attention to themselves, classical narrative cues desires and expectations that distract from its formal repetitions, lulling us into not noticing them. The following analysis of *Mildred Pierce* will, like Bellour's work, pick out the principles of repetition that structure the film. But the aim is not, like Bellour's, or Tyler's, to arrive at an underlying psychoanalytic interpretation revealed by the repetitive structure. Instead, the analysis aims to establish between this repetitive structure and the murder mystery genre a profound connection. And, insofar as the murder mystery serves as a narrative template, to posit a link between the murder scene and classical narrative cinema more broadly.

In *Mildred Pierce*, the storied reconstruction of the crime coincides with its discursive reconstruction: just as the police take the corpse and attempt to piece together its story to "make" the murderer, the filmic discourse takes the murder and assembles the causal events behind it to make the story. Both processes have a chiastic form: each returns to the place where it started, the murder scene, but upon return, our knowledge of the place changes. Inspector Peterson says that to catch a murderer entails putting together the pieces, and piece number 1 is the corpse. But the flashbacks to scenes from Mildred's life are also "pieces"; they have the same status as Monte's corpse; they do not exist as ends in themselves, but as means to the solution of a puzzle. The film "corpses"[17] scenes of life, reducing them to pieces of narrative information, subordinated to one end. The inspector's odd comparison between the assembly-line production of an automobile and the police production of a murderer makes sense only if he is talking about the murderer as an assembly of information. Peterson's lines inscribe the stakes of the formalism specific to the Hollywood murder mystery: it replaces not only experience, but also persons with information. It is as the central scene to which all this information refers that murder "pulls the film together."

*Repetition*

Murder violently imposes closure on a life. In *Mildred Pierce*, the murder that ends Monte's life also almost ends the plot. Since it starts, and nearly ends, the plot, it frames, or contains, not only Monte's life, but most of the scenes in the film. It provides closure both in the story world and on the level of narrative form. The murder "contains" the film's scenes in a more profound way: we refer each scene back to it as we seek information that will shed light on the identity and motives of the killer. The murder defines the

143    144

145    146

meaning, or importance, of the other scenes. In articulating these scenes, the film adheres so closely to the parameters of classical Hollywood style that these very parameters begin to appear intricately connected to the murder that "pulls the film together." The film's classical découpage and continuity editing echo the chiastic structure of the murder-framed narrative.

As in theater, several scenes begin with an arrival and end with a departure. Characters arrive; their words and actions reveal a bit of narrative information; they depart. The bits of narrative information thus produced appear discrete and neatly articulated, framed by an entrance and an exit. Since characters leave the scene in a fashion similar to the way they enter, scenes begin and end with graphically similar shots, creating a visual chiasmus. Graphic matches frame the opening murder scene, for instance. Of its six shots, the first, second (fig. 143), and sixth (fig. 144) feature a parked car, in extreme long shot, with its headlights on. On the sound track we hear ocean waves, which also accompanied the credit sequence and continue into the film via a soundbridge. (The credits show the names of those involved in the production over a background of sand. Surf appears to flow over them, washing them away to make room for the next list of names in an extradiegetic realization of the figure of chiasmus.) A gunshot sounds, spurring a cut from the parked car to a man in evening dress, who performs a "clutch and fall" (fig. 145). The camera reframes to follow his pitch forward, and the shot, which began with a medium shot of the man standing, ends with a medium shot of him lying on the floor. We hear and see a gun fall onto the floor next to his hand (fig. 146). The fourth shot is a cut in to a medium close-up; the dying man whispers, "Mildred," and goes limp; the camera tracks to a mirror marred by bullet holes, and we hear a door close, signaling the dis-appearance of the murderer we never saw. The fifth shot cuts to a long shot of the dead man, stretched out on the floor in front of a sofa, the gun next to him. From the corpse we cut back to the car, in long shot, which now pulls away (again, fig. 144). The lights have been turned off inside the house, the loss of light echoing the loss of life.

Perhaps what is most remarkable about this scene is the very unremark-ableness of its form. The chiasmus (from one long shot of the car to another) contains the first visual realization of the murder. The graphics of the mur-der itself—a medium long shot of a vertical man becomes a medium long shot of a horizontal man—are simple and clear. The scene neatly motivates the plot through its ostentatious refusal to disclose the murderer: it gives us the shot of the victim, but withholds the reverse shot of the killer until the film's end. The entire film is made up of scenes like the opening: neatly con-tained, each advances the plot, providing bits of information in a clear fash-ion. Beyond the structure of the individual scene, the arrangement of scenes entails larger patterns of repetition and return. The murder happens once in the story but appears twice in the plot; and these two iterations of the same event frame all but the ending, in which Mildred leaves the Los Ange-les Hall of Justice. Her arrival at the Hall of Justice early in the morning of the night of the murder and her departure later that same morning form an-other chiasmus which houses the flashback structure and interweaves with the two scenes of the murder. Within these two larger patterns of repeti-tion are the more minute patterns of departure and return. A chiastic syn-tax pervades the film.

To demonstrate this structure, let us closely examine the rest of the film's noirish overture, up until Mildred's arrival at the Hall of Justice where the flashbacks begin. The second scene also takes the form of a chiasmus: shots 8, 9, and 10 feature the heroine walking onto a pier toward a shed painted with a sign that says "Live Bait"; shot 23 shows her walking back off the pier away from the same shed (figs. 147–148). The sign on the pier, with which the scene begins and ends, retrospectively acquires significance: Mildred unwittingly functions as live bait for the police to catch her daughter. In between her walk onto, and off, the pier, she tries to commit suicide, but the strike of a policeman's baton on the metal railing of the pier keeps her from

leaping. A whip pan along the rail registers the shock of the baton strike in Mildred's hands as she starts at the noise (figs. 149–50). In the context of the film's other modes of repetition, the repetition of devices becomes more apparent; thus, the film's one other whip, or swish, pan also stands out. It occurs when Mildred's first husband, Bert (Bruce Bennett), shows up at her restaurant after its successful opening night and agrees to the divorce. Monte insults him by proposing to drink to the divorce, and Bert knocks the drink out of Monte's hand and departs, leaving a two-shot of Mildred and Monte, Mildred's face half in shadow. At that moment, a whip pan motivates our return to the police station, ending the film's first long flashback. Together the two whip pans suggest that the police—the baton, the murder investigation—were that which snaps the head to wakefulness and away from the dream of the past.

The opening murder and the next two settings, in which Mildred tries to frame Wally for the crime, commence a pattern of interscenic repetition. As Mildred walks away from the pier, Wally lures her inside his restaurant, hoping to seduce her. Inside the cocktail lounge, the camera pans to follow them to their table, then starts to follow a couple of strangers, coming to rest on a cabaret singer in extreme long shot. The shot of the singer serves to connect this moment with one that occurs later in the plot, but earlier in the story: Bert takes Mildred to Wally's lounge in order to show her that Veda performs there, attracting catcalls from sailors.[18] The cabaret singer thus doubles for Veda. While the two scenes have different editing and framings—the camera, for instance, cuts in much closer to Veda rather than panning and framing her from a distance—the setting and the presence of Mildred and Wally serve to make the two tableaux semiduplicates, suggesting a weaving, or interlocking, of almost interchangeable parts. The dialogue entails a similar repetition. It establishes that Wally has long been trying to seduce Mildred, and that Mildred "didn't always drink whiskey straight." This line has its echo in another scene that also occurs earlier in the story but later in the plot: shortly after Mildred's first husband leaves her, Wally tries to engage her in a sexual affair. He and Mildred sit on the sofa with whiskies, and Mildred, not used to the strong flavor, cannot drink hers. The two seductions resemble each other except that, in the present one, Mildred's second husband's murder replaces her first husband's departure; and Mildred, not Wally, now plays the role of temptress with the line "There's better stuff to drink at the beach house."[19]

Two dissolves take us from Wally's restaurant to the fateful beach house, where Mildred carries out her plan to frame Wally. First we dissolve to a car, its headlights on, pulling up to the same place we saw in the first scene (fig. 151). Here, too, the film is building a series of repetitions that house differences: same night, same setting, but now it is Mildred and Wally in the car. Their nocturnal trip resembles another visit to the beach house that the two of them made earlier in the story, but later in the plot. Then, as now, Monte awaits them; only then he wasn't a corpse. And it was a sunny day, not a dark night. Wally was accompanying Mildred as she went to buy her first property from Monte, so that she could start a restaurant (fig. 152).

151

152

153

Except for the light, the sunny establishing shot of the beach house scarcely deviates from the shots that show the same place on the night of the murder (fig. 153). In the sunny scene we dissolve to a close-up of Monte's hands mixing drinks (fig. 154); in the nocturnal scene we dissolve to a close-up of Wally's hands doing the same, but momentarily superimposed over Monte's corpse (fig. 155). In both scenes, Mildred sits in the same place in relation to the bar (figs. 156–157).

In order to emphasize, in the frame-up scene, that this is the same place on the same night, the camera does not follow Mildred and Wally as they head to the spiral stairs inside the house; instead it pans to the right and then cuts to show the corpse, now lying from left to right, shot from the opposite angle from which we had previously seen it. This return to the corpse from the other side of the 180-degree line from which we last saw it also fits a pattern of chiastic repetition. From Monte's corpse, the film dissolves to the close-up of Wally's hands mixing drinks. The camera does not tarry with the dead body; the pacing of the editing cues us to assimilate the corpse as a fact, not to pause for reflection.

Carrying out her scheme to frame Wally, Mildred leaves, locking him inside with the body. Wally, realizing Mildred has abandoned him, stumbles around the house looking for a way out. Details from the first scene reappear, informing us that he is nearing the dead man. We reencounter a painting of sailboats that furnished the opening scene, and we again see the bullet holes left in the mirror. Wally bumps into a lamp, and the camera reframes to follow the fall of the lamp, ending on a high-angle medium shot that shows the corpse, the fallen lamp under its left arm. The fall of the lamp echoes the fall of the man. Through such returns, the film enunciates the story of the murder.

After framing Wally, Mildred arrives home, where the police and her daughter await her; she leaves with the police. The shots of arrival and departure are remarkably similar. Mildred arrives in a light-colored taxi that moves from right to left; she leaves in a dark-colored police car that moves from left to right. Both shots have matching camera setups. Upon her arrival, a long shot frames Mildred through the taxi from approximately a forty-five-degree angle to the left of the perpendicular (fig. 158). The taxi pulls away, leaving a long shot of her approaching the door of her luxurious home (fig. 159). Upon departure, a medium long shot from approximately a forty-five-degree angle to the right of the perpendicular frames Mildred and the two policemen at the doorstep (fig. 160). Between them and the camera, the dark police car intervenes (fig. 161). The scene that takes place inside, between this arrival and departure, ends with the camera moving, as Mildred exits with the police, to capture Veda on the stairs, subtly signaling her guilt.

A catalog of the kinds of repetition we see in *Mildred Pierce* would include graphic repetition, where the opening and closing shots of a scene resemble each other on a purely visual level (e.g., shots of the same object or person involve similar framing or camera setup). Such graphic repetition arises easily from the action, particularly the arrivals and departures that begin and end many scenes. These graphic matches render the scenes as discrete pieces, neatly stylized rather than spontaneous. The narrative information

154

155

156

157

each scene provides comes, as it were, packaged in a frame of matching shots. As discrete parts, such scenes suggest the kind of "pieces" the detective implies when he talks about making automobiles and murderers.

The film also builds on interscenic or situational repetitions, as when Mildred twice goes to Wally's cocktail lounge and hears a cabaret singer; when Monte seduces first Mildred, then Veda at the beach house; or when Veda receives presents (a dress, a car), which simultaneously give rise to a quarrel between Mildred and a man (Bert, Monte).[20] Such recurring situations again allow for graphic similarities between shots. Other examples include the two close-ups where Mildred takes a revolver from a drawer when going over her accounts (the first time after Bert has left, the second time after Monte has sold her business out from under her; figs. 162–163), the two scenes where Mildred buys property from Monte, and the two quarrels between Mildred and Bert followed by the arrival of their daughters.

Finally, as Bordwell notes, characterization in classical Hollywood cinema entails repetition. We can see this, for instance, with Kay (Jo Ann Marlowe). Before her entrance, Bert mentions the athletics she enjoys. We first see her playing football in the street with neighborhood boys. Veda scolds her for not looking after her appearance. And when Kay arrives home from school, she tells her mother, "I should have been a boy." Similarly, before

162                                        163

Veda's entrance, Bert criticizes her snobbishness and greed, traits which Veda's words and actions repeatedly confirm. (A different kind of character repetition occurs when through the window of Mildred's first restaurant on its opening night we see the titles of two other Warners films on the cinema marquee across the street: *Mr. Skeffington* and *God Is My Co-pilot*. Here the film associates Crawford's Mildred with what might be called her interfilmic doppelgänger : *Mr. Skeffington* features Bette Davis, who is commonly constructed as Crawford's star rival.)

Bordwell writes of classical Hollywood style, "The fundamental plenitude and linearity of Hollywood narrative culminate in metaphors of knitting, linking, and filling."[21] *Mildred Pierce* adheres so tightly to the principles of classical découpage and continuity editing that it literalizes these metaphors. The graphic rhymes with which scenes often begin and end, the interscenic graphic similarities, the situational and characterological repetitions create rings within rings. The visual and narrative repetitions of *Mildred Pierce* suggest a deep relationship between the structural function of the murder (as a formal element) and the grammar of its representation. They frame, or articulate, each scene as a discrete bit of information about the crime, and at the same time ensure that each scene is uniform with the whole.

*Character*

These various conventional forms of repetition—graphic, situational, characterological—can have a petrifying effect on filmed persons. Consider the scene following Mildred's arrival at the Hall of Justice. We see a low-angle long profile shot of a police officer, who sits on a bench smoking. Mildred enters the office, gives the night duty sergeant her name, and leaves. The brief scene ends with the same low-angle profile shot of the man smoking as Mildred exits (figs. 164–67). The framing and mise-en-scène transform the smoking

164

165

166

167

police officer into a fixture. He functions as another pair of eyes watching
Mildred and as a framing element. This brief episode, which serves only to
mark Mildred's arrival at the station and reveal that she has had two husbands, serves as a paradigm for most of the scenes. Within a frame formed by
opening and closing shots that are partial graphic duplications, it contains
its kernel of explicit narrative information, neatly articulated as a separate
piece, or building block, within a larger whole. The smoking police officer is
more a border than a character. A graphic enhancement disguised as a casual
detail, his momentary appearance in the film emblematizes the reifying effect of the classical style as the generic plot line brushes past him.

Situational repetition occasions renewed displays of the same character traits just as these iterated traits, in turn, remotivate the same situations. Mildred dotes on her daughter, justifying repeated scenes where she
gives Veda gifts; these scenes, in turn, reemphasize her excessively indul-
gent mothering. This convention of repeating information about characters pigeonholes them, reducing them to a set of legible traits. The story
world of *Mildred Pierce* calls the categorization of persons into question. In
the job-hunting sequence we see a list of job titles—saleswomen, drapers,
cashiers—arranged as alphabetical tabs in a file case behind a barred window through which Mildred gazes, desperately hoping to fit one of the cat-

egories (figs. 168–169). These shots suggest the incommensurability between a person and a job description. With her waitress uniform, Mildred
fits a role, and this fit has social consequences. Veda tells her, "Your people
degrade us." Monte, speaking admiringly of Veda (and, by implication, dis-
paragingly of Mildred) reproaches Mildred: "You'll never make a waitress
out of *her*." But while the story world at times reveals the anxiety and shame
caused by relentless vocational and social categorization, the discourse
reinforces prejudice. A crass kind of stereotyping is intertwined with a
more pervasive form of derealization within a film grammar that, for Eisenstein and Bordwell, recalls the layering of bricks. We see this, most predict-
ably, in the portrayal of Mildred's black maid Lottie (played by the uncredited Butterfly McQueen). This caricature is but an extreme manifestation of
the classical construction of characters as a fixed set of repeatedly signified
traits. But just as, in Soviet montage, where "the entire work of the living
man" exists in tension with "the pieces [the director] requires," in classical
Hollywood, the body of the actor also takes an antithetical position in relation to the film grammar. The performer does not simply disappear into the
traits of the character; the role bends to the contours of the actor. Stanley
Cavell writes, "This is the movies' way of creating individuals: they create *in-
dividualities*. For what makes someone a type is not his similarity with other
members of that type but his striking separateness from other people."[22]
Despite its different ideology, classical Hollywood's abstraction of persons
into types is, like that of classical Soviet cinema, dialectical.

*Mildred Pierce*, as both novel and film, received criticism for its portrayal
of Americans. Hoopes reports that Cain responded to "all those who said
that the unattractive people in *Mildred Pierce* [the novel] simply did not exist"
by saying, "I can only say, as Shaw said of Pinero, 'Doesn't this fellow meet
anybody?'"[23] James McManus called the film's characters "the slimy tera-
tology of a literary monster-monger," and Hoopes writes that many agreed

168

169

with McManus. But McManus did not want the characters to have more depth—he simply wanted them to appear more positive for propaganda purposes. Thus, Max Lerner rebutted McManus's criticism of Cain's characters, writing, "What I am objecting to is an art-for-Eric Johnston or the OWI's approach to movies."[24] Agee also attacks McManus: "John McManus of *PM* and doubtless many others regard [*Mildred Pierce*] as a bad advertisement for this country abroad. As movies go, it is one of the few anywhere near honest ones, if that is of any importance; and should be signally helpful in holding down immigration to the kind of people we appear to want."[25] In this review, Agee's sense of honesty seems not to require any absence of explanation, but rather coincides with Jerry Wald's conception of realism: "Realism for Wald meant . . . an explicitness about sex and topics forbidden by the production code, a certain decadence that allowed a glimpse of the underside of life."[26] But it is not only prudishness and nationalism that gives rise to dissatisfaction with the people in *Mildred Pierce*. The work of Parker Tyler (and later feminist critics)[27] suggests an unease with the way that instrumentalized and instrumentalizing characters, devoid of self-reflection, *can* seem acceptably real to a mass audience, even when—or, perhaps, precisely because—those characters are so blatantly stylized, their lives trimmed and parceled out into a series of discrete, subtly repetitive scenes that serve primarily to inform us about a murder.

Building a theory of the popular murder mystery aound *Mildred Pierce*, Tyler writes:

> In the form of the detective story meaning is purely rational and mechanical; the wheels of justice grind until the person of the criminal is turned up from the maze of the world. However, as we well know, the identity of the criminal and the establishment of his motive constitute the most superficial conception of the meaning of a crime. Take either Oedipus or Raskolnikoff. We . . . know their identity from the beginning. . . . The point of each of their stories is the quality of their guilt, its claim to forgiveness, and even the question of a fundamental innocence. That is to say, no story of crime is meaningful unless it brings into question the very nature of guilt itself. What is the responsibility of the criminal?[28]

In Tyler's literary examples, violence takes place before even the murderer understands it. Raskolnikov does not understand the why of his crime; Oedipus does not know the who. And even when these questions find their answers (Raskolnikov never settles on a satisfactory explanation for why he killed), they give rise to new, irresolvable questions of guilt and innocence. The persistence of irresolvable questions, or ambiguity, makes the crime story "meaningful." Tyler thus distinguishes between a "mechanical" meaning, which only produces knowledge of the killer's identity, motives, and comeuppance; and the "meaningful," which troubles the concepts of guilt, innocence, and justice. The realism of the crime story depends on the "meaningful": "Neither Mildred nor Veda is guilty enough to strike from the depths of human emotion any powerful reaction. This is merely because of Hollywood's lack of realism. Indeed, in this case I should say that the lack of artistry lies much less in the form than in the substance. Both Mildred and Veda are too shallow as human beings to be conscious of their guilt roles, and only consciousness of the ambiguous logic of guilt can give a character the majestic stature of true crime."[29] Tyler's association of realism with characters who are simultaneously self-conscious and self-blind reflects back on his psychoanalytic approach to film.[30] Psychoanalysis fosters a critical awareness of the ways that self and world elude conscious mastery. Realist art, for Tyler, shows how consciousness fails fully to grasp the world; it does not reduce the world to information.

Depleted of any existence for themselves, *Mildred Pierce's* characters are defined by their relation to the murder. It configures them like a magnet configures a dusting of iron filings; they succumb to its force, shifting away from, but perhaps not entirely out of, other potential generic modes such as melodrama. Inserting a murder at the beginning of its plot and ostentatiously hiding the identity of the killer, *Mildred Pierce* motivates its flashback structure and cues us to watch the scenes with an eye to learning who killed Monte and why. The pursuit of this information might entail dead ends, or retardation, but we can expect, at the end, to conclude with what Geoffrey Hartman calls the "ocular proof" of "one definitively visualized scene to which everything else might be referred."[31] This inevitable arrival at "proof," or at withheld facts, cancels the possibility of a more complex portrayal of character. As in early Soviet montage, the representation of interiority is not a textual dominant.

But even the organizational force of Eisenstein's montage does not necessarily block the projection of interiority (by a public still familiar with Dostoevsky)[32] onto screened persons. Ironically, a Hollywood film like *Mildred Pierce*, which, from its title on, putatively emphasizes the individual, can evacuate interiority from its portrayals even more definitively than a film like *The Battleship Potemkin*. Like many classical Hollywood films, it does this by reducing characters to information, and interiority to discrete desires: Mildred desires a luxurious life for Veda; Veda desires an expensive dress, a swimsuit, a car, a house, a boyfriend, her mother's husband, revenge; Wally Fay desires Mildred and her lucrative chain of restaurants;

170

Inspector Peterson desires the facts of the murder and the proof to convict the murderer; and so on. With the exception of Peterson, these characters primarily crave consumer goods such as luxurious clothing, furnishing, and housing.[33] Tyler observes: "Symbolic of their shallowness—and here Hollywood must be praised for its substance—is the concentration of Mildred and Veda on the manner in which they are housed. Everything seems to devolve on the luxury of the living quarters, of which the luxurious restaurant chain that Mildred creates is a direct symbol."[34] The things at which Mildred and Veda grasp—clothing, housing, a car—contain the characters literally and metaphorically; their desires define them. The automobile that Mildred gives Veda for her seventeenth birthday has Veda's initials painted on it (fig. 170), a detail that resonates with Inspector Peterson's line about putting the pieces together to get "an automobile, or a murderer." Bordwell writes of classical Hollywood film, "The character assumes a causal role because of his or her desires."[35] *Mildred Pierce*, like many other films in the classical style, transforms the complexity and instability of desire into a determinant, legible causality. Murder is a vehicle for this "deinteriorization" (or formalization), and yet, as we can see in that equation between murder detection and automobile production, it is also its sign.

*

Montage fragments the body through close-ups, giving rise to frequent associations between murder and montage; découpage articulates not primarily the pieces of the body, but the temporal segments of the life. Of the Hollywood montage sequence, Max Horkheimer writes in a 1942 letter to Leo Lowenthal: "You will remember those terrible scenes in the movies when some years of a hero's life are pictured in a series of shots which take about one or two minutes, just to show how he grew up or old, how a war started and passed by, a[nd] s[o] o[n]. This trimming of existence into some futile moments which can be characterized schematically symbolizes the disso-lution of humanity into elements of administration."[36] In regard to *Mildred Pierce*, we can expand Horkheimer's claim beyond the montage sequence to the découpage itself. For Horkheimer, the synecdochic summary of a life in the Hollywood montage sequence devalues the quality of duration: "Mass culture in its different branches reflects the fact that the human being is cheated out of his own entity which Bergson so justly called 'durée.'"[37] Robert Ray elaborates: Hollywood's "sustained use of narratively motivated abridge-ments encouraged the spectator to regard the vast majority of his own wak-ing hours as insignificant—indeed all hours that did not fit immediately into some ongoing 'plot.'"[38] But it is the hours that "fit" the plot which suffer a straitened significance: *Mildred Pierce* demonstrates the powerful collusion between the paradigmatic structure of the murder mystery and the style of classical découpage to reduce characters to cogs. The catalytic murder scene channels the meaning of every other scene of their lives into information about the origins of the crime. Repetitions, visual and narrative, impart a mechanistic quality to the screen realization of their being. And their eas-ily specifiable desires make them instruments of the plot. Thus, Hollywood might be said to reenact the automaticity that was the goal of the most ex-treme manifestations of the Soviet cult of the machine, not through a crude materialism, but through a reductive psychologism.

Opposite duration is the deadline, the marking of a before and an after. Essential to the orderly functioning of mass society, deadlines are also cru-cial to its motion picture narratives. Starting, as we learn from Gunning, with the ticking clock of *The Fatal Hour*, they form the finalizing points of convergence for Griffith's parallel lines. (A paragon of classical narrative [it is used as a textbook case of the classical Hollywood style by Bordwell and Thompson], Howard Hawks's *His Girl Friday* [1940] depends on a confluence of deadlines: the hanging, the train schedule that has Hildy and Bruce im-minently departing for Albany, the election.)[39] The ultimate deadline is im-pending death. Murder imposes this deadline abruptly. The murder mys-tery typically begins with such a deadline passing, or already past; it leaves behind necessity and impossibility in its wake. Similarly, Freud's descrip-tion of the primal scene suggests a deadline that passes before we are pre-pared to meet it; we suffer the consequences of missing it until, through analysis, we finally piece together what eludes us. It is this structure of a violence that happens "too fast to be spotted," and so must be reconstructed, that leads Tyler, Hartman, and Bordwell to draw parallels between murder mysteries and psychoanalysis. In "A History of an Infantile Neurosis," Freud posits a primal scene to which every last detail of his patient's case history

refers. His analysis aims to give the man his life, to free him from the unconscious ramifications of a childhood trauma that cause him to suffer repetitive behaviors and situations. But this same analysis, in the thoroughness
of its execution, also takes from the man his life, understood as something
irreducible and unfinalized: Freud explains his patient's every peculiarity. If
the murder mystery resembles the psychoanalytic discovery of the primal
scene, it does so in this double sense of potentially giving and taking life.
The murder scene can restore life to a character encased in the repetitive,
automatized conventions of representation, but as the focus of an investigation it can also petrify, as it does in *Mildred Pierce*, by predetermining the
parameters of every character's significance.

## Style and the Man

Consider the famous medium close-up of the bandit firing at the camera in
*The Great Train Robbery* (Edwin S. Porter, 1903; fig. 171). The shot provides no
essential narrative information. Indeed, its ties to the story are so loose that
its exact placement entailed an option. Charles Musser writes, "Labeled 'Realism' in the catalog, this extra shot could be placed at either the beginning or
end of the film. At the beginning, it introduced the leading character just like
the opening shot in Edison's earlier *Laura Comstock's Bag-Punching Dog*. Shown
at the end as an 'apotheosis,' it abstracted a single moment from the narrative as had been done with *Rube and Mandy at Coney Island*."[40] This shot of gun
violence as stylistic flourish well predates the Hollywood aestheticization of
Western violence remarked by numerous critics and historians—for example, David Cook, Stephen Prince, and Richard Slotkin—during and after the
Vietnam War.[41] And while a far cry from the exploding squibs and the slow-
motion flight of hurled bodies that characterizes the ultraviolent films of the
post-Vietnam era, this early example of violent spectacle suggests that the
tension between violence that predominantly functions as stylized attraction
and violence whose graphic realization has less importance than its narrative
motivations and meanings inheres in the film Western from its inception.

Even in Westerns where every scene of violence has explicit thematic significance, the spectacle of the individual man who appears skilled and calm
under circumstances where he might have to shoot or be shot competes with
more integrated narrative meanings for our attention. Robert Warshow emphasizes the power of this spectacle when he writes:

> Those values [we seek in the Western] are in the image of a single man who
> wears a gun on his thigh. . . . The drama is one of self-restraint: the moment of

171

violence must come in its own time and according to its special laws, or else it is valueless. . . . Our eyes are not focused on the sufferings of the defeated but on the deportment of the hero. Really, it is not violence at all which is the "point" of the Western movie, but a certain image of man, *a style*, which expresses itself most clearly in violence. Watch a child with his toy guns and you will see: what most interests him is not . . . the fantasy of hurting others, but to work out how a man might look when he shoots or is shot. A hero is one who looks like a hero.[42]

The spectacle that Warshow calls "a certain image of man, a style, which expresses itself most clearly in violence" differs from the spectacle that David Cook, writing of *The Wild Bunch*, calls "ballistic balletics": the stylized representation of the violence done to men's bodies is not the same as the stylized representation of the violent man. As spectacle, however, the style that Warshow describes can, like graphic images of bullets tearing holes through flesh, distract attention from narrative cues that call for reflective judgment. Thus, John Wayne projects "a certain image of man, a style" that makes him attractive even when he plays a tyrant in *Red River* (Howard Hawks, 1947), a racist and possibly a criminal in *The Searchers* (John Ford, 1956), and a man who does what he is told even when he knows it to be unjust in *Fort Apache* (John Ford, 1948).

Why does this particular style express itself most clearly in violence? Why is it important how a man *looks* specifically when he shoots or is shot, or, potentially, kills or is killed? And might we not extend Warshow's claim about style and guns to other forms of violence—and hence dilute his argument, which specifies the Western genre? Is not the style with which Errol Flynn wields a sword, or Ewan McGregor a light saber, equally important? Perhaps, but there is an important difference: in gunfighting, opponents duel from a distance. While accuracy and speed are skills crucial to the gunfighter, seeing and being seen take precedence over strength and agility. The moves are often slight: draw the gun, aim, fire. This is why Sergio Leone develops his elaborate gunfight montages, which lovingly dwell on the gunfighters' motionless bodies, breaking them down into parts with special emphasis on the eyes. It is Leone's shots, and not the bodies of the actors, which move rapidly and rhythmically. Only at the end of such sequences comes the brief movement and briefer shot, which breaks the spell. A gunfighter's look (in both senses of the word) thus takes on a different importance relative to fights with swords or fists, which require direct contact. In a showdown the drama is, finally, in the stance, the suspense of the hand hovering at the hip, and, most important, the eyes; the fall is often anticlimactic. (Classical Hollywood's reluctance to focus long on falling and fallen bodies has made an impression on critics as diverse as Mikhail Yampolsky and Stephen Prince.) The enunciation accords death itself little or no space; the way a man faces death is paramount.

The structure of the showdown—the distanced and primarily visual engagement of gunfighters with one another—also differentiates the dominant Western form of violence from, say, the drive-by and other surprise shootings of the gangster film. Gunfighters, even though they might begin by strategically using the various covers afforded by a western town or landscape, often study each other, like poker players looking for a tell. The very term "showdown" primarily means to display one's hand at poker. In the Western showdown, the player stakes his life. And more than in any other genre, life and death hinge on how well one sees, and how well, or poorly, one is seen. But the aim is not necessarily to see without being seen, to be a subject rather than an object. (Indeed, in *West of Everything*, Jane Tompkins goes so far as to claim that the hero aims to be an object.)[43] The gunfight is often as much a matter of self display—the display of oneself as indifferent to death, or at least as willing to stake one's life—as it is a matter of keeping one's opponent in one's sights. What Warshow calls "style" is precisely this *display* of indifference to killing and to being killed. The Western hero tends to approach gun violence impersonally. Ideally he shows neither fear of death nor eagerness to kill. The man he kills may have done him a grievous wrong, but if he takes vengeance through gunfighting, he appears to do so coldly, dispassionately. In *Ride Lonesome* (Budd Boetticher, 1959), the hero, Ben Brigade (Randolph Scott), a former sheriff turned bounty hunter, deliberately reveals himself and his route as he takes outlaw Billy John (James Best) to Santa Cruz for certain execution by hanging. He stays out in the open in order to lure Billy's brother Frank (Lee Van Cleef) to a showdown. Frank killed Brigade's wife many years before. In making no attempt to cover his trail or take a safer path, Brigade expresses a clear challenge to Frank, which Frank grasps. Brigade forces Frank into a showdown, and Frank meets him on Brigade's terms. Brigade coolly kills Frank. The man killed, if it is not the hero himself, can show himself a worthy adversary of the hero by similarly casting a cold eye on death, even if it is to be his own. We might read into Brigade's impassive, matter-of-fact demeanor duty, honor, or principle; but certainly not openly displayed passion. If Brigade overtly expresses any strong emotion at killing his wife's murderer, he does so only by burning down the tree on which Frank hanged her. In the tree-burning scene, Brigade appears in an extreme long shot. We can see his erect, motionless stance, but not his face.

A film like Anthony Mann's *The Tin Star* (1957) might rationalize the coolness of the gunfighter—Morg Hickman (Henry Fonda) teaches the inexperienced Sheriff Ben Owens (Anthony Perkins) that a man needs to be confident so that he can be calm enough to take an extra moment to decide whether force is necessary, and, if necessary, to aim well. But this lesson, while it ostensibly corrects the cliché of the seemingly impassive gunfighter, ultimately only sets the pattern in relief: Ben, who buys into the cliché, might display some awkwardness (thanks to Perkins's nuanced performance), even when he kills town bully Bart Bogardus (Neville Brand) in a final showdown at film's end; but his mentor, Morg, never appears anything other than completely indifferent and unquestionably competent in scenes where he might be called upon to take violent action.

If the style that Warshow finds at the heart of the Western lies, as I argue, in the *display* of indifference to killing and being killed, then clearly some Western heroes lack this style, and many manifest it only in complicated ways. Tompkins locates a moment where such indifference fails in one Western prototype, Owen Wister's novel *The Virginian* (1902). The Virginian breaks down and cries after hanging his friend Steve for cattle rustling. It is important that the hero is presiding over an execution here—and not engaging in a gunfight. (And Tompkins notes, "This is the only Western novel I have read in which the hero cries.")[44] In the scene where the Virginian kills his archenemy, Trampas, he again sobs, but not at the prospect of killing or being killed; instead, he cries because he mistakenly believes that by engaging in this duel, to which he is honor bound, he forfeits his lover, who has demanded that he choose between fighting and her. Prior to the showdown, Trampas, full of hatred and fear, turns to alcohol for courage, but in the description of the gunfight itself, we see nothing of hatred or fear—only the wind from Trampas's bullet. After killing Trampas, the Virginian hides his thoughts and feelings from his friends:

A wind seemed to blow his sleeve off his arm, and he replied to it, and saw Trampas pitch forward. He saw Trampas raise his arm from the ground and fall again, and lie there this time, still. A little smoke was rising from the pistol on the ground, and he looked at his own, and saw the smoke flowing upward out of it.

"I expect that's all," he said aloud. . . .

He had scarcely noticed that he was being surrounded and congratulated. His hand was being shaken, and he saw it was Scipio in tears. Scipio's joy made his heart like lead within him. He was near telling his friends everything, but he did not.

"If anybody wants me about this," he said, "I will be at the hotel."

"Who'll want you?" said Scipio. "Three of us saw his gun out." And he vented his admiration. "You were that cool! That quick!"

"I'll see you boys again," said the Virginian, heavily, and he walked away.

Scipio looked after him, astonished. "Yu' might suppose he was in poor luck."[45]

The basic structure of this standard Western scene, the showdown—two men stand in the middle of the street and aim guns at one another, usually in front of at least one witness—undeniably demands of them impassive self-display precisely when such display is hardest to achieve. The Western showdown thematizes the assertion of disposability that characterizes the murder scene more generally: the Western gunfighter, in order to be true to type, must demonstrate a calm willingness to forfeit his own life. He must assert the disposability of his life in order for that life to retain any value. As we shall see, this willingness to stake one's life is also, in Hegel's influential dialectic of lordship and bondage, a crucial step in the process of becoming an individual self-consciousness. But before we compare the structure of the Western showdown to Hegel's narrative of a life-and-death struggle for recognition, let us juxtapose the Western's "duel plot" with the novel's marriage plot, to which Hegel's contemporary, Jane Austen, gave new form. A recent work on the social content of Austen's style by D. A. Miller has far-reaching implications for the consideration of style more generally; in particular, Miller's essay helps to illuminate my argument that the style of the Western, while expressed "most clearly in violence," necessarily precludes the full realization of murder.[46]

*

Initially, it seems perverse to imagine that we can compare an Austen heroine, negotiating the treacherous social terrain of marriage, with a Budd Boetticher hero, making his way through a violent Western frontier. (Laura

Mulvey famously cites Boetticher's sexist characterization of movie heroines in her canonical essay "Visual Pleasure and Narrative Cinema": "What
counts is what the heroine provokes, or rather what she represents. She is
the one, or rather the love or fear she inspires in the hero, or else the concern
he feels for her, who makes him act the way he does. In herself the woman
has not the slightest importance.")[47] But the love scene rivals that of murder in terms of its effects on narrative (and film) form; the romantic kiss is
as iconic as the showdown. And Miller's work, when considered along with
Warshow's 1954 "Movie Chronicle: The Westerner," makes possible a productive juxtaposition of the marriage plot and Hollywood Westerns. Specifically, we can see how the style of both the Austen heroine (an influential,
if never equaled, model for the heroines of subsequent courtship plots) and
the Western hero arises out of the negation, renunciation, or repression of
personal desire or self-interest.

In order to conceptualize the problematic of the murder scene, we have,
thus far, posited a universal subject as the victim of murder. The comparison of the Western and the marriage plot allows us to see more clearly the
role of difference. In individual murder scenes, the subject is always particular (a particular race, ethnicity, gender, class, age, sexual orientation, etc.).
The murder scene defines and/or obscures difference as it follows and revises various social and cultural patterns of recognition. We can see the way
the murder scene is implicated in larger patterns of recognition in Melvin
Van Peebles's anecdote about the Atlanta premiere of *Sweet Sweetback's Baadasssss Song* at the Coronet Theater in 1971. He recalls sitting next to "a little
old black lady" who, during the scene where the hero is in the desert, was
praying out loud, "Oh Lord, let him die . . . let him die on his own." Van Peebles explained her prayer: until this film, if a black man "did anything majestic or defiant in a movie, he was going to die." Since everyone is equal
before nature, the woman preferred the hero to die by exposure to the harsh
conditions of the desert rather than be murdered by the white men chasing
him. At least he would have "the dignity that he died on his own and they
didn't kill him."[48] The point of Van Peebles's film was to create a resourceful
and assertive black hero whose story is not abruptly ended by murder, and
whose significance is not markedly curtailed because he disappears from the
discourse. As Van Peebles and the woman next to him understood, reductive
aesthetic representation coincides with reductive political representation.

*

Miller focuses on Austen's development of free indirect style, through which
the narrative discourse easily moves in and out of the consciousness of the

heroines. He provides the following negative definition of style: "'All style and no substance': the formula helps us recognize not that style is different, or even opposite, to substance (and hence capable of being united with it . . . but that the one is incompatible with, and even corrosive of the other. Style can only emerge at the expense of substance, as though it sucked up the latter into the vacuum swollen only with the 'airs' it gives itself."[49] "Substance," in Miller's analysis, has a specific meaning; it is the "person" as defined by the parameters (married, unmarried, landed, impoverished, etc.) of her social position. Actual subjects do not always fit comfortably within these parameters and their social implications: "Behind the glory of style's willed evacuation of substance lies the ignominy of a subject's *hopelessly insufficient social realization*."[50] The failure of a woman to marry—her rejection by and of available men—entails shame. To avoid this shame, or potential shame, Austen's heroines must initially display indifference to it through displaying indifference to their own marriage prospects. It is precisely this initial show of indifference that helps heroines such as Elizabeth Bennett and Emma, in the end, to marry "appropriately," just as the Western hero's ability to repress personal feelings perfects his aim and timing. In regard to such heroines, we might paraphrase Warshow's description of the Western hero: "The drama is one of self-restraint: the moment of [violence/conjugality] must come in its own time and according to its special laws, or else it is valueless." The Austen heroine must display lack of interest in the determination of her conjugal fate; the Western hero must remain impassive as he prepares to kill or be killed. In the Western's violent story world, style can, quite literally, evacuate substance.

As in the moment when the Western hero takes violent action, the moment when Emma or Elizabeth consents to marry the appropriate suitor entails exposure of the self as vulnerable. Indeed, it even entails a certain self-erasure marked by the woman's giving up her family name to adopt the name of her husband. Miller writes of the Austen heroine at this moment, "She becomes Woman at last, compelled both to accept the state of lack that makes her a well-functioning subject, and to represent this lack to men so that, at her expense, they may imagine themselves exempt from it."[51] It may seem that here the comparison with the Western hero reaches an impasse. As Lee Clark Mitchell demonstrates, Westerns tend to immunize the male hero against lack.[52] And in the Western, the male hero can reject conjugality without facing the shame this rejection would entail for the Austen heroine. But this impasse is only apparent: style, in both cases, emerges out of social alienation, or a desire to break out of the delimited role or value one would occupy or have within a community. And in both cases, gender roles can be subverted. Miller's analysis of Austen novels suggests that for the greater part of the novel the heroine negates projected lack through forging a style of reflection which keeps her from becoming "woman at last" too hastily. Conversely, Mitchell observes that the cowboy's body-accentuating costume invites the spectator to see him as spectacle or object of desire—a position coded as feminine:

> The cowboy's sign-laden costume permits the eye to roam across the male body without seeming to focus on that body as actual flesh. In Western films, the eye is trapped and held up by fetish items associated with parts of the body, as our gaze is directed from eyes, chins, chests, legs, and muscle groups to articles instead that either cover or exaggerate them. Hats of assorted shapes and tilts . . . handkerchiefs knotted round the neck; ornate buckles, gun belts worn low, and, of course, an array of holsters and six-shooters; pearl-buttoned shirts, fringed jackets; leather gloves carefully fitted and as carefully stripped off; leggings, chaps (with the groin area duly uncovered and framed), and tight-fitting Levi's or leather pants (in the only genre that allows men to wear them); long, stylized linen dusters; pointed, high-heeled boots and spurs: all the way up and down, the cowboy's costume invites and deflects our gaze.[53]

According to Mitchell, Western violence is the price paid by, or the punishment meted out to, the male body for being a desirable spectacle. Ultimately, however, the hero's body is made vulnerable, wounded, or "lacking" only so that its masculine invulnerability can be recuperated all the more forcefully: "Western heroes are knocked down, made supine, then variously tortured so that they can recover from harm in order to rise again. Or rather, the process of beating occurs so that we can see men recover, regaining their strength and resources in the process of once again making themselves into men. The paradox lies in the fact that we watch them become what they already are, as we exult in the culturally encoded confirmation of a man again becoming a man."[54] Marriage allows the Austen heroine to become "woman at last"; violence enables the Western hero "to become," to paraphrase Miller, "man at last." And style, defined as the displayed renunciation of self-interest or desire, emerges as a response to, or symptom of, the social pressure that imposes on the subject such repressive gender, and other, roles. One mechanism by which social pressure operates is shame. The Austen heroine incurs shame by failing to marry; the Western hero, by walking away from a fight. Miller calls "the extraordinary sensitivity to shame" the "basic operating equipment" of style.[55] We might define shame as the desire to be invisible, even, temporarily, to be dead. There is a suicidal impulse to shame.

Suicide is a form of murder (and sometimes murder is a form of suicide).[56] Style forestalls shame by rendering the desiring self already invisible; it "kills" the desiring self, leaving only the seemingly impersonal or indifferent subject. The Western hero keeps shame at bay by exercising enormous self-control in relation to violence. He is not a loose gun. But the sequence of events ultimately forces him, in order to vanquish shame, to enter an arena where he must either kill or be killed.

Paradoxically, grasping too quickly at a chance to kill, or marry, incurs shame just as does the failure to marry, kill, or be killed at the appropriate moment. Style, for both the Austen heroine and the Western hero, entails self-restraint, while a too open display of one's desires incurs shame. Austen novels often reveal the consequences of a lack of self-restraint through various characters—Lydia Bennett's foolhardy elopement with Wickham, Charlotte Lucas's compromise to marry a man far beneath her in judgment, Mary Crawford's excessive and off-putting wit. Westerns feature secondary characters who lack self-restraint when it comes to violence—the sociopathic juvenile delinquents Billy Jack (Skip Homeier) and Chink (Henry Silva) of *The Tall T* (Budd Boetticher, 1957); the excitable Stumpy (Walter Brennan), who mistakes his friend Dude (Dean Martin) for the enemy and nearly kills him in *Rio Bravo* (Howard Hawks, 1959); the blustery Frank "Stonewall" Torrey (Elisha Cook, Jr.) of *Shane* (George Stevens, 1953), who, too quick to draw on professional gunslinger Jack Wilson (Jack Palance), is shot dead in the muddy street.

Austen's heroines partake of their author's style through free indirect discourse, but in the end, they marry and she does not; they lose their style while she maintains it. Miller writes: "Behind the glory of a style's willed evacuation of substance lies the ignominy of a subject's hopelessly insufficient social realization, just as behind style's ahistorical impersonality lies the historical impasse of someone whose social representation doubles for social humiliation. . . . Austen Style . . . presupposes, and enforces, its author's own 'under-representability,' a condition I can describe most simply for the moment by observing that the realism of her works allows no one like Jane Austen to appear in them. Amid the happy wives and pathetic old maids, there is no successfully unmarried woman."[57] For Miller, as for Warshow, style emerges in conjunction with risk to the self. The stylized moment is the moment of intensified bodily and social vulnerability. Style, which requires a seemingly cool disregard for one's person—its needs and desires—receives its starkest expression in murder scenes. The murderless Western is rare. (Even Fred Zinneman's 1955 Western musical *Oklahoma* and Mel Brooks's 1974 Western comedy *Blazing Saddles* show killing.) But while almost every Western has a murder, few, if any, approach showing it fully.

This generic mitigation of murder appears most clearly when we contrast the hero's calm under fire with rarer scenes where all such self-control momentarily evaporates. Consider *The Man from Laramie* (Anthony Mann, 1955). Confronted by Dave Waggoman (Alex Nicol), a man to whom style means nothing, the hero Will Lockhart (James Stewart) is momentarily reduced to his wounded body. Unprepared for his dishonorable adversary, he is forced to hold out his hand to be shot point blank. He staggers, gaping and cringing in agonizing pain, amazed and crippled. To show the violence—which is not fatal, even though it is more disturbing than many of Hollywood's deadly showdowns—the film must dispense, at least momentarily, with the style.

\*

Critics writing on the Western tease out the ways it responds to various desires for recognition. Robert Ray, for instance, locates in the genre a repeated refusal to choose between an "outlaw" individuality and an official hero who stands for community values. In Ray's reading, this myth of reconciliation between these two positions answers to an American anxiety about giving up a cherished myth of American exceptionalism and individualism in an increasingly globalized world. He further argues that we can map this reconciled binary opposition between the freedom of the individual and the responsibilities and encumbrances of community, so starkly dramatized in the Western as a matter of life-and-death struggle, onto other genres. Jane Tompkins claims that the Western arises as a male backlash against American Victorian domestic novels and the female-dominated worlds they create.[58] For Richard Slotkin, the Western's variations on the frontier myth often serve to cement, or subvert, the repression of aspects of American history, or American society, that threaten its claim to legitimacy. For Gilberto Perez, "the Ford Western celebrates a democracy emergent on the frontier. Through the encounter with the wilderness, civilization in Ford undergoes a breakdown of classes and snobberies and a renewal of the democratic spirit."[59] In their varied conjoining of insufficient social recognition (which is linked to shame), heightened self-risk, and a fight to the death in a struggle for mastery, Westerns, as well as the critical literature surrounding them, recall, in multiple ways, a more abstract narrative produced roughly contemporaneously with Austen's novels: Hegel's dialectic of master and slave.

\*

If Eisenstein had proposed a film adaptation of Hegel's *Phenomenology* instead of Marx's *Capital*, or if Jacques Feyder had imagined a film treatment of Hegel rather than Montesquieu, they would have found, in the Western showdown, a ready dramatization of the fight to the death described in the master-slave dialectic; it has the key elements—the staking of one's life and consciousness of the self as an object for the other in a struggle for recognition. In the dialectic between lordship and bondage, we find the scene of the showdown itself: the fight to the death constitutes the site where both the Western hero and Hegel's individual self-consciousness claim, and sometimes irrevocably lose, the recognition they desire. To invoke Hegel here does not mean to subscribe to his totalizing view of history. Rather than read him strictly as a philosopher, this comparison aims to read him as a narrator, whose story is, like Miller's, about a subject's search for recognition.

The murder scene can have various effects on the character of the victim—murder can reduce the victim to a mere narrative function or symbol; conversely, the murder victim can appear more real or important precisely through being killed off. The Western gunfight (and specifically the showdown) elaborates the murder scene from another angle: through the prism of the self-consciously staked life. Let us return to the "floating" close-up that could be inserted either at the beginning or end of *The Great Train Robbery*. Unanchored to any particular space and time in the story world, and aiming at the camera, the man in the shot stages himself, and is framed, as pure presence. The shot suggests continuity between the space of the man firing the gun and the space of spectator, even though both performer and spectator know themselves to be separated in space and time. Charles Musser writes, "The shot added realism to the film by intensifying the spectators' identification with the victimized travelers. It reiterated and intensified the viewer-as-passenger convention of the railroad subgenre."[60] By placing the spectator in the imaginary position of facing death, the shot functions as what Tom Gunning defines as an attraction.[61] Like Eisenstein's attractions—and like contemporary film spectacles of violence, with their booming stereo sound and abrupt edits—it assaults the audience, aiming not primarily for a cognitive, but for an emotional, even bodily, effect. But what is so attractive about imagining oneself—from a safe position, of course—facing death?

The staking of one's own life famously appears as a crucial phase in Hegel's story of the development of self-consciousness, leading into the dialectic of lordship and bondage: "And it is solely by risking life that freedom is obtained; only thus is it tried and proved that the essential nature of self-consciousness is not bare existence, is not merely the immediate form in which it at first makes its appearance, is not its mere absorption in the expanse of life."[62] For Hegel, to stand apart from oneself in order to stake one's own life "proves" that the self-consciousness which stands apart exceeds the biological existence that is its medium. Hegel continues: "The individual, who has not staked his life, may, no doubt, be recognized as a Person; but he has not attained the truth of this recognition as an independent self-consciousness."[63] Only through staking its life can self-consciousness assert its independence from that life, which is, nevertheless, necessary to it. Moreover, only the freedom and power to engage in violence outside the law, to declare oneself independent of communal bonds and regulations, can, for Hegel, permit the disavowal of violence in favor of community to be a free choice; otherwise it remains merely a response to coercion or an automatic effect of a deterministic rationality. Where Ray sees Hollywood's withdrawal of the necessity to choose between individual and community we might also see a realization of what, for Hegel, is the necessity to keep both terms—outlaw individual and community—in play. The movies, and not just Westerns, have long made possible the vicarious experience of a highly visible self-assertion against both death and the need for communal bonds. The sheer frequency of scenes of such heroism speaks to their popularity and attests to a desire among consumers of mass culture for the imaginary experience of life-and-death struggle.

Many Western showdowns dramatize, in starkest terms, the structure of the dialectic between lordship and bondage at the stage where two self-consciousnesses stake their lives, prior to assuming the roles of lord and bondsman, and prior to the mutual recognition that constitutes an ideal society. In Hegel's narrative, each self-consciousness seeks recognition from the other, so that it can exist as an independent self-consciousness not only for itself, but for the other as well. Similarly, in Westerns, shooting and being shot at entail reflection and self-consciousness: the gunfighter both sees and sees himself being seen by the one he sees.

Seeing and seeing oneself being seen go beyond the purely visual tactics of the shooting contest. Consider, for instance, the final showdown between Pat Brennan (Randolph Scott) and Frank Usher (Richard Boone) in The Tall T. Usher and his accomplices Billy Jack and Chink have taken Brennan and Doretta Mims (Maureen O'Sullivan) hostage in order to gain ransom money from Doretta's wealthy father. While holding them captive, Usher distinguishes himself from his sociopathic accomplices, expressing admiration for Brennan and sharing his desire to settle down on a ranch of his own. To share the other's desire is, for Hegel, to move beyond the life-and-death struggle to the middle term, the social, where the two extremes—the two self-consciousnesses—each mutually desire what the other desires. Unfortunately, Usher cannot make this leap. He must prove himself to Brennan and to himself by staking his life. Brennan manages to kill Usher's two accomplices while Usher is away, and Usher returns to enter a life-and-death struggle with Brennan, which he loses. Boetticher says of Boone's Usher, "I felt that Boone [Usher] really loved Randy [Brennan] in the picture, to the point of being terribly attracted to him physically. He would have liked to have been Randy."[64] Hegel writes that self-consciousness "sees its own self in the other," which is why it feels "it must cancel this its other."[65] Similarly, Boetticher says of the films he made with Randolph Scott more generally, "In every one of the Scott pictures, I felt that I could have traded Randy's part with the villain's."[66] In the same interview, Boetticher addresses Usher's need to stake his life:

> Q. Why does Boone come back and try to kill Scott at the end of *The Tall T*? Could he have kept going and escaped the situation?
>
> A. I think he had to come back. When Boone gets wrapped up in that burlap outside the cave, so that he can't even see, it's like putting a hood over Susan Hayward's head in *I Want to Live*. No matter how many steps you have to take, when they cover your head up, you're dead. Also, remember that Boone's last cry was for Randy. In dying, he wanted to see him.[67]

Usher dies because he acts on his desire for Brennan. The importance of Brennan's view of Usher to Usher's sense of self resonates with Hegel's narrative of *individual* self-consciousness as it seeks recognition. But it also points up the strictures of the Western's heteronormativity: instead of acting on his physical attraction to Scott and revealing his own desire, Boone must assert "masculine" wholeness and deny feminized "lack." Instead of expressing love, he must die of it. In this light, Hegel's story about the separation of self-consciousnesses into masters and slaves, so influential within Western political thought, also appears to be a parable about gender division and sexual desire in a patriarchal society.

*

While the larger social stakes in the contest between Brennan and Usher lie well in the background of their story world, Hegel conceptualizes the dialectic between individual lordship and bondage as a framework through which to analyze the historical progress of entire societies. And in many Westerns, the gun duel also expresses broader social tensions.[68] We find this implication reflected in Warshow's essay, beginning with its epigraph, the first eight lines of Shakespeare's sonnet 94:

> They that have power to hurt and will do none,
> That do not do the thing they most do show,

Who, moving others, are themselves as stone,
Unmoved, cold, and to temptation slow;
They rightly do inherit heaven's graces,
And husband nature's riches from expense;
They are the lords and owners of their faces,
Others but stewards of their excellence.

For Warshow, the self-restrained and virtuous Western heroes are the "lords" and "others but stewards"; the gangster "desperately wants to 'get ahead'" whereas "the Westerner is the last gentleman."[69] Warshow never explicitly invokes Hegel, but we can detect in his understanding of the Western a view of history and class relations that we can trace back to *The Phenomenology of Mind*. For Warshow, the Western hero's stylized violence has nothing to do with labor.

> The Westerner is *par excellence* a man of leisure. Even when he wears the badge of a marshal or, more rarely, owns a ranch, he appears to be unemployed. We see him standing at a bar, or playing poker. . . .
>
> Employment of some kind—usually unproductive—is always open to the Westerner, but when he accepts it, it is not because he needs to make a living, much less from any idea of "getting ahead." Where could he want to "get ahead" to? By the time we see him, he is already "there."[70]

Warshow's insistence on the Western hero's freedom from ordinary labor coincides with his emphasis on the hero's style: style, by definition, conceals the labor that produces it. The stylist makes it "look like but a moment's thought." Complicating Warshow's argument, Jane Tompkins writes of a life-and-death struggle in Louis L'Amour's *Heller with a Gun* (1955):

> Though it reproduces with amazing thoroughness and intensity the emotional experience of performing intolerable labor, it removes the feelings associated with doing work from their usual surroundings and places them in a locale and a set of circumstances that expand their meaning, endow them with an overriding purpose, and fill them with excitement. In short, hard work is transformed here from the necessity one wants to escape into the most desirable of human endeavors: action that totally saturates the present moment, totally absorbs the body and mind, and directs one's life to the service of an unquestioned goal.
>
> Rather than offering an alternative to work, the novels of Louis L'Amour make work their subject. They transfer the feelings of effort and struggle that belong to daily life into a situation that gives them a point, usually the preservation of life itself. . . . Although the settings are exotic and the

circumstances extreme, these situations call on the same qualities that get people out of bed to go to work, morning after morning. They require endurance more than anything else; not so much the ability to make an effort as the ability to sustain it. It isn't pain that these novels turn away from. It isn't self-discipline or a sense of responsibility. Least of all is it the will to persevere in the face of difficulty. What these novels offer that life does not offer is the opposite of a recreational spirit. It is seriousness.[71]

For Warshow, the Western hero avoids the indignity of the "rat race" to "get ahead" or, more simply, make ends meet. In this the cowboy differs from the gangster, who directs his unrestrained violence to that end. But as Tompkins compellingly argues, the L'Amour hero—and, by implication, many other Western heroes—replaces the indignity of alienated labor with work that enables the hero to direct his very "life to the service of an unquestioned goal." Rather than work that deadens the possibility of experience through mind-numbing repetition, the hero's work "totally saturates the present moment, totally absorbs the body and mind." If we situate Tompkins's and Warshow's images of the Western hero in relation to Hegel's dialectic of lord and bondsman, we see that the hero has the best of both worlds. He appears as independent self-consciousness and lord, willing and able to stake his life. And yet, unlike the lord of Hegel's dialectic, he also seems to reap the benefits of labor, which accrue to the bondsman. With a foot in both camps, lord's and bondsman's, he stalls the change motivated by the dialectic. To stake one's life means to labor; mastery is slavery.

Using Hegelian language, but rejecting the Hegelian trajectory, Tompkins claims that in performing his violent labor, the Western hero aims to divest himself of self-consciousness:

> By becoming a solid object, not only is a man relieved of the burden of relatedness and responsiveness to others, he is relieved of consciousness itself, which is to say, primarily, consciousness *of* self.
>
> At this point, we come upon the intersection between the Western's rejection of language and its emphasis on landscape. Not fissured by self-consciousness, nature is what the hero aspires to emulate: perfect being-in-itself.[72]

For Tompkins, rather than asserting his self-consciousness and seeking its recognition (like Hegel's' individual self-consciousness), the Western hero seeks to retreat into—and here Tompkins uses Hegel's terminology—"being-in-itself." While Tompkins's connection between landscape and hero is compelling, she overstates her case. The hero may seek to display indifference, or an objectlike woodenness, but many of the scenes in which he displays this remarkable impassivity imply just the opposite: that under such circumstances it is impossible not to feel strongly moved. And, indeed, in one of Tompkins's own case studies, Owen Wister's novel *The Virginian*, the narrative makes clear that despite the Virginian's impassive facade, he experiences a great deal of anxiety, despair, rage, and so on. Indeed, returning to Warshow's concept of style, we might say that the greater the mismatch between the hero's cool exterior and the clear power of the circumstances to call forth extreme emotion, the greater the hero's style. This is why this particular form of style, for Warshow, "expresses itself most clearly in violence." Miller discovers in Austen's style a story—like Hegel's dialectic of lordship and bondage—about a violence intricately bound with selfhood. Hegel presents consciousness with a stark choice: accept to murder or be murdered; or accept being an unessential, unrecognized slave. Austen's style, for Miller, already constitutes such a choice: in its strict impersonality and indifference, it forestalls the violence of insufficient social recognition by apparently killing off the self that expresses the need for recognition. In contrast, the Western hero refuses to relinquish his demand for recognition, even if it means he has to kill or be killed.

Despite the seeming strangeness of comparing the Western and the marriage plot, we can find many resonances between them. But these resonances do not mean that we can neglect the differences between an Elizabeth Bennett and a Ben Brigade. Murder scenes and marriage plots emphasize and/ or contain difference according to political, social, and cultural patterns of recognition and exclusion. The critics we examine in this chapter all consider the way characters fit, or chafe against, such patterns. The critical approaches to the Western covered here bifurcate along two separate strands: criticism that decodes the homoerotic subtext of the genre, and that which sees its generic plots and characters as the framework for the telling and retelling of myths and allegories about the legitimacy and intricacies of United States political power. On the one hand we have a critical understanding of Western violence and murder as a subtle pattern of punishment meted out to men for gazing meaningfully at one another while making spectacles of their bodies.[73] On the other we have critics concerned with the political implications of the climactic gunfights that define the long history of the genre. These approaches do not cancel one another; together they tell a larger story about nation building, political power, and gendering. And we can locate their roots in two classic midcentury essays on the Western: Warshow's essay on style, discussed above, and Bazin's on the Western as an epic form.

Bazin describes the Western as "the only genre whose origins are almost identical with those of the cinema itself." He compares it, in its epic and historical quality, to the films of the Soviet avant-garde and speculates that cinema is "the specifically epic art." Notably, the murder scene—the showdown in the Western, martyrdom in the classics of the Soviet montage era—occupies an important role in the syntax of these epic cinemas. And Hegel's narrative of a ritual fight to the death in a struggle for recognition underlies both Hollywood's Western showdown and the Soviet myth of the martyr which develops out of Marx's Hegelian conceptualization of class struggle. Bazin writes that "[the Western] must possess some . . . secret that somehow identifies it with the essence of cinema."[74] One component of this "secret" must be the showdown, or gunfight, the genre's key iconographic element. It lies at the intersection, or nodal point, of many threads that have historically constituted "filmness." As a murder scene, it starkly dramatizes the tensions between registering and cutting person and world in story and discourse, which lie at the crux of photography-based narrative film. Around this crux swirl the Western's particular reflections and refractions of cinema's historic ties to the nation-state and its role as a purveyor of national myths concerning origins, power, and social hierarchies.

Warshow, we have seen, locates the Western's "secret" in a style best expressed through violence. One of his key case studies is Henry King's *The Gunfighter*. He writes: "No matter what he has done, he looks right, and he remains invulnerable because, without acknowledging anyone else's right to judge him, he has judged his own failure and has already assimilated it, understanding . . . that he can do nothing but play out the drama of the gun fight again and again until the time comes when it will be he who gets killed. What 'redeems' him is that he no longer believes in this drama and nevertheless will continue to play his role perfectly: the pattern is all. The proper function of realism in the Western movie can only be to deepen the lines of this pattern."[75] "Again and again," "the pattern is all": Warshow's description of Gregory Peck's Jimmy Ringo makes him sound a little like Marilyn Monroe in Bruce Conner's *Marilyn Times Five* (1973), a sad and tedious loop of an old stag film featuring Monroe rolling a Coca-Cola bottle over her almost naked body. Some of Monroe's camp iconicity tempers the figure of the gunfighter. If camp revises popular culture to suit marginalized tastes, the classical Western, at first glance, might seem more like camp in reverse: it typically represents a culturally dominant image—the strong, silent, individualist white man—as a marginalized figure within its story world. But so much of Warshow's description resonates with the discourse on camp: "he has judged his own failure" suggests camp's "failed serious-ness," identified by Clement Greenberg and Susan Sontag; "the pattern is all" suggests the radical separation of substance from style mentioned by Miller, but it also suggests the foregrounding, if not exaggeration, of pop-cultural devices (here the genre's basic syntax and semantics) that defines the camp aesthetic; "again and again" recalls the tedium that often marks camp; "he no longer believes in this drama" points up the dissolution of the gunfighter's aura; and that he "will continue to play his role perfectly" reso-nates with camp's insistence on self-conscious performance and masquer-ade. The mainstream Western hero, Warshow's man of a certain style, tee-ters on the brink of camp. In doing so, he threatens to undercut with irony the seriousness of the master-slave dialectic, so reliably played out in Hol-lywood cinema's foundational epic form.

"You can't camp about something you don't take seriously," Christopher Isherwood writes in *The World in the Evening*. Few things are more serious than murder, particularly when it functions as a primal scene, central to the foundation of everything from society to manliness. But if the political aim of camp is to ironize or undercut the things mainstream culture takes seriously, then Isherwood's statement means that camp is doomed either to failure (because mainstream culture continues to take the camped ob-ject seriously), or self-destruction (when camp destroys its own object, so that no one takes it seriously). In regard to the Western, camp fails. The style that best expresses itself through violence remains compelling and the fig-ure of the gunfighter proliferates, migrating to other genres and national cinemas.

The generic gunfighter short-circuits, while Hegel's self-consciousness moves on: "As soon as the warring individuals stop and think (as soon as they carry out that 'comparison' of their standing vis-à-vis each other) vi-olence must come to an end, for it appears to them as entirely counterpro-ductive—instead of asserting his difference and uniqueness, each individ-ual finds himself doing exactly the same thing as the others; and so instead of finding his own unique identity he loses himself in the crowd. Violence—or at least the blind, unconditional violence of exclusion—now ceases to make any sense."[76] In contrast to Hegel's evolving individuals, Hollywood's gunfighters keep replaying the same scene. Their generic style, like the duel to the death through which it realizes its apotheosis, suggests distinctive-ness *and* disposability: unique within the fictional world, the gunfighter is commonplace, or replaceable, within the genre. Laying claim to an individ-uality, and masculinity, that are at once exclusive and illusive, he figures the pathos of genre.

## Murder in the Mirror: *The Shining* (1980) and *Dead Man* (1995)

*Is the secret to murder to be found in a reflection?*
*She sits by the mirror and waits.*

SALLY POTTER, *Thriller*

Consider the scene from Lev Kulijanov's film adaptation of *Crime and Punishment* (1970) where Raskolnikov (Georgi Taratorkin) murders Elizaveta (Lyubov' Sokolova): after Elizaveta falls, we are left with the distorted image of Raskolnikov in the window of the cabinet that was behind her (figs. 172–75). A reflection needs to be brought in; otherwise, the scene cannot be represented in its full consequence. The distorted image in the glass expresses Dostoevsky's theme that in killing the pawnbroker and her sister, Raskolnikov destroys himself. Felling the other, he leaves himself with nothing but his own distorted self-image. His gaze can only turn inward, just as the mirror on-screen, with its self-reflexive overtones, turns the film in on itself, reminding the viewer that the image on the screen is but a reflection, a stylized representation.[77]

Dostoevsky's novel gives rise to a cinematic scene that demonstrates how the event of murder can strike at a central problematic of film form: the coordination of point of view, which is fundamental to film syntax. At stake in this particular scene is the shot-reverse-shot sequence, a crucial syntactic device that often stabilizes filmic perspective by clearly establishing a spatial relationship between persons. Kulijanov's "reverse shot" (the absented victim's point of view) must take place in the story world, as a reflection, since it has lost all motivation in the editing or enunciation. Murder, the abolition of one of the potential points of view (the victim's), disrupts the stabilizing "suture" of conventional editing.[78]

The problem of representing murder permeates Hollywood cinema, from the level of the classic shot-reverse-shot sequence to the large systems of genre, which entail decisions about point of view in a broader sense. Genres such as the horror film, the combat film, and the Western, in stylizing violence, inevitably transform, or deform, the real violence they reference. Correspondingly, numerous scholars have described them as ideologically suspect distortions of a violent past.[79] We have seen, for instance, Agee's criticism that combat films trivialize the suffering undergone by those fighting in World War II. Ralph and Natasha Friar's *The Only Good Indian . . . : The Hollywood Gospel* charges the Western with distorting racial violence. Film historians have panned their book for its historical inaccuracies and overgeneralization,[80] but in working to provide a more nuanced

172

173

174

175

picture of Hollywood's portrayal of Native Americans, scholars continue to acknowledge that images of Indians as bloodthirsty savages mark one historically misleading extreme of a diverse representational practice.[81] Just as Westerns can distort racial violence, many horror films of the fifties distort and displace the perceived threats of the atomic era and the cold war.[82] The war in Vietnam and televised genre serials catalyzed a growing awareness of such distortions. This awareness coincided with a breakdown of the old studio system, creating conditions for genre revision and pastiche.[83]

In his essay on *The Shining* Frederic Jameson also locates these conditions in the breakdown of a communal sense of reality that accompanies what he calls "late capitalism."[84] This social atomization prevents a shared vision of reality and of history. The basis for consensus on what constitutes, at a given moment, a realist aesthetic begins to crumble and ceases to sustain wide-spread authority. And yet the problem of confronting a history of violence and a history of its cinematic misrepresentation, or occlusion, remains. Genre pastiche can serve as privileged strategy for such confrontation. On a formal level, narrativity and continuity editing give way to greater self-reflexivity. The horror film often features elements of camp and self-parody, from the hyperbolic revenge of Meir Zarchi's *I Spit on Your Grave* (1978) to the sex-or-the-saw phallicism of Tobe Hooper's *The Texas Chainsaw Massacre* (1974). Stanley Kubrick's *The Shining* (1980) is, of course, as Jameson points out, a horror-film pastiche par excellence. Revised and parodying Westerns include Robert Altman's films *McCabe and Mrs. Miller* (1971) and *Buffalo Bill and the Indians* (1976) and Jim Jarmusch's *Dead Man* (1995), which we might describe as an art film created in the style of a Western. A foundational re-vised Western is Sam Peckinpah's *The Wild Bunch* (1969). Unable directly to represent the violence of Vietnam, Peckinpah displaces it into the Western. And the genre, historically so important for distorting the history of Amer-ican colonial violence, implodes.

If Kulijanov, in *Crime and Punishment*, introduces a mirror in order to shoot a murder, thus inscribing a double point of view within a single shot, Kubrick's *The Shining* memorably puts the actual word "murder" in the mir-ror, signaling the film's self-consciousness about these problems of repre-sentation. In *The Shining*, and in *Dead Man*, we can find a demonstration of how genre pastiche works: it does not aim to create a positive representa-tion to combat other positive representations (as does, for instance, Arthur Penn's 1970 film *Little Big Man*); instead, it opts for a negative approach that reveals how any cinematic representation fails to do justice to its referent.

In *Dead Man* William Blake (Johnny Depp), an accountant from Cleve-land, spends his last money traveling west to the town of Machine, where a metalworking firm has supposedly hired him as an accountant. When he gets there, he finds out that the firm has already given his job to some-one else. Penniless and with nowhere to go, he befriends a flower seller, Thel (Mili Avital), who takes him in for the night. Thel's former beau Char-lie Dickinson (Gabriel Byrne), son of the owner of the metal works (Robert Mitchum), surprises the two of them together in bed the following morn-ing. Charlie shoots and kills Thel, and the bullet passes through her body, wounding Blake. Blake shoots Charlie dead and flees, stealing a horse. He is rescued (temporarily) from death by an Indian named Nobody (Gary Farmer). Meanwhile Charlie's father offers a reward to any man who can find Blake and kill him. The film then pieces together the journey of the hunt-ers and the hunted in a series of short, crosscutting episodes, each framed by fades to black, except in a crucial instance when the screen fades to white.

We might interpret *Dead Man* as an explicit rendering of the stylization which is always implicit within genre films. The relationship between stylization and genre, the dialectic between form and reference at the heart of genre, is also a preoccupation of Jarmusch's *Ghost Dog* (1999), a Mafia movie presented through a similarly hyperstylized prism. Perhaps Jarmusch's chief formal technique for foregrounding stylization is rhythmic repetition. In *Dead Man*, repetitive fades frame equally repetitive travel sequences—William Blake on a train, William Blake on foot in a street in the town of Machine, William Blake on horseback riding with Nobody. In these sequences, the same point-of-view structure continually recurs: a shot of Blake, a point-of-view shot, showing us what he sees, another shot of Blake, showing his reaction, or, more precisely, his stone-faced nonreaction (Jonathan Rosenbaum compares Depp to Buster Keaton).[85] This basic structure becomes a theme on which Jarmusch plays his variations.

With its regular fades, *Dead Man* breaks down the building blocks of cinematic narrative and in this manner distances itself from narrativity. The screenplay frequently weaves Blake's poetry into the dialogue, especially into Nobody's speeches. Jarmusch thus accentuates a formal lyricism. The film's brief episodes, separated from one another by a black screen, seem more analogous to lines of poetry rather than linear narrative, an analogy appropriate to a film whose central character shares his name with a major romantic poet. The Russian formalist distinction between a poetic and a prose cinema primarily lies in the motivation for the joining of shots. In prose cinema, the advancement of the plot serves as the primary motivation for shot organization: each shot reveals new narrative information. In poetic cinema, the ordered revelation of narrative knowledge does not serve as the dominant logic behind shot arrangement: other factors such as rhythm, metaphor, and graphic rhymes between shots take precedence over specifically narrative conventions.[86] Poetic cinema has often opposed, aesthetically and politically, the narrative modes of filmmaking that dominate national and global markets.[87] *Dead Man* is no exception. A mixture of poetry and prose, art film and Western, it short-circuits the narrative trajectory of manifest destiny: its hero, a maltreated clerk turned accidental gunslinger, is already dead. He does not "advance" westward; his movement toward the Pacific coincides with the approach of death. With nothing to conquer and nothing to civilize (in short, with no future), his witnessing of a violence that has already taken place takes precedence over his destination. Relieved of the pressure to advance a desire-driven plot, the images of Blake's and Nobody's visions demand reflection rather than a passing "read." The hyperformalization that encourages this reflective spectatorship implicates the Western genre more broadly in a practice of distorting stylization.

Not only is the narrative fragmented by unusually regular and frequent fades; it is impossible to reconstruct a definitive version of its story. The precredit sequence opens with a title attributed to Henri Michaux, a twentieth-century French writer drawn toward mysticism. We read, "It is preferable not to travel with a dead man." From this moment, the temporal relation between Blake's death and the story we see unfolding starts to become ambiguous. The narrative "travels" with William Blake. And while the plot shows him suffering a serious gunshot wound upon his arrival in Machine, the almost hallucinatory point-of-view shots, separated by fades that potentially suggest movement in and out of consciousness, raise the possibility that, from the beginning, the film is showing us a dying man's vision. There are scenes without Blake, of which he could have no conscious memory, and these suggest a more straightforwardly linear plot, but small, strange details evoke a persistent temporal confusion. In the precredit train ride sequence, for instance, the fireman (Crispin Glover) enters Blake's car, sits opposite Blake, and says, "Look out the window. And doesn't it remind you of when you're in a boat, and then later that night you're lying, looking up at the ceiling, and the water in your head was not dissimilar from the landscape, and you think to yourself, 'Why is it that the landscape is moving, but the boat is still?' "[88] At the beginning of the film his words seem surreal, but when Blake lies dying in a canoe in the final scenes of the film, the words acquire uncanny significance. They suggest that the entire film may consist in the unfolding of a murdered man's perspective. Another such detail occurs when Nobody rescues Blake and asks him, "Did you kill the man who killed you?" These words, like the title, imply that Blake is already dead.

The austere black-and-white photography and almost stately rhythm of its fades set in relief some of *Dead Man's* scenes of violence. Consider the aftermath of the scene where Blake kills two marshals, Lee (Mark Bringleson) and Marvin (Jimmie Ray Weeks), who are trying to kill Blake in order to collect the reward money offered by Dickinson. The men initially hired by Dickinson come upon the corpses of these marshals, and the meanest, Cole Wilson (Lance Henrikson) crushes one of the heads beneath his heel. The conflict between the following shots is at the heart of the film's aesthetics: in the first shot we see an image of a man's head lying at the center of sticks arranged for a campfire; the sticks form a sort of halo, making the picture

176

177

look like an icon (fig. 176). In a subsequent shot we witness the squashing of the head: brains ooze out of the skull and blood spurts from the nostrils in an image of violence typical of a slasher film (fig. 177). This Eisensteinian collision of shots has an element of self-parody appropriate to this art film *cum* Western. Like these juxtaposed shots of the beautiful and the gore, the film's lines of dialogue collide with one another as Blake's poetry (itself full of similar contrasts) is met with banalities. When Nobody, for instance, tells Blake, "Rise now and drag your cart and plow over the bones of the dead," Blake responds, "Do you have my eyeglasses?"

Through such ironic juxtapositions, which set it apart from conventional Western films, *Dead Man* addresses colonialist racism and its continuation by other means in many Hollywood Westerns. The most sustained representation of such violence occurs in the minor plot line of the flashback that fills in Nobody's past. We see images of him kept in a cage as he is taken to the East Coast and Europe and placed on display as a specimen. By making him a specimen, his captors obscure his particularity as a subject. Nobody opposes this strategy when, given access to a library, he commits to memory the poet William Blake's lyric realization of subjectivity. As he journeys back home, we see him witness destroyed teepees and burning canoes. Here the crucial fades to white, instead of black, appear. When Nobody returns to his people they refuse to believe his story and give him the name He-Who-Talks-Loud-and-Says-Nothing. This anecdote of how Nobody got his name can be read as an allegory of the film's aesthetic philosophy. When Nobody tries to tell his story directly to his people, he fails to represent it. It is only when he styles himself as Nobody, forsaking himself as subject, that his story gets communicated through indirection; indeed, perhaps its very communication is only the vision of a dead man. It is this same indirection that is characteristic of genre pastiche.

*

Stanley Kubrick's films—his political satire *Dr. Strangelove* (1964), his science fiction *2001: A Space Odyssey* (1968), his war films *Paths of Glory* (1957) and *Full Metal Jacket* (1987), his adaptation of Thackeray's historical novel *Barry Lyndon* (1975), and *The Shining*—provide ample material for exploring the tension, heightened in violent genres, between mimesis and stylization. In fact, we would be hard pressed to find another filmmaker who pushes both violence and stylization—the contradiction so legibly probed in *Dead Man*—to such extremes. In Kubrick, the representation of the world's violence, from nuclear warfare to adolescent crime sprees, from World War I trenches to eighteenth-century duels, is profoundly implicated in artistic formalism, in an austerity which seems to cut the films off from a referenced world. The mirror of art and particularly the distorting mirror of generic stylization thus seems constantly both to picture violence and to negate it as nonreferential—as pictured only within formalized generic codes.

We can use the famous "redrum" episode in *The Shining* to think through the mechanics of genre pastiche. Danny Torrance (Danny Lloyd), using his mother's lipstick, writes the word "murder" on the door next to his sleeping mother, Wendy (Shelley Duvall), but he writes it in reverse (fig. 178). Danny is not talking in his "own" voice, but in the weird, high-pitched rasp of Tony, whom Danny describes as "the little boy who lives in my mouth." Scared out of his wits in the haunted hotel where his father Jack (Jack Nicholson) has taken a job as a winter caretaker, Danny loses his voice. (Jack Nicholson, like Danny Lloyd, shares his name with the character he plays.) Danny/Tony alerts Wendy to the impending attack by her insane and murderous husband. Tony repeats the word "murder" in reverse, getting shriller and louder once the word has been written. Only when Wendy awakens and looks into the bedroom mirror, does she (and we, since it is a point-of-view shot) see the actual word "murder" (fig. 179). Along with the nondiegetic violins that allude to *Psycho*, we hear the bang of the murderer's ax. We then cut to Jack, swinging an ax against the locked door of their room.

178

179

It is in this mirror, where the reversal of the word "murder" is reversed, thus negating a negation, that we can locate an allegory for the mechanics of genre pastiche in terms of the way it registers historical violence. If genres themselves distort and displace the real violence entailed in colonizing the United States or in conducting the cold war, genre pastiche, like the mirror in *The Shining*, is a negation of that distortion. The pastiche of genre, in other words, does not seek directly to reinscribe the violence that has been excluded, but to represent the occlusion that has taken place. But this negation of a negation seems particularly appropriate for violence, and especially murder: in so far as murder revolves around the elision of a point of view, how would it be possible to bring this fully to light? Any representation of murder is itself going to be the negation of a negation. But a film might represent the very way that murder is never fully seen, just as genre pastiche "represents" and thus disrupts the stylization of genre which often serves, quite literally, to cover over violence (and actual killing).

Returning to *The Shining*, we can note that in the "redrum" scene, the act of murder itself is not played out. Instead, we have merely the writing of the word "murder," which replaces the scene of murder. In this sense we have a film representation of a linguistic representation of an event. Danny (or "Tony") writes the word "murder" in reverse, so that we initially see it as a signifier turned backwards. It is only when Wendy wakes up and glances in the mirror that she (and we) in the subsequent point-of-view shot, can read the word "directly."

This double reversal of the word is a precise negation of negation: an inverted representation of something is itself inverted to reveal the thing itself. In this sense we do not get at murder directly, but only in a doubly displaced form: it might look like the same word but it is not. Why not? Because it becomes legible as murder only as it appears to us as a reflection, as something, in other words, which it is not. In this sense, the scene is also a filmic representation of filmic representation. As in Kulijanov's *Crime and Punishment*, the mirror serves in two contradictory ways: it is both a vehicle for representation (it turns a nonsensical word into a meaningful one) and a self-reflexive reminder that we are only watching a film (any shot of a mirror, after all, makes us aware that the filmic screen itself is only an indirect reimaging of an actual event). This scene is thus a cinematic crux: the word "murder" gets translated into a referent only as, simultaneously, the film inscribes its own mediated referentiality. This mediated referentiality occurs in *The Shining* precisely in terms of genre, which stylizes and distorts histories of violence, and genre pastiche, which calls our attention to, and actually disrupts, this system of stylization. The actuality of murder is multiply displaced (represented in a backwards word, then in a word in a mirror, then in the story world of the film).

The mirror is the most traditional of metaphors for artistic mimesis. But a genre pastiche like *The Shining* does not believe in direct mimesis. The mirror in *The Shining*, confronting the unrepresentability of violence (of the threatened violence of a husband against his wife and child), becomes an emblem for self-reflexivity rather than mimesis. On this level the film resonates with the feminist critique of cinematic realism, which revolves around demonstrating that the mirror cannot be dissociated from the gaze (just as mimesis often serves as a screen for projection rather than replication). The best of genre pastiche recuperates reference as something other than gaze, but only indirectly: it holds up the mirror to genre itself.

Throughout *The Shining*, reflections in mirrors, with their discursive, self-reflexive overtones, are repeatedly shown to be more truthful than the mimetic world that lies outside these mirror scenes. There are three major mirror scenes in addition to the "redrum" scene. The first occurs before the family moves to the fateful Overlook Hotel. Danny stands before a sink and a mirror to brush his teeth. He asks his "imaginary" friend Tony to show him what staying at the Overlook Hotel will be like. The camera tracks in toward Danny's reflection, so that we can almost mistake the bathroom mirror for

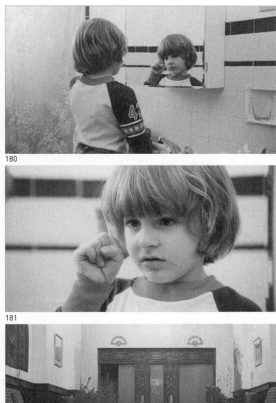

180

181

182

the screen. Still looking in the mirror, Danny sees a river of blood cascading down an elevator shaft and spilling into the lobby with a force so strong it moves the furniture before covering up the lens of the camera and thus motivating the black screen (figs. 180–82). Rapidly intercut with the cascading blood are the twin girls who, we eventually learn, were murdered by their father, Delbert Grady (Philip Stone), a former winter caretaker of the hotel. The image of the twins appropriately suggests the uncanniness of twinning, doubles, and mirrors. And the ending of the film realizes Danny's prescient vision of the bloody hotel, which he first sees in the mirror.

In the second important mirror scene, Wendy brings Jack breakfast in bed and the camera briefly shows us the mirror that reflects the couple

183

184

185

before zooming in on it so that its edges disappear beyond the frame. The dialogue then continues for over forty-five seconds, allowing sufficient time, perhaps, to forget that the camera is focused on the reflection in the mirror and not directly on the two actors. When the film finally cuts and focuses directly on Wendy, and then on Wendy and Jack, it initially seems as though the 180-degree rule, a linchpin of continuity editing, is being broken. In the cut from the reflection of the actors in the mirror to the actors themselves, the actors appear to switch places in a way that is unmotivated and jarring (figs. 183–85). The self-reflexive functioning of the mirror in this scene, while not technically breaking the rules of continuity editing, serves, by seeming to break the rule, to remind us of the truth of the film's remove from referentiality. The dialogue that occurs while the camera focuses on the mirror also reflects the latent aggression in the marriage that erupts later in the film.

The third significant mirror scene occurs when Jack enters room 237 and a naked woman emerges from the bathtub and awaits his embrace. As he kisses her, Jack glances in the mirror behind her and sees that he's not embracing a beautiful young woman but the rotting flesh of an aged female zombie (figs. 186–187). The mirror again provides a more accurate reflection than the naked eye: the woman is dead; the hotel, haunted. The mirror reveals the untruth of what Jack, the eventual murderer, thinks he sees. In the bedroom scene, where the use of a mirror creates the effect of breaking the 180-degree rule, the mirror reveals the untruth of mimetic representation. (The pattern, followed in each of these scenes, of tracking toward the mirror so that its edges align with, or disappear beyond, the frame, lulls us, or demonstrates how easily we can be lulled, into forgetting that what we are seeing is a mere reflection.) In the initial scene, the mirror provides a glimpse of great violence which has no clear referent. The cascading blood is an abstraction, a symbol of violence. But to what violence is this image alluding? The hotel is the architectural embodiment of a violent history. It was built over a Native American burial ground; more Native Americans were killed

186

187

when they tried to stop the building of the hotel in 1907; and the hotel has been haunted ever since, resulting in repeat instances of domestic violence among its winter caretakers.

*

In the "redrum" scene, a child wakes his sleeping parent to warn her of a violence that has already happened and is happening even at that moment. But it is, in a sense, the absent child who wakes his sleeping parent. Unable to speak since entering room 237, where his father had the sexual encounter with the dead woman, Danny has ceded his voice to Tony. Thus, we have a child who is not really there attempting to wake a sleeping parent with news of a violence that has taken place, and is taking place, even as the waking takes place. The scene has a profound resonance with the dream of the burning child described by Freud in *The Interpretation of Dreams*.

In Freud's account, a father whose young son has just died of fever leaves an old man to guard the corpse, which is surrounded by burning candles, and goes to sleep in the next room. He is awakened by a dream. In the dream his dead son is again alive and tugging at his sleeve saying, "Father, can't you see I'm burning?" The father wakes up, banishing this longed-for apparition of the once-again-living child, and goes into the next room, where he discovers that the old man has fallen asleep and that a candle has tipped over, starting a fire in the bedclothes and burning the dead child's arm.

There are obvious differences between the dream of the burning child and the "redrum" scene. The mother falls asleep, not the father. Indeed, the father in *The Shining* wants his son dead, not alive—a far cry from the grief-stricken father of the dream of the burning child. The film does not indicate whether Wendy is dreaming, much less show the content of that dream. And Wendy awakens to confront not her child's death, but a threat to his life—and her own. But it is this awakening to read the word "murder" in the mirror that resonates with Freud's classic example.

Freud's analysis of the dream of the burning child (and Jacques Lacan's interpretation of this analysis) has been further developed by Cathy Caruth as a model for the missing of experience that constitutes trauma. Caruth's explication of the dream (and of Freud's and Lacan's readings of it) emphasizes the belatedness of the father's seeing and the repetition of this belatedness. Within the dream, the child appears to reproach his father for not seeing that he is burning—burning, perhaps, with the fever that killed him. And the father again fails to see this burning of his child by awakening too late to prevent the fallen candle from burning the corpse. Caruth locates the trauma in the father's inability to witness the child's dying as it occurred—

in the child's call to his father to respond to his burning, to respond, in essence, to his death; and in the impossibility of such a response.[89] The "red-rum" scene as well contains these same elements of awakening, belated seeing, and repetition (e.g., the repeated visions of an earlier scene of violence that prompt Danny to withdraw into himself and the repetition of the domestic violence which Delbert Grady transmits to Jack). Finally, the film itself, as a genre pastiche, is precisely about the necessity and impossibility of witnessing to a violent past, and an other's death, that traditional Hollywood genres missed, distorted, and erased.

Stephen King's choice for the very name of the hotel, the Overlook, implies the missing of something. But to "overlook" can also mean to look at from above, as when Jack looks down on the model of the hedge maze. The film cuts to an overhead shot of the actual maze, where his wife and child are currently playing. It seems like a point-of-view shot, but it is not Jack's point of view. The threat implicit in Jack's gaze is transferred across this cut to the camera, realizing the classic feminist critique of the gaze. In addition to this instance of overlooking, there are several shots in the film, such as the many tracking shots following Danny on his Big Wheel, which are suggestive of some presence in the hotel itself overlooking the winter inhabitants.

No one in the story world really sees what underlies the Overlook, a Native American burial ground. Such burial grounds are a commonplace in Stephen King novels and have their roots in the American gothic. There is a kind of return of the repressed in the mise-en-scène of the hotel. The very tiles and carpets of the floors are covered, the hotel manager (Barry Nelson) announces to Wendy, with Apache and Navaho "designs." But the Torrance family pays little attention to these constant visual reminders of a population that was annihilated. The metonymic significance of the designs is too subtle and easily missed.

As Jameson points out, the ghostly society that emerges during the hotel's winter months is the unapologetically class-conscious aristocracy of 1920s America.[90] The underlying violence of this class-based social structure is made directly apparent when Grady incites Jack against his son by telling him of his son's attempts to contact the hotel cook, Hallorann (Scatman Crothers), who winters in Miami. Grady implies that Hallorann's race and class make him inferior and that his "interference" with Jack's son is a disgrace to Jack. Hallorann is the only murder victim in the diegetic present tense of the film (and the only major black character), and it is difficult not to read this violence against him referentially in terms of a history of racial violence.

Besides the murder of Hallorann, the only other violence the film actually shows is Jack's attempts to murder Wendy and Danny with the ax and Wendy's attempts to repel Jack's violence with a baseball bat and knife. Domestic violence, racist violence, and colonialist violence converge. Blood cascades down the elevator shaft. This river of blood suggests a history of violence, and not just Grady's freakish murder of himself and his family. But this larger violence remains at the level of allusion. The allusions to and representations of violence occur in the context of an exceedingly playful pastiche. The film is filled, for instance with ludic allusions to Hitchcock's *Psycho* (1960). In addition, when violence does erupt between Jack and Wendy, Nicholson and Duvall's performances occasionally cross the line into comedy. Their performances are exaggerated; the actors become caricatures of the roles they are playing.

Space, too, is exaggerated. The credit sequence consists of a series of overhead tracking shots of a car traveling through various landscapes. All are relatively long takes, and the overall effect is to create a sense of journey into a vast and removed space. The interior space of the hotel is also made to appear vast, through the use of a wide-angle lens. In the "redrum" scene, for instance, Danny, when he writes "redrum," appears to be standing much farther from his sleeping mother than he actually is. Ironically, in telling Jack about the former winter caretaker's murder of his wife and children, the hotel manager cites "cabin fever," a "claustrophobic reaction that can occur when people are shut in together over long periods of time." The incongruity between a comment like this and the deep, empty spaces depicted on the screen is ironic.

It is uncomfortable to be confronted with representations of violence and murder—particularly if those representations have some basis in history, but it is more uncomfortable when these representations of murder and allusions to violence are presented in such a way that we cannot quite take them seriously. This is precisely what happens when violence and murder are restylized in Kubrick's pastiche of the horror film. This incongruity between an ironic, playful, and even humorous discourse and a gruesome story that references an even more gruesome history has led to widely diverging interpretations of the film, with some critics seeing it as apolitical or even reactionary and others seeing it as having ominous import for patriarchal structures of family and society.[91] The very undecidability of the film's final significance reflects back on the impossibility of direct referentiality, particularly in representing murder.[92] The negation, through murder, of a character's perspective, and the history of the negation of a people's perspective through culture and, specifically, through traditional Hollywood genres, both calls for representation and confronts the filmmaker with the impossibility of that task except in forms such as genre pastiche. Such a form does not move closer to referentiality, but simply negates the negation of earlier attempts at realism.

Kubrick's art conveys a sense of resigned hopelessness at this referential remove, which is why a film like Jarmusch's *Dead Man* makes such an interesting contrast to *The Shining*. Both films tell the story of gruesome violence—both historical and fictional—through the playful, even humorous form of pastiche. But the relentless narrativity and lush color images of Kubrick's film stand in stark contrast to the black-and-white photography and the pauses afforded by the fades that are so central to the lyricism, the resistance to narrative in Jarmusch's film. If, to paraphrase James Joyce's *Ulysses*, history is a nightmare from which one tries to awaken, then Jarmusch's fragmentation of the narrative, sometimes into pure filmic moments, at least allows some escape; whereas *The Shining* perhaps leaves us in the disoriented state between nightmare and waking life, so that we do not know whether history is what we wake from or wake into, whether historical violence is inscribed or evaded.

# Conclusion: Hitchcock's Aerial Views

We have seen how film form—montage techniques and generic syntax—took shape around scenes of killing. In conclusion, let us consider Jean-Luc Godard's account of cinema's demise, which locates the "death" of cinema in its *failure* to confront murder. In *Histoire(s) du cinéma*, Godard contends that cinema declined toward death when it neglected to bear witness to the Holocaust and to address the problems of representation that such witnessing would entail. In chapter 3 (a), "Currency of the Absolute," for instance, we hear:

> the fact that cinema was made initially for thinking
> will be forgotten straight away
> but that's another story
> the flame was finally extinguished at Auschwitz[1]

In the same work, however, even as Godard charges that by failing to show the Holocaust, cinema ceased to be a living, relevant art form, he describes Alfred Hitchcock as "master of the universe," a position that connotes life's prime, not its collapse:

> Alfred Hitchcock succeeded
> where Alexander, Julius Caesar, Hitler, and Napoleon
> had all failed
> by taking control of the universe[2]

The propaganda film *Bon Voyage* (1944) and *Lifeboat* (1944) are as close as Hitchcock ever came to directly addressing World War II, but his reflexive films certainly do not ignore the violence of the twentieth century. The history and technology of this violence intertwine with cinema from its inception, transforming Hitchcock's specialties, scenes of murder and attempted murder, into sites of concentrated reflection on the violence implicit in cinematic seeing.

To understand this paradoxical "mastery of the universe," which Hitchcock achieves by creating murder scenes *in* an art form that is "dying" because it fails to confront the murder happening *outside* it, let us consider one of his signature moves: the cut, in and around scenes of murder, to an overhead perspective. Despite their god's-eye view, these are not the shots that lead Godard to bestow upon Hitchcock the title "master."[3] But ask Hitchcock fans about these shots and they will rattle them off—the scene on the polar-bear rug in *Murder!* (1930) when Sir John (Herbert Marshall) catches Handel Fane (Esme Percy) in his "mousetrap," the Mount Rushmore scene in *North by Northwest* (1959), the scene of Madeleine's fall in *Vertigo* (1958), that of Arbogast's murder in *Psycho* (1960), the shot from the Statue of Liberty in *Saboteur* (1942)—and so on.

The aerial perspective, or overhead shot, places Hitchcock firmly in the modernist tradition, which writers as varied as Ernest Hemingway, Evelyn Waugh, and Gertrude Stein, early on linked to the sight of the earth from an airplane. Summarizing the connections typically made between aerial views and modernism, Paul K. Saint-Amour writes:

> One might say that bios surrenders to logos as the landscape offers itself to be read . . . as a planned text. The sharpened lines, clarified structure and geometric shapes of the planned text, in turn, might be said to resonate with cubist mechano-morphism. . . . From sufficient altitudes, the individual organism dwindles to the vanishing point, bodies recede to exteriorized and genderless dots circulating as particles in the fluid dynamics of the urban mass, made visually contiguous with the material fabric of the city as viewed from above. Alternately, the body diminishes to a data point in the emerging statistical epistemes that were cognate with the aerial perspective in their shared claims to spatially arrayed overviews of an aggregate of such points.[4]

In its reduction of the "individual organism" to a "data point" indistinguishable from other data points, modernism enacts a violence whose extreme literalization characterizes the view of the bomber pilot and the individuality-erasing practices of twentieth-century genocides.[5] In Hitchcock's bird's-eye views, too, the abstraction of a scenic totality replaces individual details, faces go unseen, and people appear, if not as "genderless dots," then certainly more objectified. But as Stein, Hemingway, and Waugh attest, aerial perspective permits a creative seeing as well as a destructive one; while heightened abstraction may characterize artistic modernism, so too does intensified self-questioning.

Hitchcock's sudden move to the markedly different overhead perspective takes us by surprise. The other shots have oriented us *in* the scene. We are with Scotty as he struggles against vertigo in an effort to climb the stairs of the bell tower and save Madeleine. We stay closely focused on Arbogast's face as he climbs the stairs of the house behind the Bates motel.[6] After the overhead shot that shows us Handel Fane, forced to reenact the scene of his crime, we cut to a straight-on medium shot that shows him slumped, exhausted by the traumatic repetition. If a cubist painting queries the very concept of perspective and its representation by aiming simultaneously to show an object from multiple points of view, the arrangement of shots in film allows for startling perspectival shifts that emphasize, precisely, the shock of difference. Hitchcock's Eisensteinian collisions between angles of vision evoke a split, volatile subjectivity, at once in the scene and outside it. These sudden moves to a place above and beyond rend the subjectivity implicit not only in the spectatorial position, but also in that of the character.

That spectators identify with characters is commonly acknowledged, but film criticism far more rarely recognizes that a character might identify with the spectator, or might *be* a spectator of himself. And yet William Rothman makes precisely this Bakhtinian move when he writes of the overhead shot where Arbogast nears the top of the stairs (and his death) in *Psycho* that the rectangular space framed by the camera is emblematic of the character's interiority: "At this moment, there is a cut to an extraordinary shot that invokes the perspective of a bird. Viewed from this perch, Arbogast appears imprisoned, the space of the landing as frighteningly confined. . . . But this space also resonates with the empty theater in *Stage Fright*, emblematic of Jonathan's interiority. The space in which Arbogast is trapped comes alive, in effect as an inner space."[7] But how can Arbogast or Jonathan see when they are in the scene? If the overhead view emblematizes the character's interiority, that means the character is aware of how things look from up there, where he is not. Rothman's and numerous other scholarly interpretations of this scene place us in multiple subject positions—Arbogast's, Norman/Mother's, the camera's—at once. But only Rothman sees Arbogast seeing, and implicitly resisting, his own confinement. Perhaps this is an effect of the interpreter's own dispersed subjectivity, which he projects onto the character. But the very possibility that we might see Arbogast seeing himself framed in this tight space, and the fact that Rothman has seen it that way, constitutes a negative moment. The film frame contains the stairwell frame that contains Arbogast. But in Rothman's interpretation, the framed man frames, the pictured man pictures—he sees, or contains, the frame, or picture, that contains him. This is the moment latent—but of course not always sufficiently realized—in every scene of murder.[8]

We might expect the god's-eye view to suggest omniscience. In Hitchcock's hands, as it punctuates a violent scene or marks, in Handel Fane's case, a traumatic memory, the overhead shot points up a tragic blindness. Opposite the overhead shot in that it orients us within the scene rather than taking us out of it, the shot-reverse-shot, a staple of classical Hollywood style, has served as a focal point for critiques of Hollywood cinema. Jean-Pierre Oudart, Noël Burch, and others have described the shot-reverse-shot as a primary device behind the "illusionist" power of Hollywood films. When Godard talks about a "real reverse-shot," he has something else in mind: "We don't know what a real reverse-shot is. Lévinas often has good ideas, but when he talks about the gaze of the other that cannot be killed, the other who is such that he can't be killed, he is doing a bad reverse-shot."[9] Godard's coupling of Levinas's "gaze of the other that cannot be killed" with the "bad" reverse shot reminds us that the shot-reverse-shot often undergoes deformation in murder scenes. We have seen how, in Kulijanov's *Crime and Punishment*, Raskolnikov's reflection in a distorting mirror replaces the impossible reverse shot that would have shown the murdered Elizaveta's view of her killer. By abolishing a key point of view, murder disrupts the stabilizing "suture" of conventional editing. We see other disruptions in John Ford's variations on reverse shots in murder scenes from *Stagecoach* (1939) and *The Man Who Shot Liberty Valence* (1962); murder mysteries that withhold the reverse shot of the murderer such as *The Maltese Falcon* (John Huston, 1941) and *Mildred Pierce* (Michael Curtiz, 1945); and important art films such as *The Crime of Monsieur Lange* (1936), where, as we have seen, Jean Renoir uses a now famous pan in place of a reverse shot to show Lange's murder of Batala.[10]

Godard's proposal for envisioning a "real reverse-shot" focuses not on murder, but on love: "I have a project for a short film on lovers meeting in the various *arrondissements*. . . . I'd call it 'Champ contre champ.' It features a girl called Adrienne Champ and a boy called Ludovic Champ." The family name of Godard's protagonists emphasizes the crucial problem of the reverse shot: in the conventional shot-reverse-shot, placing one field of vision against another both defines difference (between two distinct points of view) and denies it, positing the same contiguous, objective space and time.

But early in his career, well before this imagined project, Godard achieved a reverse shot that admitted an absolute distance between two gazes. This happens in the scene in *My Life to Live* when Nana (Anna Karina) goes to a movie theater and sees Dreyer's *The Passion of Joan of Arc*. Godard frames Karina in close-up so that she rhymes, graphically, with Dreyer's close-ups of Renée Falconetti as Joan. Joan appears against a white background; Nana appears against the blackness of the movie theater. When the priest (Antonin Artaud) tells Joan she will die on the stake, Godard inserts a close-up of Nana into Dreyer's shot-reverse-shot sequence. Nana, like Joan, stares ahead. We return to a close-up of Nana at one other point in the sequence, after Joan tells the priest that death will be her deliverance. Here, too, Nana's facial movements match Joan's: tears well in the eyes of both actors. Nana remains clearly outside the shot-reverse-shot structure of Dreyer's film: she is not *in* the scene. But as one character weeping for another, who is in the film within the film, she is closer to Dreyer's Joan than the spectator of Godard's film, who is at one further remove. Kaja Silverman and Harun Farocki interpret Nana's closeness to Joan as a foreshadowing of Nana's own death; the two women maintain their difference and specificity, and yet Nana's fate (violent death) mirrors Joan's.[11]

In addition to the scene's foreshadowing function within the narrative, we might, taking up Godard's problem of the "real reverse-shot," ask what happens if we consider the inserted close-ups of Nana looking at Joan as a deformation of the conventional reverse shot. If, as Farocki and Silverman convincingly argue, the structure of the scene suggests that Nana's fate is written on that screen, then Dreyer's film is looking back at her, even if Nana does not fully understand the implications of its regard.[12] Technically, we do not have here a reverse shot. The two women do not occupy the same space, and Joan never looks directly at the camera, which would make her seem to be seeing Nana as Nana sees her. But it is the technically "correct" reverse shot that, according to Godard, has never achieved the status of a "real reverse-shot." For Godard, Levinas's reverse shot—"the face of the other that cannot be killed"—is not "unreal"; it is "bad." "The face of the other that cannot be killed" takes on literal meaning in this scene. In looking at Joan's face, Nana is looking at once at a referenced historical figure and an actor who are both dead. The "other," whose visage Nana regards, cannot be killed, because it has already departed from the image left in its stead. And if the screen "looks back" at Nana, its look, at her, likewise signals her own immanent departure.

If the conventional shot-reverse-shot disavows the difference it asserts—two points of view, same world—this "deformed" reverse shot maintains an absolute distance not simply between points of view, but between their worlds. In weeping for Joan precisely as Joan contemplates her impending death, Nana posits and mourns a perspective she cannot grasp. She occupies, and realizes, the paradigmatic position of the film spectator at that nodal point, in or around the murder scene, where human reference emerges only to be obliterated. Her spectatorship recalls Rothman's view of Arbogast: Rothman does not assume the perspective of the victim; he responds as if the victim has, impossibly, usurped his, and the camera's, point of view. For Hitchcock and Godard, the murder scene's stark negation of a particular perspective produces paradox: the bird's-eye view that evokes blindness, the movie screen that returns the gaze.

# Notes

## Introduction

1. Sergei M. Eisenstein, "The Method of Making a Workers' Film" (1925), in *Selected Works*, vol. 1, *Writings, 1922–1934*, ed. and trans. Richard Taylor (London: British Film Institute, 1988), 65.

2. In a suggestive reading, Anne Nesbet points out that the film's juxtapositions of strikers with animals presents the spectator with a choice between being treated like an animal and being treated like a political subject. *Savage Junctures: Sergei Eisenstein and the Shape of Thinking* (London: I. B. Tauris, 2003), 21–47.

3. "Montage," in the Soviet context, initially meant, broadly, the arrangement of shots to produce meaning. In the late twenties and thirties, Eisenstein began to locate montage within shots, as well; he also found its principles operative within other art forms, such as poetry. From the start he emphasized that montage should produce not only meaning, but also physiological and emotional responses. Soviet montage theorists often describe specific techniques also found in Hollywood cinema—the use of close-ups, the match on action, the manipulation of shot duration to produce various rhythms. Both montage and continuity editing aim, primarily, to produce signification, but they have different stylistic emphases. David Bordwell writes: "What Soviet filmmakers of the 1920's called montage—shot assembling as the basic constructional activity—Hollywood filmmakers called cutting or editing, terms associated with trimming off unwanted material. The best term for the Hollywood practice is another French one, découpage: the parceling out of images in accordance with the script, the mapping of the narrative action onto the cinematic material." David Bordwell, "The Classical Hollywood Style, 1917–60," in *The Classical Hollywood Cinema: Film Style and Mode of Production to 1960*, by David Bordwell, Janet Staiger, and Kristin Thompson (New York: Columbia University Press, 1985), 60. For a detailed definition of découpage, see Noël Burch, *Theory of Film Practice*, trans. Helen R. Lane (New York: Praeger Publishers, 1973), 3–4. I observe these distinctions made by Bordwell and Burch and also, where possible, follow the usage of the given writer.

4. André Bazin, "Will CinemaScope Save the Film Industry?" in *Bazin at Work: Major Essays and Reviews from the Forties and Fifites*, ed. Bert Cardullo, trans. Alain Piette and Bert Cardullo (New York: Routledge, 1997), 90–91.

5. Kracauer writes, "If film grows out of photography, the realistic and formative tendencies must be operative in it also. Is it by sheer accident that the two tendencies manifested themselves side by side immediately after the rise of the medium? As if to encompass the whole range of cinematic endeavors at the outset, each went the limit in exhausting its own possibilities. Their prototypes were Lumière, a strict realist, and Méliès, who gave free rein to his artistic imagination. The films they made embody, so to speak, thesis and antithesis in a Hegelian sense." Siegfried Kracauer, *Theory of Film: The Redemption of Physical Reality* (Princeton, NJ: Princeton University Press, 1997), 30. Kracauer footnotes the following texts, which make a similar argument: Maurice Caveing, "Dialectique du concept du cinéma," *Revue Internationale de Filmologie* 1, no. 1 (July–August 1947): 71–78; Edgar Morin, *Le Cinéma ou l'homme imaginaire* (Paris: Éditions de minuit, 1956), 58; and Georges Sadoul, *Histoire d'un art: Le Cinéma des origines à nos jours* (Paris, 1949), 31.

6. Mary Ann Doane, *The Emergence of Cinematic Time* (Cambridge, MA: Harvard University Press, 2002), 208.

7. See Mary Ann Doane, "The Object of Theory," in *Rites of Realism: Essays on Corporeal Cinema*, ed. Ivone Margulies (Durham, NC: Duke University Press, 2003), 80–92. In particular, Doane turns to Miriam Hansen's introduction to Kracauer, *Theory of Film*, vii–xlv; and Paul Willemen, *Looks and Frictions: Essays in Cultural Studies and Film Theory* (Bloomington: Indiana University Press, 1994), esp. 223–57.

8. Vsevolod Illarionovich Pudovkin, *Film Technique and Film Acting*, trans. Ivor Montagu (New York: Bonanza Books, 1949), 139.

9. Eisenstein, *Selected Works*, vol. 1, *Writings, 1922–1934*, 178–79.

10. Indeed, other objects do serve as examples, but they do not appear with the same frequency across the writings of several theorists and are often less compelling.

11. In his study of minor characters and their relation to the protagonist, Alex Woloch shows how the coordination of a person in a narrative, and the significance that we derive from him or her, is posited against the human being implied by that discursive realization. Woloch calls this "intersection of an implied human personality . . . with the definitively circumscribed form of a narrative" a "character-space" and describes it as "that particular and charged encounter between an individual human personality and a determined space and position within the narrative as a whole." Woloch formulates this theory of characterization primarily in reference to the heavily populated nineteenth-century novel, which leads him to elaborate the concept of a "character-system," which he defines as: "the arrangement of multiple and differentiated character-spaces—differentiated configurations and manipulations of the human figure—into a unified narrative structure." These concepts—character-space and character-system—provide the framework for an examination of the way that narratives distribute attention among character spaces. The protagonist emerges at the expense of the minor characters; reference inheres in form: fictional narratives, like society, give more attention to some characters than others. Alex Woloch, *The One vs. the Many: Minor Characters and the Space of the Protagonist in the Novel* (Princeton, NJ: Princeton University Press, 2003), 13–14. My understanding of the murder scene shares this sense of representation as always negotiating the tension between external reference and internal form.

12. Devin McKinney, "Violence: The Strong and the Weak," *Screening Violence*, ed. Stephen Prince (New Brunswick, NJ: Rutgers University Press, 2000), 108–9 (originally published in *Film Quarterly* 46, no. 4 [Summer 1993]: 16–22).

13. André Bazin, "Theater and Cinema—Part One," in *What Is Cinema?* trans. Hugh Gray, 2 vols. (Berkeley: University of California Press, 1967), 1:89.

14. See, for instance, Stephen Prince, *Classical Hollywood Violence: Designing and Regulating Brutality in Hollywood Cinema, 1930–1968* (New Brunswick, NJ: Rutgers University Press, 2003). In relation to the kiss, see, Linda Williams, "Of Kisses and Ellipses: The Long Adolescence of American Movies," *Critical Inquiry* 32, no. 2 (Winter 2006): 288–340. If murder suggests the cut and the kiss suggests suture, the iconic image of the racing train also has a reflexive power. Reflecting on the railroad long before the invention of cinema, Ralph Waldo Emerson, in "Nature" (1836), observed that by destabilizing the materiality of things (by, for instance, seeing them through the moving window of a train), we can recognize a more fundamental immateriality: "A man who seldom rides, needs only to get into a coach and traverse his own town, to turn the street into a puppet-show. The men, the women,—talking, running, bartering, fighting,—the earnest mechanic, the lounger, the beggar, the boys, the dogs, are unrealized at once, or, at least, wholly detached from all relation to the observer, and seen as apparent, not substantial beings. What new thoughts are suggested by seeing a face of country quite familiar, in the rapid movement of the railroad car!" Emerson, *Selected Essays*, ed. Larzer Ziff [New York: Penguin, 1982], 64. Like the train window, cinema enables us to recognize a fundamental immateriality in material things.

15. Obviously missing from this list is Dziga Vertov, who, in his documentary practice, allergically avoids anything approaching the melodrama of a murder scene.

16. See Vladimir Nizhny, *Lessons with Eisenstein*, ed. and trans. Ivor Montagu and Jay Leyda (London: George Allen and Unwin, 1962), 93–139. Interestingly, all the problems covered in the three seminars transcribed by Nizhny center around scenes of violence. The book begins with an assignment to visualize the filming of Vautrin's arrest in Balzac's *Le Père Goriot*, a novel whose own questions concerning murder serve as subtext to Dostoevsky's *Crime and Punishment*, written over thirty years later. The other seminar concerns the dramatic story, told by John W. Vannercook in *Black Majesty: The Life of Christophe, King of Haiti* (New York: Harper and Bros., 1928), of the failed French colonizers' attempt to capture the revolutionary Haitian General Jean-Jacques Dessalines and deport him to France for execution. Eisenstein's 1941 seminar on the short fiction scenario also revolves around scenes of killing. It takes as its primary example a violent short story by Ambrose Bierce, "The Affair at Coulter's Notch." Set during the American Civil War, the story tells of a corrupt general who forces a young artillery captain to fire on his own home and thus kill his wife and child. The story serves as a model from which Eisenstein goes on to critique scripts of a story about a Ukrainian grandmother who poisons herself in order to trick invading German soldiers into eating her poisoned food. During this seminar, Eisenstein gives an explanation for why so many of his films and seminars show murder: "You will see that essentially all the secrets of composition are contained in the detective novel. Even the fact that in every detective novel there is a death or murder is an example of using a situation that makes the strongest physiological impact." Sergei M. Eisenstein, *On the*

*Composition of the Short Fiction Scenario*, trans. Alan Y. Upchurch (Calcutta: Seagull Books and Eisenstein Cine Club, 1985), 13.

17. Grigorii Kozintsev, "A Child of the Revolution," in *Cinema in Revolution: The Heroic Era in Soviet Film*, ed. Luda Schnitzer, Jean Schnitzer, and Marcel Martin, trans. David Robinson (London: Secker and Warburg, 1966), 91–92.

18. Jay Leyda, *Kino: A History of the Russian and Soviet Film* (Princeton, NJ: Princeton University Press, 1960), 132, 154.

19. Barbara Leaming, *Grigorii Kozintsev* (Boston: Twayne Publishers, 1980), 18.

20. For a qualification of Eisenstein's argument, see Tom Gunning, *D. W. Griffith and the Origins of American Narrative Film* (Urbana and Chicago: Univesity of Illinois Press, 1991),134–38.

21. Stephen Prince makes a similar claim: "I regard violence as an essential component of cinema: part of its deep formal structure." *Classical Film Violence*, 3. For Prince, *Classical Film Violence* is the "prequel" to his earlier *Savage Cinema: Sam Peckinpah and the Rise of Ultraviolent Movies* (Austin: University of Texas Press, 1998). It focuses on the way the Production Code fostered formal innovation in the representation of violence. Whereas Prince deliberately excludes discussion of screen violence "at the more abstracted level of film as society's mirror" (4), I try to show how film "grammar" develops through the representation of violence *and* in dialogue with the history that grounds the popular reception of screened murder.

22. Locating Griffith's originality not in his editing techniques per se, but rather in the harnessing of those techniques in the service of film narrative, Gunning writes of the revolver-clock contraption in *The Fatal Hour*, "Although such machinery of revenge has a long heritage in stage melodrama, this fatal clock inscribes time itself into the narrative and determines the form of the film's parallel-edited climax." *D. W. Griffith and the Origins of American Narrative Film*, 98–99.

23. Karl Marx, *The Poverty of Philosophy* (New York: International Publishers, 1963), 58–59. Quoted in Georg Lukács, "Reification and the Consciousness of the Proletariat," in *History and Class Consciousness: Studies in Marxist Dialectics*, trans. Rodney Livingstone (Cambridge, MA: MIT Press, 1968), 89.

24. Georg Simmel, *The Sociology of Georg Simmel*, trans. and ed. Kurt Wolff (Glencoe, IL: Free Press, 1950), 409–24.

25. Kristi McKim suggests that cinematic love scenes, too, can have this power, particularly when the love shown is framed by death. "The Astounded Soul: Cinematic Aesthetics of Time and Love" (PhD diss., Emory University, 2005).

26. Herbert Eagle draws a connection between martyrdom and murderous tendencies, remarking in relation to Dušan Makavejev's parodic character Luv Bakunin (Pierre Clémenti) in *Sweet Movie*, "Why is the urge toward martyrdom so strong in revolutionaries? Is their acceptance of their own destruction related to their willingness to destroy others?" In "Yugoslav Marxist Humanism and the Films of Dušan Makavejev," in *Politics, Art and Commitment in the East European Cinema*, ed. David W. Paul (London: Macmillan, 1983), 146. In the film, as Eagle notes, Luv is actually Vakulinchuk, identified as "the sailor from the Potemkin" and costumed as in Eisenstein's film. In stark contrast to his contemporaries Eisenstein and Pudovkin, Dovzhenko emphasizes that the Ukrainians of *Arsenal* (1928) are

already leading meaningful lives before the disruptions of World War I and the Revolution. Although *Arsenal* expresses a qualified sympathy for the Bolshevik cause, the violent deaths suffered by members of all social groups and political factions do not bring glory; they leave a void. This exceptional film, as Vance Kepley points out, refuses to make an absolute distinction between the brutality of the war and that of the Revolution. See Vance Kepley, *In the Service of the State: The Cinema of Alexander Dovzhenko* (Madison: University of Wisconsin Press, 1986), 62–74.

27. Kristen Thompson, *Eisenstein's "Ivan the Terrible": A Neoformalist Analysis* (Princeton, NJ: Princeton University Press, 1981), 286. In *Savage Junctures*, Anne Nesbet demonstrates that such disjunctive excess exists in Eisenstein's theory and practice of montage more generally.

28. Thompson, *Eisenstein's "Ivan the Terrible,"* 286.

29. Mikhail Yampolsky, "Kuleshov's Experiments and the New Anthropology of the Actor," in *Inside the Film Factory: New Approaches to Russian and Soviet Cinema*, ed. Richard Taylor and Ian Christie (London: Routledge, 1991), 31–50.

30. For a detailed discussion of early reception of the close-up and shot distance more generally, see Yuri Tsivian, *Early Cinema in Russia and Its Cultural Reception*, trans. Alan Bodger (Chicago: University of Chicago Press, 1998), 188–207.

31. Suture theory describes the mechanisms by which narrative films distract spectators from the potential awareness of their own bodily absence from the story world and the site of production. According to theorists such as Jean-Pierre Oudart and Jean-Louis Baudry, this absence produces unease because it means that the apparatus, not the viewer, controls the gaze and only reveals part of the story world, but not the whole. Oudart associates the viewer's lack of control over the site of production with castration, the central figure for lack in Lacanian and Freudian psychoanalysis. The psychoanalytically inflected feminist film theory of Laura Mulvey, Kaja Silverman, and others argues that castration anxiety and the male subject's desire for wholeness results in a projection of lack onto female bodies in an effort to place a distance between male subjects and lack.

32. Mikhail Bakhtin, *Problems of Dostoevsky's Poetics*, ed. and trans. Caryl Emerson (Minneapolis: University of Minnesota Press, 1984), 59.

33. Emmanuel Levinas, *Totality and Infinity: An Essay on Exteriority*, trans. Alphonso Lingis (Pittsburgh, PA: Duquesne University Press, 1969), 55.

34. In contrast to Pudovkin's courage-cowardice dichotomy, Bazin, at a very different historical moment, writes: "L'homme bogartien ne se définit pas . . . par son courage ou sa lâcheté, mais d'abord par cette maturité existentielle qui transforme peu à peu la vie en une ironie tenace aux dépens de la mort." "Mort d' Humphrey Bogart," *Cahiers du Cinéma* 68 (February 1957): 8.

35. Lev Kuleshov, "Chto nado delat' v kinematograficheskikh shkolakh" (ca. 1921), quoted in Mikhail Yampolsky, "Kuleshov's Experiments and the New Anthropology of the Actor," 44.

36. Jean Epstein, "Magnification," in *French Film Theory and Criticism: A History/Anthology, 1907–1939*, vol. 1, *1907–1929*, ed. Richard Abel (Princeton, NJ: Princeton University Press, 1988), 236. Abel reprints, with changes, Stuart Liebman's translation, which

appeared in *October* 3 (Spring 1977): 9–15. The original, "Grossissement," was published in *Bonjour cinéma* (Paris: Editions de la sirène, 1921), 93–108.

37. André Bazin, "The Evolution of the Language of Cinema," in Bazin, *What Is Cinema?* 36.

38. Anne Nesbet makes a similar point in relation to the gods sequence in Eisenstein's *October*. In this sequence Eisenstein juxtaposes Christian images of the divine with images of gods produced by other cultures in order to discredit all religious concepts of the deity. Nesbet writes that Eisenstein "would seem to be deconstructing . . . all hope of getting images to communicate particular concepts in a consciously controllable manner. If image and concept are fundamentally slippery, no longer held in any kind of tight correspondence, then perhaps we should see the 'Gods' sequence not as evidence that '*Capital*—the Movie' is possible (as Noel Carroll does), but as a warning that most likely such a project will prove impossible." *Savage Junctures*, 93.

39. Cinema's nineteenth-century forerunners include cameras built by Pierre Jules César Janssen and Etienne-Jules Marey, with photographic plates that revolved like gun chambers in order to capture both the slow motion of planets and the fast flight of birds. Eadweard Muybridge likewise froze human and animal movement with revolving photographic plates and strings that triggered the opening of camera shutters. Paul Virilio's *War and Cinema* traces the tandem historical development of military and cinematic technology. *War and Cinema: The Logistics of Perception*, trans. Patrick Camiller (London: Verso, 1989). Harun Farocki's film *Images of the World and the Inscription of War* (1989) provides a cinematic demonstration, and elaboration, of Virilio's claims. Many writers note the metaphorical correspondence of photography, cinema, and the gun. In *Camera Lucida*, Roland Barthes famously argues that it is photography—not cinema—that is an instrument of death. He writes, "Photography transformed subject into object. . . . The Photograph . . . represents that very subtle moment when, to tell the truth, I am neither subject nor object but a subject who feels he is becoming an object: I then experience a micro-version of death . . . I am truly becoming a specter." *Camera Lucida: Reflections on Photography*, trans. Richard Howard (New York: Hill and Wang, 1981), 13–14. Garrett Stewart extends Barthes's comparison of photographing and killing to analyses of cinema's repressed photogram—the stilled image that subtends cinema's illusion of movement. See Stewart, *Between Film and Screen: Modernism's Photo Synthesis* (Chicago: University of Chicago Press, 1999), 36–39. Alluding to the parallels between camera and gun, Michael Powell's *Peeping Tom* (1960) kills off its protagonist by having him charge toward impalement through what Laura Mulvey, in her commentary on the 1999 Criterion Collection DVD of the movie, calls "a Muybridgean gauntlet of cameras that freeze his movement even as they are triggered by it" (Mulvey, "Audio Essay," *Peeping Tom*, DVD, directed by Michael Powell [New York: Criterion Collection, 1999]); Michelangelo Antonioni's *Blow-Up* (1966) constructs a parallel between camera and gun; and Sam Peckinpah's *The Wild Bunch* (1969) credits the director immediately after the line "If they move, kill 'em."

40. Robert Warshow, *The Immediate Experience: Movies, Comics, Theatre, and Other Aspects of Popular Culture* (Cambridge, MA: Harvard University Press, 2001), 123.

41. Jeanine Bassinger, *The World War II Combat Film: Anatomy of a Genre* (New York: Columbia University Press, 1986), 64–66.

42. I borrow this phrase from Greg Taylor, *Artists in the Audience: Cults, Camp and American Film Criticism* (Princeton, NJ: Princeton University Press, 1999), 33.

43. Paul Fussell, *Wartime: Understanding and Behavior in the Second World War* (New York: Oxford University Press, 1989). See esp. 66–78. Fussell takes up James Dickey's observation of the facelessness of the soldiers in Randall Jarrell's poems about the war and writes, "Because Jarrell's servicemen are 'just collective Objects . . . or Killable Puppets,' the reader observes their frustration or destruction with an apparently inappropriate detachment. 'You care very little what happens to them,' says Dickey, 'and that is terrible.' But terrible or not, that is precisely the effect of the wartime anonymity Jarrell is pointing to. The detachment may be heartless, but it makes it possible for sensitive people to survive the war relatively undamaged." *Wartime*, 67.

44. The *Cambridge Dictionary of Philosophy* describes the tension between left and right Hegelians thus:

> In the decades following his death . . . most of the prominent academic defenders of Hegel were interested in theology, and many of these were interested in defending an interpretation of Hegel consistent with traditional Christian views of a personal God and personal immortality. This began to change with the work of "young Hegelians" such as D. F. Strauss (1808–74), Feuerbach (1804–72), Bruno Bauer (1809–82), and Arnold Ruge (1803–80), who emphasized the humanistic and historical dimensions of Hegel's account of religion, rejected the Old Hegelian tendencies toward a reconciliation with contemporary political life, and began to reinterpret and expand Hegel's account of the productive activity of human spirit (eventually focusing on labor rather than intellectual and cultural life). Strauss himself characterized the fight as between "left," "center," and "right" Hegelians, depending on whether one was critical or conservative politically, or had a theistic or a humanistic view of Hegelian *Geist*.

Robert B. Pippin, "Hegel," in *The Cambridge Dictionary of Philosophy*, ed. Robert Audi (Cambridge: Cambridge University Press, 1995), 369.

George Lichtheim writes: "To the best known of France's neo-Hegelians, M. Alexandre Kojève, Hegel's work has come to signify the arrival of a form of historical self-consciousness equally present in the two rival totalitarian movements of communism and fascism; it has been suggested, and not only by M. Kojève, that the European civil war of the nineteen thirties and forties can in one aspect be regarded as an internecine conflict between right-wing and left-wing Hegelians." George Lichtheim, introduction to *The Phenomenology of Mind*, by G. W. F. Hegel, trans. J. B. Baillie (New York: Harper and Row Publishers, 1967), xxxi.

## Chapter 1

1. Jean Epstein, "Magnification and Other Writings on Film," trans. Stuart Liebman, *October* 3 (1977): 13.

2. Béla Balázs, *Theory of the Film (Character and Growth of a New Art)*, trans. Edith Bone (New York: Roy Publishers, 1953), 62.

3. André Bazin, "The Passion of Joan of Arc," in *The Cinema of Cruelty: From Buñuel to Hitchcock*, ed. François Truffaut, trans. Sabine d'Estrée (New York: Seaver Books, 1982), 20. Originally published in *Radio-Cinéma* (1952).

4. Nesbet, *Savage Junctures*, 27–29.

5. Gilles Deleuze, *Cinema 1: The Movement Image*, trans. Hugh Tomlinson and Barbara Habberjam (Minnesota: University of Minnesota Press, 1986), 100.

6. See *Hugo Münsterberg on Film*, ed. Allan Langdale (New York: Routledge, 2002), 62, 86–91; and *Kuleshov on Film: Writings of Lev Kuleshov*, trans. and ed. Ron Levaco (Berkeley: University of California Press, 1974), 49–50.

7. See, for instance, S. M. Eisenstein, "The Montage of Film Attractions" (1924) and "The Dramaturgy of Film Form" (1929), in Eisenstein, *Selected Works*, vol. 1, *Writings, 1922–1934*, 41, 47, 179.

8. Bazin, *What Is Cinema?* 1:105 (my emphasis).

9. Christian Metz, *Film Language: A Semiotics of the Cinema*, trans. Michael Taylor (Chicago: University of Chicago Press, 1974), 67.

10. Münsterberg, *Hugo Münsterberg on Film*, 62.

11. Münsterberg, *Hugo Münsterberg on Film*, 86–91. If Münsterberg has in mind the assassination of Lincoln in Griffith's *Birth of a Nation*, then he is using the term "close-up" for an iris-in. The revolver becomes the center of attention because the rest of the frame is masked, and not because the revolver fills the screen.

12. "The room must have wallpaper, flowered wallpaper, let's paper the walls. Paintings are hung on the walls. Flowers are placed on the windowsills. There must be a chest and a stove. . . . The desk has writing implements, just as in reality." Kuleshov, *Kuleshov on Film*, 49.

13. Kuleshov, *Kuleshov on Film*, 49–50.

14. In "Beyond the Shot" (1929) Eisenstein rejects the term "fragment," adopting, instead, "cell." *Selected Works*, vol. 1, *Writings, 1922–1934*, 144.

15. S. M. Eisenstein, "The Montage of Film Attractions," 41.

16. For Eisenstein's description of this production, see "The Cinema as an Outgrowth of Theater: Through Theater to Cinema," in *Film Form: Essays in Film Theory*, ed. and trans. Jay Leyda (New York: Harcourt, Brace, Jovanovich, 1949).

17. These three passages come, respectively, from the following three essays: "The Montage of Film Attractions" (1924), "Constanţa (Whither 'The Battleship Potemkin')" (1926), and "The Problem of the Materialist Approach to Form" (1925), in Eisenstein, *Selected Works*, vol. 1, *Writings, 1922–1934*, 39, 70, 64 (emphasis in original).

18. Eisenstein, "The Montage of Film Attractions,"41–42.

19. Eisenstein, "The Montage of Film Attractions," 47.

20. Pudovkin, *Film Technique and Film Acting*, 78.

21. This is an instance where montage, meant more broadly as editing, is in tension with the concept of montage as a style of filmmaking in which discontinuity is emphasized rather than concealed.

22. Both here and in *The Mother*, where montage metaphorically aligns revolutionary protest with the spring thaw, Pudovkin represents Marxist revolt as a force of nature rather than as human violence that is consciously undertaken, against an oppressor.

23. Pudovkin's attention to the details of a gunshot wound is all the more remarkable when compared to the conventions governing the representation of gun violence in Hollywood cinema for the better part of the century. Despite the explosion of cinematic violence in the mid-1960s David Cook is still able to write that, "for all of their graphic letting of stage blood and piling up of corpses, when it came to showing actual gunshot wounds, the spaghetti Westerns and their American clones were remarkably old-fashioned: however riddled with bullets a character might be, and at whatever range, there was little or no representation of entry and exit wounds. . . . As late as mid-1967, then, American films that contemporary critics could describe as 'brutally realistic' were refusing to represent the physiological effects of violence by suppressing the clinical pathology of gunshots and other wounds." "Ballistic Balletics: Styles of Violent Representation in *The Wild Bunch* and After," in *Sam Peckinpah's "The Wild Bunch,"* ed. Stephen Prince (Cambridge: Cambridge University Press, 1999), 138.

24. André Bazin, "The Ontology of the Photographic Image," in Bazin, *What Is Cinema?* 1:15.

25. S. M. Eisenstein, "Montage 1937," in Eisenstein, *Selected Works*, vol. 2, *Towards a Theory of Montage*, ed. Michael Glenny and Richard Taylor (London: British Film Institute, 1991), 16. For the Russian see Sergei M. Eisenstein, *Izbrannye proizvedeniia v shesti tomakh* (Moskva: Izdatel'stvo iskusstvo, 1964), 2:339.

26. Jacques Aumont, "Griffith: The Frame, the Figure," in *Early Cinema: Space, Frame, Narrative*, ed. Thomas Elsaesser (London: British Film Institute, 1990), 354.

27. André Bazin, *Jean Renoir*, trans. W.W. Halsey II and William H. Simon (New York: Simon and Schuster, 1973), 87. Except where noted, all reference's to Bazin's *Jean Renoir* are to this English edition.

28. Nizhny, *Lessons with Eisenstein*, 127.

29. Nizhny, *Lessons with Eisenstein*, 138.

30. Nizhny, *Lessons with Eisenstein*, 105.

31. Nizhny, *Lessons with Eisenstein*, 141.

32. Since Eisenstein was unable to edit this film, I restrict my analysis to editing within the shots. I work from Grigory Alexandrov's reconstruction of the film, which he made with the aid of Eisenstein's sketches and notes. Although some of the shots I analyze may have been cut by Eisenstein, I try to maintain a focus on pronounced patterns that occur across several shots, both in Alexandrov's version and in the film *Sergei Eisenstein: Meksikanskaia fantasia* (Oleg Kovalev, 1998).

33. For additional details on this opening shot, see David Bordwell, *The Cinema of Eisenstein* (Cambridge, MA: Harvard University Press, 1993), 81. The classic text on this sequence is, of course, Marie-Claire Ropars's "L'Ouverture d'*Octobre* ou les conditions théoriques de la Révolution," in *Octobre: Ecriture et idéologie* (Paris: Editions Albatros, 1976), 27–66. The essay appears in English as "The Overture of *October*," trans. Larry Crawford and Kimball Lockhart, *Enclitic* 2, no. 2 (1978): 50–72; 2, no. 3 (1978): 35–47. Future references will be to the English translation.

34. See Sergei M. Eisenstein, "The Dramaturgy of Film Form" (1929), in Eistenstein, *Selected Works*, vol. 1, *Writings, 1922–34*, 168. This essay's taxonomy of conflicts found in film form helps describe the vast differences between the sizes of human figures in the frames

of *¡Que viva México!* which was filmed approximately two years after the essay was written. The contrasting sizes of individuals in close-up and long shot combine "conflict between planes," "conflict between volumes," and "spatial conflict." David Bordwell takes issue with the entire taxonomy, arguing that Eisenstein is really talking about mere difference rather than conflict. See *The Cinema of Eisenstein*, 130. But these formal "differences" in *¡Que viva México!* reflect the story world conflicts that they enunciate.

35. It is, of course, problematic to assert that camera angle ever did, on its own, connote power relations, since there are so many exceptions to the principle that low-angle shots suggest the power of the person framed, and high-angle shots, the opposite. David Bordwell and Kristin Thompson point this out in their introductory textbook, *Film Art: An Introduction*, 8th ed. (New York: McGraw-Hill, 2008), 192. See also Bazin's discussion of the low angle in *Citizen Kane* in *Orson Welles: A Critical View*, trans. Jonathan Rosenbaum (New York: Harper and Row, 1978), 75. In *¡Que viva México!* camera angle is used sufficiently consistently with other factors (such as size within the frame and characterization within the diegesis) to make the case that it does pertain to power relations.

36. Bruno Dumont, whose style, dominated by the long take, has little in common with the aesthetics of montage, employs a similar tactic in *The Life of Jesus* (1997), where racial intolerance in a provincial town results in the "crucifixion" of a minor character, a young Muslim man.

37. Marie Seton, *S. M. Eisenstein* (New York: Grove Press, 1960), 205.

38. Seton, *S. M. Eisenstein*, 205.

39. Metz, *Film Language*, 80.

40. Peter Wollen, *Signs and Meaning in the Cinema* (London: British Film Institute, 1998), 105. Wollen is arguing that the Peircean concept of the sign, as opposed to the Saussurian, constitutes the best model for the analysis of cinematic signification. He therefore needs to establish that there are instances of objectively coded symbolic signs in the cinema, and Metz's seemingly subjective reading of connotation clouds the issue.

41. *¡Que viva México!* DVD, directed by Sergei Eisenstein, reconstructed by Grigory Alexandrov and Nikita Orlov, 1931/1979 (New York: Kino Video, 2001).

42. Joan Neuberger, "Multimedia Essay on the History of *Ivan the Terrible*." *Ivan the Terrible Parts I and II*, DVD, directed by S. M. Eisenstein (New York: Criterion Collection, 2001).

## Chapter 2

1. Balázs, *Theory of the Film*, 34–35.

2. Jürgen Habermas, "The Debate on the Ethical Self-Understanding of the Species," in *The Future of Human Nature*, trans. Hella Beister and Max Pensky (Cambridge, MA: Polity Press, 2003), 50. Quoted in Jay M. Bernstein, "Suffering Injustice: Misrecognition as Moral Injury in Critical Theory," paper presented at Emory University's 10th Annual Graduate Student Philosophy Conference, Emory University, Atlanta, March 25, 2005. Bernstein adds in his footnote, "The idea of being a body and at the same time having a body . . . is an idea Habermas borrows from Helmuth Plessner."

3. Bernstein, "Suffering Injustice," 17. See also Jay M. Bernstein, "Intact and Fragmented Bodies: Versions of Ethics 'after Auschwitz,'" *New German Critique* 33, no. 1 (Winter 2006): 31–52.

4. Sergei M. Eisenstein, *Nonindifferent Nature: Film and the Structure of Things*, trans. Herbert Marshall (Cambridge: Cambridge University Press, 1988),136–37.

5. Maurice Merleau-Ponty, *Phenomenology of Perception*, trans. Colin Smith (London: Routledge, 2001), 98. Quoted in Mikhail Yampolsky, "Death in Cinema," *Re-entering the Sign: Articulating New Russian Culture*, ed. Ellen E. Berry and Anesa Miller-Pogacar (Ann Arbor: University of Michigan Press, 1995), 275.

6. Boris Bilinsky, "Le Costume," *L'Art Cinématographique* 6 (1929): 33: "Car au cinéma, les objets acquièrent tous une vie individuelle, une puissance d'expression dynamique. Á l'écran, plus de nature morte: c'est autant le revolver que la main et la cravate du meurtrier qui commettent le crime."

7. Jean Epstein, "On Certain Characteristics of *Photogénie*," in Abel, *French Film Theory and Criticism*, vol. 1, 1907-1929, 317. Abel provides the publication history at the head of the article, which first appeared on August 15, 1924.

8. Pudovkin, *Film Technique and Film Acting*, 115.

9. Pudovkin, *Film Technique and Film Acting*, 24.

10. Balázs, *Theory of the Film*, 58.

11. Yuri Tsivian, "Homeless Images: D.W. Griffith in the Eye of Soviet Filmmakers," *Griffithiana* 16, nos. 60–61 (October 1997): 51.

12. Tsivian, "Homeless Images," 53. The original is Victor Shklovsky, "The End of the Baroque: A Letter to Eisenstein," in *Za sorok let* (Moscow: Iskusstvo, 1965), 119. We might productively place this classical discourse concerning things in early cinema in dialogue with what Bill Brown calls "thing theory." See Bill Brown, ed., "Thing Theory," special issue, *Critical Inquiry* 28, no. 1 (Autumn 2001).

13. Ropars, "The Overture of *October*," pt. 1, p. 52.

14. In one instance, Ropars overstates the displacement of people, describing shot 34 of the film as "a long shot to a medium shot which only leaves the soldiers' arms and raised rifles." We can still discern faces in this thicket of vertical lines. "The Overture of *October*," pt. 1, p. 63.

15. Ropars, "The Overture of *October*," pt. 1, pp. 63, 64. Ropars's claim that the opening sequence does not primarily show particular people overthrowing a particular ruler, but, rather, one set of power symbols opposing another is in tension with her analysis of the sequence's intertitle "February." She writes: "The year is not mentioned, only the month: the implied reference does not appeal to the time of established history which is fixed in an exterior chronology, but to that of a history still in the process of being made, since it comes back to the spectator to spontaneously complete and read this date in terms of his/her close at hand experience; the dates of the tsar belong to the space of the statue, those of the revolution to the space of the spectator" (65). The Soviet government commissioned Eisenstein to make this film for the tenth anniversary of the October Revolution. An official version of the Revolution's history is already taking shape and Eisenstein's task is to cement it on celluloid. (After Trotsky's 1927 clash with Stalin, Eisenstein had to cut sequences in which Trotsky appeared in order to make the film officially acceptable.) As

Ropars shows, the decade between the Revolution and the film suffices to transform the people of 1917 into symbols. This symbolization counters the "close at hand experience" the hypothetical spectator might associate with "February." Ropars abstracts the spectator rather than maintaining her focus on the abstraction which takes place through the conjunction between formal compositional abridgement and the creation of a history.

16. Colin Crisp, *The Classic French Cinema, 1930–1960* (Bloomington: Indiana University Press, 1993),171–72.

17. André Bazin, "An Aesthetic of Reality" (1948), in Bazin, *What Is Cinema?* 2:38.

18. Roberta Pearson has traced the intricacies of Delsarte's influence on Griffith and his actors. In her study of acting in Griffith's Biograph films, she identifies two codes of acting, the histrionic and the verisimilar, both of which influenced the work of actors in Griffith's Biograph films between 1908 and 1913. Pearson observes the irony that, while Delsarte aimed to make the histrionic code more verisimilar by observing real-life movements and using them to replace the code's unabashedly exaggerated gestures, the introduction of his method to the United States led to its perversion: it became associated precisely with the histrionic code it aimed to modify or replace. Pearson argues that Griffith and his actors gradually distanced themselves from the histrionic code (and thus from Delsarte's method as it had been debased) to favor a verisimilar mode of acting. In making this shift, they followed a path similar to Delsarte's, photographing and observing ordinary persons and applying what they learned from these observations to their acting. *Eloquent Gestures: The Transformation of Performance Style in the Griffith Biograph Films* (Berkeley: University of California Press, 1992), see esp. 22–23, 92–94. Yampolsky's work tracing the path from Delsarte to Kuleshov might be supplemented by considering the more diffuse influence of Delsarte on early Soviet cinema via the films of Griffith. Yuri Tsivian begins a consideration of performance in Griffith and its influence on Soviet filmmakers and critics with an observation of several Soviet elaborations "on the role of hands in Griffith's films." "Homeless Images," 69.

19. For an instance of the machine aesthetic in American cinema, see Gaylyn Studlar, *This Mad Masquerade: Stardom and Masculinity in the Jazz Age* (New York: Columbia University Press, 1996), 52. Studlar claims that this aesthetic, though detectable in the performances of Douglas Fairbanks, here takes a decidedly antimodernist turn toward "nostalgic primitivism."

20. Kuleshov, *Kuleshov on Film*, 112. Kuleshov's concept of a repertoire of signifying gestures is in tension with his suggestion that cinematic montage renders facial expression almost irrelevant.

21. S. M. Eisenstein, "The Montage of Film Attractions," in Eisenstein, *Selected Works*, vol. 1, *Writings, 1922–1934*, 53. (Ironically, Delsarte himself believed that the emotional state of the performer *should* correspond to the external gesture.)

22. James Agee, "Comedy's Greatest Era" (1949), in *Agee on Film: Criticism and Comment on the Movies* (New York: Modern Library, 2000), 394.

23. See Studlar, *This Mad Masquerade*, 41.

24. Lev Kuleshov, *Selected Works: Fifty Years in Films*, trans. Dmitri Agrachev and Nina Belenkaya (Moscow: Raduga Publishers, 1987), 174: "Etudes with wrestling and fighting are very helpful in acquiring technique. It is best when these are done by people familiar with

acrobatics, boxing, wrestling and gymnastics. Every future film model must be trained in athletics and the above-mentioned physical disciplines; instruction in these fields of sport should be made obligatory in all film schools."

25. Metz, *Film Language*, 35–36 (my emphasis). La machine a dégossé le langage humain, l'a débité en tranches bien nettoyées où plus aucune chair n'adhère. . . . C'est une grande fête pour l'esprit syntagmatique. . . . On [l'objet naturel] analyse, au proper ou au figuré, on isole ses éléments constitutifs, c'est le moment du *découpage*, comme au cinéma. Puis ces éléments sont répartis en catégories isofonctionnelles (1): d'un côté les rails droits de l'autre les rails courbes. C'est le moment de la paradigmatique. Mais tout cela n'est que préparatif, comme l'était pour Eisenstein le tournage séparé de chaque «plan». Le grand moment . . . c'est le moment syntagmatique. On reconstitue un double de l'objet initial, un double totalement pensable puisque pur produit de la pensée: c'est l'intelligibilité de l'objet devenue elle-même un objet. . . . Cette reconstruction n'a pas pour but de représenter le réel, ce n'est pas une *reproduction* . . . c'est une simulation. . . . Squelette structural de l'objet érigé en un second objet, c'est toujours une sorte de prothèse. *Essais sur la signification au cinema* (Paris: Éditions Klincksieck, 1978), 1:43–44 (emphasis in original).

26. Lev Kuleshov, "*Mr. West—Ray—By the Law*" (1926), in Kuleshov, *Selected Works*, 66–67 (my emphasis). For Kuleshov's discussion of the model actor, or *naturshchik*, see "Spravka o naturshchike" (ca. early 1920s), "Programma kinematograficheskoi eksperimental'noi masterskoi kollektiva prepodavatelei po klassu naturshchikov" (1923), and "Xarakter proizvodstvennoi raboty naturshchikov i rezhissera" (1923), all in Lev Kuleshov, *Sobranie sochinenii v trekh tomakh*, vol. 1, *Teoriia, kritika, pedagogika*, ed. R. N. Iurenev (Moscow: Iskusstvo, 1987),86–87, 349–56.

27. Kuleshov, "*Mr. West—Ray—By the Law*," 67.

28. Kuleshov, "*Mr. West—Ray—By the Law*," 67.

29. Kuleshov, "*Mr. West—Ray—By the Law*," 67.

30. Jean Mitry, *Aesthetics and Psychology of the Cinema*, trans. Christopher King (Bloomington: Indiana University Press, 1997), 38–43.

31. The final sentence of Jack London's "The Unexpected" (1905), from which Kuleshov and Shklovsky adapted the film, also focuses, from an alienating perspective, on the feet of the hanged man. After the hanging, Hans and Edith return to the cabin, but the Native Americans who witness the hanging stay at the scene: "But the Indians remained solemnly to watch the working of the white man's law that compelled a man to dance upon the air." In London's story, Dennin does not survive the hanging.

32. Prince, *Classical Hollywood Violence*, 207.

33. Prince, *Classical Hollywood Violence*, 209.

34. Kuleshov, *Kuleshov on Film*,62–63.

35. For a discussion of the making and unmaking of statues, and the Medusa figure in Eisenstein's *The Battleship Potemkin* and *October*, see Nesbet, *Savage Junctures*, 67–73 and 86–87.

36. Vance Kepley makes a similar observation in his companion book to the film but argues the antithesis to my thesis (or the thesis to my antithesis), writing that the monuments "start to *resemble* humans rather than looming up over them as powerful objects." *The End of St. Petersburg: The Film Companion* (London: I. B. Tauris, 2003), 93.

Together our experiences of these images echo the claims of early film theorists that silent cinema makes the inanimate appear animate while revealing the human body as thinglike.

37. On the topic of living actors made to resemble statues, we might also think here of Griffith, who asked the actors in the Babylonian scenes of *Intolerance* to imitate certain postures of human figures in recently discovered Mesopotamian antiquities. See Joyce Jesionowski, "Performance and Characterization in *Intolerance*," in *The Griffith Project*, vol. 9, *The Films Produced in 1916–18*, ed. Paolo Cherchi Usai (London: British Film Institute, 2005), 65–66. Early cinema's fascination with statues and friezes suggests its "Pygmalian complex": it revels in its ability to bring petrified objects to life and to freeze and preserve the animate. At the opposite end of the spectrum from the motionless body are the frenetic bodies of Pudovkin's stock traders in *The End of St. Petersburg* and F. W. Murnau's jazz musicians in *Sunrise* (1927). These rapid, mechanical movements, far from being lively, can also suggest the violent, involuntary twitchings of the dying.

38. Kepley astutely observes that the Communist Worker, "shown in silhouette with his arm raised," "answers" the pose of the Bronze Horseman. *The End of St. Petersburg*, 93.

39. Pudovkin, *Film Technique and Film Acting*, 118.

40. See Richard Taylor and Ian Christie, eds., *The Film Factory: Russian and Soviet Documents, 1896–1939* (London: Routledge, 1988),234–35.

41. Although it was possible to mix two tracks as early as 1929, Pudovkin was not using this technology. He could, however, have recorded gunfire and voice onto a single track.

42. Warshow, *The Immediate Experience*, 240.

43. Warshow, *The Immediate Experience*, 227–28.

44. Konstantin Stanislavsky, *My Life in Art* (New York: Theatre Arts Books, 1987), 465.

45. In a footnote to *Eloquent Gestures*, Roberta Pearson writes, "In a private communication, James Naremore has pointed out that Griffith's rehearsal methods bear a resemblance to Stanislavski's. But because Stanislavski, according to Naremore, was 'not conscientiously studied in America until the late twenties,' there is no question of direct influence" (see James Naremore, *Acting in the Cinema: The American Screen to 1907* [Berkeley: University of California Press, 1990], 52). Quoted in Pearson, *Eloquent Gestures*, 160.

46. Lillian Gish, *The Movies, Mr. Griffith, and Me* (Englewood Cliffs, NJ: Prentice-Hall, 1969), 37. Quoted in Pearson, *Eloquent Gestures*, 90.

47. Linda Arvidson, *When the Movies Were Young* (New York: E. P. Dutton and Company, ca. 1925), 217. Recounted in Pearson, *Eloquent Gestures*, 90.

48. Myrtle Gebhardt, "The Unknown Quantity," *Picture Play*, July 1926, in *The Scarlet Letter* clipping file, New York Public Library for the Performing Arts at Lincoln Center. Quoted in Pearson, *Eloquent Gestures*, 102 (my emphasis).

49. Daniel Gerould, "Russian Formalism and Theories of Melodrama," in *Imitations of Life: A Reader on Film and Television Melodrama*, ed. Marcia Landy (Detroit: Wayne State University Press, 1991), 160. Quoted in Pearson, *Eloquent Gestures*, 53.

50. In *Moving Picture World* of April 15, 1911, Hanford C. Judson, in an article called "What Gets Over," expresses the following Kuleshovian viewpoint: "Nothing that is not clear and plain as daylight will be wholly effective as drama. The pantomime actor can picture the emotion perfectly; the audience will see it and sympathize, but like one who

sees another man in grief and doesn't know why he looks so sad; it can guess the reason but guessing isn't knowing." In the November 13, 1909, *New York Dramatic Mirror*, Frank Woods, in "Spectator's Comments," puts his finger on the tension between realism (the verisimilar code) and meaning: "The whole problem . . . is one of approximating reality and at the same time making the story clear." Pearson, *Eloquent Gestures*, 55–56.

51. Dorothy Donnell, "I Remember When," *Motion Picture Classic*, November 1925, 40. Quoted in Pearson, *Eloquent Gestures*, 102.

52. In a 1926 article tellingly called "Hands and Arms," for instance, Kuleshov writes:

> The "psychological work" of joints in films was pioneered by D. W. Griffith who made tremendous progress, having undoubtedly used the studies of Delsarte and his disciple Etienne Giradot as a starting point.
> The staggeringly expressive hands and arms of some film actresses from beyond the Atlantic are the product of Griffith's method. Recall the modern story in *Intolerance*, *Way Down East* and *Broken Blossoms*, and you will realize the scope of this great director's attainment regarding the creative use of hands and arms.

Kuleshov, *Selected Works*, 64–65. Similarly, Pudovkin twice refers to Mae Marsh's hands in the trial scene of *Intolerance*: "Suddenly the spectator sees for an instant her hands, only her hands, the fingers convulsively gripping the skin. This is one of the most powerful moments in the film." *Film Technique and Film Acting*, 65. And "when Griffith shot the hands of Mae Marsh in the trial scene, the actress was probably crying when she pinched the skin of her hands; she lived a full and real experience and was completely in the grip of the necessary emotion as a whole, but the director, for the film, picked out only her hands." *Film Technique and Film Acting*, 118–19. Eisenstein focuses on the way Griffith uses props for characterization: "I remember the way Griffith 'introduced' the 'Musketeer,' the gang-leader in Intolerance: he showed us a wall of his room completely covered with naked women and then showed the man himself. How much more powerful and more cinematic this is, we submit, than the introduction of the workhouse supervisor in Oliver Twist in a scene where he pushes two cripples around: i.e. he is shown through his deeds (a purely theatrical method of sketching character through action) and not through provoking the necessary associations." "The Montage of Film Attractions," 42. Eisenstein's observation resonates with Kuleshov's use of props in *By the Law* and, more generally, with the sense that cinema, more than theater, can give to inanimate objects a "presence" as powerful as that possessed by the actors.

53. Jesionowski, "Performance and Characterization in *Intolerance*," 69.

54. One of the conclusions Pudovkin draws in *Film Technique and Film Acting* is that "the Stanislavski school, which emphasizes (more truly, emphasized) most particularly the initial process of deep 'absorption' by the actor of the image, even at the expense of the 'theatricalisation' of its content, is nearest of all to the film actor" (152).

55. Edward R. Branigan, *Point of View in the Cinema: A Theory of Narration and Subjectivity in Classical Film* (The Hague: Mouton, 1984).

56. As Pudovkin and others note, the colonel repeatedly appears in low-angle—even extremely low-angle—shots while the pleading mother, her close-ups intercut with those of the colonel, inversely appears in high-angle shots indicative of her downtrodden state.

57. Perhaps Metz is alluding to this when he writes, "Straight tracks to one side, curved to the other." *Film Language*, 35–36.

58. For Vygotsky, "speech for oneself," or inner speech, "originates through differentiation from speech for others." *Thought and Language*, ed. and trans. Eugenia Hanfmann and Gertrude Vakar (New York: MIT Press, 1962), 133. (*Thought and Language*, a collection of Vygotsky's essays, was published posthumously in 1934, the year of Vygotsky's death. Eisenstein describes an encounter with Vygotsky's student A. R. Luria as early as 1929 in "Beyond the Shot." See *Selected Works*, vol. 1, *Writings, 1922-1934*, 141. The later publication date for *Thought and Language* does not mean that Eisenstein was unaware of Vygotsky's work prior to 1934.) In "Help Yourself!" Eisenstein echoes Vygotsky, asking, "How do you talk 'within yourself' as distinct from 'outside yourself'? What is the syntax of inner language, as distinct from external?" *Selected Works*, vol. 1, *Writings, 1922-1934*, 236.

59. Eikhenbaum theorized inner speech as the precondition that enables the accretion of film images to form a unified, signifying whole in the spectator's mind. See Boris Eikhenbaum, "Problems of Cinema Stylistics," in *Russian Formalist Film Theory*, ed. and trans. Herbert Eagle (Ann Arbor: University of Michigan Press, 1981).

60. See Emily Tall, "Eisenstein on Joyce: Sergei Eisenstein's Lecture on James Joyce at the State Institute of Cinematography, November 1, 1934," *James Joyce Quarterly* 24, no. 2 (Winter 1987): 133–42. For a broader discussion of inner speech and film, see Willeman, *Looks and Frictions*, 27–55. For a discussion of, specifically, Eisenstein and cinematic interior monologue, see Rachel O. Moore, *Savage Theory* (Durham, NC: Duke University Press, 2000).

61. With Ivor Montagu, Eisenstein wrote a treatment of Dreiser's novel in preparation for writing a screenplay. See Seton, *S. M. Eisenstein*, 179–80.

62. Seton, *S. M. Eisenstein*, 80.

63. Seton, *S. M. Eisenstein*, 106.

64. We might also consider here the essay "Regress—Progress" (1934), which Eisenstein begins with a consideration of Raskolnikov's interior monologue as Raskolnikov walks the streets of St. Petersburg in a trial run for his murder of the pawnbroker and compares the way that for both Raskolnikov and, more extensively, Joyce's Leopold Bloom, the outer world of the city and the inner world of reflection penetrate one another. Sergei Mikhailovich Eisenstein, *Metod*, ed. N. I. Kleiman, 2 vols. (Moscow: Muzei kino/ Eizenshtein-tsentr, 2002), 2:355.

65. Nesbet, *Savage Junctures*, 67.

66. Eisenstein, "Help Yourself!" 236.

## Chapter 3

1. Philip Rosen, *Change Mummified: Cinema, Historicity, Theory* (Minneapolis: University of Minnesota Press, 2000), 19–20.

2. Rosen, *Change Mummified*, 23.

3. Rosen, *Change Mummified*, 23.

4. André Bazin, "Death Every Afternoon," in *Rites of Realism: Essays on Corporeal Cinema*, ed. Ivone Margulies (Durham, NC: Duke University Press, 2003), 30.

5. Bazin, "Death Every Afternoon," 31.

6. Bazin, *Jean Renoir*, 87.

7. Bazin, "Erich von Stroheim: Form, Uniform, and Cruelty" (1949), in Bazin, *The Cinema of Cruelty*, 8.

8. André Bazin, "Rear Window," in Bazin, *The Cinema of Cruelty*, 163.

9. Bazin, "The Passion of Joan of Arc" (1952), in Bazin, *The Cinema of Cruelty*, 20.

10. Bazin, "*Le Journal d'un curé de campagne* and the Stylistics of Robert Bresson," in Bazin, *What Is Cinema?* 1:125–43, esp. 136, 141.

11. Bazin, *Bazin at Work*, 3–4.

12. Bazin, *Bazin at Work*, 14.

13. André Bazin, "Theater and Cinema—Part II," in Bazin *What Is Cinema?* 1:105.

14. Bazin, "Theater and Cinema—Part II," 105.

15. Bazin, "Theater and Cinema—Part II," 106.

16. Bazin's discussion of this scene resonates with Jacques Aumont's later claim that in Griffith's films "leaving the scene signifies at least potentially the death of the character." Aumont, "Griffith: The Frame, the Figure," 354. His analysis of the scene also resonates with Christian Metz's relocation—between the publication of *The Imaginary Signifier* (1977) and "Photography and Fetish" (1985)—of the absent object of film from the profilmic to the off-screen. For a discussion of this development in Metz's film theory, see Martin Jay, *Downcast Eyes: The Denigration of Vision in Twentieth-Century French Thought* (Berkeley: University of California Press, 1993), 484–85.

17. Bazin, "The Myth of Stalin in the Soviet Cinema" (1950), in Bazin, *Bazin at Work*, 32.

18. Bazin, "The Myth of Stalin in the Soviet Cinema," 33.

19. Rosen, *Change Mummified*, 34.

20. Rosen, *Change Mummified*, 36, 40.

21. André Bazin, "An Aesthetic of Reality: Neorealism (Cinematic Realism and the Italian School of the Liberation)," in Bazin, *What Is Cinema?* 2:26.

22. André Bazin, "William Wyler, or the Jansenist of Directing," in Bazin, *Bazin at Work*, 5.

23. Bazin, *What Is Cinema?* 2:35. "Un enfant pleure au milieu de ses parents morts : voilà, c'est un fait. Comment s'y sont pris les Allemands pour connaître la culpabilité des paysans? Pourquoi l'enfant est-il encore vivant? Ce n'est pas l'affaire du film." André Bazin, *Qu'est-ce que le cinema?* (Paris: Éditions du cerf, 1958), 4:31.

24. Warshow, *The Immediate Experience*, 227–29.

25. Keith Reader, "Renoir's Popular Front Films: Texts in Context," in *La Vie est à nous! French Cinema of the Popular Front, 1935–1938*, ed. Keith Reader and Ginette Vincendeau (London: British Film Institute, 1986), 44–45. Pappas's claim appears in his review of *The Crime of Monsieur Lange* for the column A Second Look, *Cineaste* 10, no. 3 (Summer 1980): 28.

26. Bazin, "An Aesthetic of Reality," 16.

27. Bazin, *What Is Cinema?* 1:39–40. "Au temps du muet, le montage *évoquait* ce que le réalisateur volulait dire, en 1938 le découpage *décrivait*, aujourd'hui enfin, on peut dire que lae metteur en scène *écrit* directement en cinéma. L'image—sa structure plastique, son organization dans le temps—parce qu'elle prend appui sur un plus grand réalisme, dispose ainsi de beaucoup plus de moyens pour infléchir, modifier du dedans la réalité." Bazin, *Qu'est-ce que le cinema?* 1:148.

28. In Bazin, *What Is Cinema?* 1:23–40. See esp. 36 and 39.

29. Bazin, *Qu'est-ce que le cinema?* 1:148 (my translation).

30. André Bazin, "The Virtues and Limitations of Montage," in Bazin, *What Is Cinema?*1:51.

31. Bazin, *What Is Cinema?* 1:39. "Mais loin d'éliminer définitivement les conquêtes du montage, (la régénérescence réaliste du récit) leur donne au contraire une relativité et un sens. Ce n'est que par rapport à un réalisme accru de l'image, qu'un supplement d'abstraction devient possible. Le repertoire stylistique d'un metteur en scène comme Hitchcock s'étend des pouvoirs du document brut aux surimpressions et aux très gros plans. Mais les gros plans de Hitchcock . . . ne sont qu'une figure de style parmi d'autres." Bazin, *Qu'est-ce que le cinema?* 1:148.

32. Bazin, *Bazin at Work*, 8 and 20n.

33. Bazin, *What Is Cinema?* 1:24.

34. Gayatri Chakravorty Spivak, "Translator's Preface," in *Of Grammatology*, by Jacques Derrida (Baltimore: Johns Hopkins University Press, 1997), xvi.

35. Christopher Faulkner, *The Social Cinema of Jean Renoir* (Princeton, NJ: Princeton University Press, 1986), 66.

36. Dudley Andrew and Steven Ungar, *Popular Front Paris and the Poetics of Culture* (Cambridge, MA: Harvard University Press, 2005),170–71.

37. Daniel Serceau, *Jean Renoir, l'insurgé* (Paris: Le Sycomore, 1981),64–65. Quoted in Reader, "Renoir's Popular Front Films," 47–48.

38. André Bazin, *Jean Renoir* (Paris: Editions Champ Libre, 1971), 42 (my translation). (All other references to Bazin's *Jean Renoir* are to the English translation.)

39. Roger Leenhardt, "Le Cinéma: Le Crime de M. Lange," *Esprit* 4, no. 42 (1 March 1936): 977. Quoted in Bazin, *Jean Renoir*, 39. Also quoted in Reader, "Renoir's Popular Front Films," 43. (I use Reader's translation here. The French is, "La réalization, avec des traits de génie, comporte le cafouillage habituel à Renoir. Oh, ces panoramiques en zigzags! Faute ou manque d'argent?")

40. Serceau, *Jean Renoir, l'insurgé*, 64 (my translation).

41. According to Martin O'Shaughnessy, Serceau's interpretation of the pan already exists in nascent form in Bazin's analysis: "Although [Bazin] has been accused of formalism, a close reading of his analysis shows that he is quite aware of how the circling camera encapsulates the sense of tight community associated with the yard." O'Shaughnessy, *Jean Renoir* (Manchester: Manchester University Press, 1988), 106. O'Shaughnessy, too, criticizes Bazin for depoliticizing Renoir. According to O'Shaughnessy, Bazin's analysis fails to "detach [the murder] from the individual." But if Bazin implies that the significance of the pan lies in realizing a circular mise-en-scène that in itself suggests a collective, then how is he *not* arguing that the shot shifts some of the focus from Lange acting alone to Lange engaging in an act of revolutionary violence for the community? Second, while the political is unthinkable without a focus on the collective or the community, does that mean that the individual can be ignored? Must not a responsible politics constantly negotiate between the particular and the collective?

42. Raymond Durgnat, *Jean Renoir* (Berkeley: University of California Press, 1974), 124.

43. Reader, "Renoir's Popular Front Films," 48.

44. Gilberto Perez, *The Material Ghost: Films and Their Medium* (Baltimore: Johns Hopkins University Press, 1998), 195.

45. Faulkner, *The Social Cinema of Jean Renoir*, 69.

46. Bazin, *Jean Renoir*, 48.

47. André-G. Brunelin, "Jacques Becker, ou la trace de l'homme," *Cinéma* 60, no. 48 (July 1960): 97. Quoted in Faulkner, *The Social Cinema of Jean Renoir*, 62 n. 2.

48. Like Faulkner, Lyall Bush also writes, "The shot-countershot technique that gives greatest rhetorical access to two-way dialogue is employed throughout. Thus the apparatus is invisible." But shots that show both speakers in the frame in dialogue scenes tend to dominate. Bush does *not* conclude, as does Faulkner, that the film leaves the spectator with the feeling that it is primarily "illusionist": "To anyone more than passingly familiar with the film . . . this rehearsal of its realism will seem inadequate to a story and form so finally strange. While the technique would persuade the viewer that it is 'classic,' and would efface itself as technique, a number of unsettlingly unrealistic moments—of camera movement, of delineation of space, and of editing—appear to be seeking different effects." Bush, "Feminine Narrative and the Law in Renoir's *Le Crime de M. Lange*," *Cinema Journal* 29, no. 1 (Fall 1989): 58–59.

49. I take the term "character-system" from Alex Woloch's *The One vs. the Many*.

50. Faulkner, *The Social Cinema of Jean Renoir*, 61.

51. Bazin, *Jean Renoir*, 46.

52. Bazin, *Jean Renoir*, 46.

53. Faulkner, *The Social Cinema of Jean Renoir*, 61.

54. Goffredo Fofi, "The Cinema of the Popular Front in France (1934–38)," *Screen* 13, no. 4 (Winter1972–73): 15.

55. Alexander Sesonske, *Jean Renoir: The French Films, 1924–1939* (Cambridge, MA: Harvard University Press, 1980), 198. Prior to this assessment of Berry's performance, Sesonske claims, without providing any supporting evidence, that "the unrelieved villainy of Batala's character might be attributed to Jacques Prévert, whose vision of the world has always been less tolerant than Renoir's." Pappas and Reader could well point to Sesonske as a critic who depoliticizes Renoir. Sesonske also makes the following statement: "Renoir's deep attachments have always been to people rather than ideologies" (18).

56. Walter Benjamin, *The Origin of German Tragic Drama*, trans. John Osborne (London: New Left Books, 1977), 233.

57. Robin Wood, *Sexual Politics and Narrative Film: Hollywood and Beyond* (New York: Columbia University Press, 1998), 83.

58. Sesonske, for instance, writes, "The scene transforms the game of love into the dance of death—and, perhaps, just that death that haunted Europe between Munich and the war." *Jean Renoir*, 399.

59. Jean Renoir, "Introduction to the Film by Jean Renoir," *The Rules of the Game*, DVD, directed by Jean Renoir (New York: Criterion Collection, 2004).

60. Wood writes, "Of all the leading characters André remains the least rounded, the least complex, the most predictable: he never surprises us." *Sexual Politics and Narrative Film*, 72.

61. S. M. Eisenstein, "The Montage of Film Attractions," 41.

62. Sesonske, *Jean Renoir*, 178.

63. Perez, *The Material Ghost*, 194.

64. Perez, *The Material Ghost*, 215.

65. Perez, *The Material Ghost*, 221.

66. This is most clear in representations of "criminals" in the "countdown" before execution. Orwell writes: "No guilty person is ever punished. So far as subjective feelings go, a person who is in a position to be punished has become the victim, and has therefore become innocent. This is perfectly well understood, internally, by everyone concerned. When a murderer is hanged, there is only one person present at the ceremony who is not guilty of murder. The hangman, the warders, the governor, the doctor, the chaplain—they are all guilty: but the man standing on the drop is innocent." "Appendix 2: Notes from Orwell's Last Literary Notebook," in *The Complete Works of George Orwell*, vol. 20, *Our Job Is to Make Life Worth Living, 1949–1950*, ed. Peter Davison (London: Secker and Warburg, 1998), 213.

67. This distinction between the universal and the particular corresponds to Renoir's goal, as described by Dudley Andrew and Steven Ungar, of "putting the background of history to the fore" and "challenging France by thrusting in its face a democratic view of the Revolution." *Popular Front Paris*, 171.

68. Otis Ferguson, "While We Were Laughing," in *The Film Criticism of Otis Ferguson*, ed. Robert Wilson (Philadelphia: Temple University Press, 1971), 22.

69. Nesbet, *Savage Junctures*, 185–208.

## Chapter 4

1. Fussell, *Wartime*, 66.

2. Taylor, *Artists in the Audience*, 33.

3. Farber suggests that part of this crisis has to do with a crisis in masculinity. In "Underground Films" he writes, "The underground directors have been saving the American male on the screen for three decades without receiving the slightest credit from critics and prize committees." *Negative Space: Manny Farber on the Movies* (New York: Praeger, 1971), 18. His assertion gives credence to Abigail Solomon-Godeau's claim that "masculinity, however defined, is, like capitalism, always in crisis. . . . The real question is how both manage to restructure, refurbish, and resurrect themselves for the next historical turn." "Male Trouble," in *Constructing Masculinity*, ed. Wallace Berger (New York: Routledge, 1995), 70.

4. Manny Farber, "Detective Story" (1951), in Farber, *Negative Space*, 42.

5. Farber, "Underground Films," 12–24. Page numbers for this work are hereafter given in the text.

6. Robert Ray uses the phrase "planned obsolescence" in describing Hollywood films:

The movie industry, and the nature of film itself, complicated the necessary forgetting process by flooding the audience with examples that were at once disposable and permanent. Indeed, the economic constraints that forced Hollywood to reproduce the traditional American mythology 300–500 times a year inherently undermined that mythology by fostering too many trivial incarnations. But those same constraints, by encouraging a *planned obsolescence*, kept that undermining slow and subtle, and prevented its effect from being felt. All but the most exceptional movies vanished after short runs, replaced by the steady stream of new versions designed to keep the traditional mythology afloat. (My emphasis)

Robert B. Ray, *A Certain Tendency of the Hollywood Cinema, 1930–1980* (Princeton, NJ: Princeton University Press, 1985), 264.

7. *The Naked City* gave rise to a television series, *The Naked City*, 1958–63. Television, more generally, forced Hollywood film to engage in its own battle against obsolescence.

8. Ironically, in order to sell Hellinger on the idea for the film, screenplay writer Malvin Wald initially had to assure him of a "safe" plot (i.e., one with a proven formula). Wald also claims that in order to talk Hellinger into producing a film out of his experimental, semi-documentary treatment of a murder story, he cited semidocumentary films of producer Louis de Rochemont: *House on 92nd Street* (Henry Hathaway, 1945), *13 Rue Madelaine* (Hathaway, 1947), and *Boomerang* (Elia Kazan, 1947). Malvin Wald, "Afterword: The Anatomy of a Hit," in *The Naked City: A Screenplay*, ed. Matthew J. Bruccoli (Carbondale: Southern Illinois University Press, 1948), 137, 144. To this list, Sarah Kozloff adds Anthony Mann's *T-Men* (1948). Sarah Kozloff, "Humanizing 'The Voice of God': Narration in *The Naked City*," *Cinema Journal* 23, no. 4 (Summer 1984): 42.

9. According to Malvin Wald, who wrote the very first treatment, the film had these two aims from its inception. Wald writes that in trying to get Hellinger to produce the story, "I explained that in combining the artistic documentary technique of Flaherty with the commercial product of Hollywood, a safe subject matter should be used—murder, a police story." And his first outline of the screenplay was "in a bastard form—using the documentary-style presentation of a divided page with one half for the visuals, the other half for the narration, for the semi-documentary form . . . then . . . full-page treatment for the dramatic sections." Wald, "Afterword: The Anatomy of a Hit," 137,141–42.

10. For the main story, he draws from the unsolved murder of Dot King, a famous model. (Mark Hellinger, the producer, was one of the newsmen who came to the murder scene of Dot King, and according to Malvin Wald, Hellinger had also known the victim.) See Wald, "Afterword: The Anatomy of a Hit," 140. Wald had access to the case files and believed that a wealthy Philadelphian with influence forced the police prematurely to drop the case. This shadowy figure finds his way into Wald's story as the fictional "Henderson," Jean Dexter's wealthy lover, supposedly from Baltimore. Henderson turns out to be the harmless Dr. Stoneman, whose character also resembles that of an actual Hollywood producer who hosted lavish parties while the homes of the invitees were robbed. Indeed, several of the characters are based on real people. Detective Halloran resembles a New York City policeman and family man described in a *Time Magazine* article. Wald took his inspiration for Frank Niles from another case file, that of an RAF man who murdered his wife: police divers found a duffle bag with the bloody RAF uniform and thus solved the murder. The minor characters who offer to help solve the case or who make false confessions also have real-life counterparts. Wald based the grocery boy who confesses, for example, on a delivery boy for a Wall Street firm who actually did commit murder. (The alcoholic writer initially suspected in this case became the inspiration for Billy Wilder's *The Lost Weekend*.) Unless otherwise noted, information concerning the story's genesis comes from Malvin Wald's "Commentary," *The Naked City*, Laserdisc, directed by Jules Dassin (New York: Roan Group, 1995). Notably, the actual people who inspired the suspicious characters—the wealthy Philadelphian

who allegedly forced the closing of the Dot King case, the RAF man, the delivery boy—actually did (or most likely did) commit murder, whereas their fictional counterparts did not.

11. As a matter of fact, Universal hesitated to distribute the film precisely because *The Naked City*'s portrayal of the police as working people who earn modest incomes and feel tired at the end of the day appeared problematic in a country increasingly in the grip of anticommunist hysteria. Wald, "Commentary." After this film, director Jules Dassin, denounced by Edward Dmytryk, went into exile in France, where he made *Rififi* with Jean Gabin. And writer Albert Maltz went to prison. In Malvin Wald's story of his first and last meeting with Maltz, he observes that Maltz's story could have been one of the eight million had it been set in New York and not Hollywood, suggesting an intricate connection between the film's makers and its characters. Wald's anecdote is worth relating: "*Photoplay* magazine selected *The Naked City* as one of the ten best pictures of the year, and, as was the custom, invited the writers to attend the awards banquet. At the time of the awards Maltz, as one of the 'Hollywood Ten,' was on his way to a federal penitentiary for contempt of Congress during the House Un-American Activities hearings. The editors of *Photoplay* were embarrassed. They could not refuse to invite Maltz, but they saw to it that he and I were seated out of sight of the photographers, behind a palm tree, near the kitchen. . . . As I recall it now, the rest of the banquet room was enthusiastically responding to the introductions of the stars who were being honored, and there sat Albert Maltz, one of America's most gifted writers, quietly sipping champagne, on his way to prison for defying Congress and pleading his First Amendment rights. If the scene were New York and not Hollywood, it could easily have been one of the 'eight million stores of The Naked City.'" Wald, "Afterword: The Anatomy of a Hit," 147.

12. See also Kozloff, "Humanizing 'The Voice of God,'" 46.

13. Indeed, Kozloff argues that Hellinger's narration in *The Naked City* is at variance with nondiegetic or disembodied narration as it has been theoretically described by Pascal Bonitzer and Mary Ann Doane. Kozloff, "Humanizing 'The Voice of God,'" esp. 48–50.

14. This is not his first commentary on a crime film—see, for instance, the opening titles, accredited to Hellinger, of *The Roaring Twenties* (Raoul Walsh, 1939).

15. Wald emphasizes how real research into police work makes his story stand out from other murder mysteries:

> The month spent with those hard-boiled New York City cops was an eye-opener. They did not greet me with open arms. . . . They brusquely informed me that they harbored little affection—or respect—for Hollywood screen writers, especially those who wrote murder mysteries based on the books of Dashiell Hammett or Raymond Chandler. In too many fictional movies, police detectives were shown as lazy, comic characters, who wore derbies indoors and spoke out of the side of their mouths like ex-cons. . . .
>
> "Look, friend," said one detective, "we don't look upon ourselves as heroes. We're hard-working civil servants trying to support families on $80 or $90 a week. We've paid our dues pounding beats as patrolmen and earned promotions to detectives the hard way."
>
> "We're no glamour boys," pointed out a neatly dressed lieutenant. "But we solve most murders and arrest the killers. And we hope to dodge enough bullets to stay alive and collect our pensions."

Wald, "Afterword: The Anatomy of a Hit," 138. (Wald is perhaps being a bit disingenuous as he makes a claim for his own realism here.)

16. For an exploration of the unease potentially generated by a corpse, see Peter Schwenger, "Corpsing the Image," *Critical Inquiry* 26, no. 3 (Spring 2000): 400.

17. This could be a pun on Dr. Stoneman's name. Like a building, he presents a facade, using his social position as a respected doctor to facilitate a burglary ring for his lover.

18. Geoffrey Hartman, "Literature High and Low: The Case of the Mystery Story," *The Fate of Reading and Other Essays* (Chicago: University of Chicago Press, 1975), 207.

19. Pascal Bonitzer, "The Silences of the Voice," in *Narrative, Apparatus, Ideology* , ed. Philip Rosen (New York: Columbia University Press, 1986), 319–34.

20. Kozloff, "Humanizing 'The Voice of God,'" 47–48.

21. Elizabeth Bronfen, *Over Her Dead Body: Death, Femininity and the Aesthetic* (Manchester: Manchester University Press, 1992), 12.

22. Malvin Wald relates his conversation with Dassin about the attention lavished on the tennis players who themselves seem so inattentive: "'Boy,' I said, 'you were lucky to have those people in white clothes playing below the bridge.'—'Lucky,' snorted Dassin indignantly, 'I planted those tennis players there—they're extras!'" Wald, "Afterword: The Anatomy of a Hit," 145. To correspond more fully to Brueghel's painting, Dassin would have to reverse foreground and background, making his Icarus, Garzah, tiny, and placing the tennis players in a plane closer to the camera.

23. Parker Tyler called it "the crime melodrama without star actors": "In *Naked City* it is Manhattan Island and its streets and landmarks that are starred. The social body is thus, through architectural symbol, laid bare ('naked')." Parker Tyler, *The Three Faces of the Film* (South Brunswick, NY: A. S. Barnes and Company, 1960). Quoted in Wald, "Afterword: The Anatomy of a Hit," 148.

24. Farber and Agee expressed admiration for one another, but they also had serious differences. Agee, for instance, admired the films of John Huston; Farber despised them.

25. James Agee, "So Proudly We Fail," *Nation*, October 30, 1943; reprinted in Agee, *Agee on Film: Criticism and Comment on the Movies*, 38–39.

26. James Agee, review, *Nation*, March 24, 1945; reprinted in Agee, *Agee on Film: Criticism and Comment on the Movies*, 139–40.

27. Agee, review, *Nation*, March 24, 1945: reprinted in Agee, *Agee on Film: Criticism and Comment on the Movies*, 139–40.

28. Frequently in his columns Agee moves from criticism of the screened world to criticism of the extrafilmic world that produces and encompasses the screened image. In a late, pessimistic summing-up of the American war film, for instance, he explicitly links American combat film aesthetics to the ethics of the American polity: "Few Americans either behind or in front of our cameras give evidence of any recognition or respect for themselves or one another as human beings, or have any desire to be themselves or to let others be themselves. On both ends of the camera you find very few people who are not essentially, instead, just promoters, little racketeers, interested in 'the angle.' I suspect it will some day be possible to deduce out of our nonfiction films alone that the supposedly strongest nation on earth collapsed with such magical speed because so few of its members honored any others, or even themselves, as human beings." James Agee, review, *Nation*, October 12, 1946; reprinted in Agee, *Agee on Film: Criticism and Comment on the Movies*, 216–17.

29. James Agee, review of *Victory through Air Power*, *Nation*, July 3, 1943; reprinted in Agee, *Agee on Film: Criticism and Comment on the Movies*, 25–28.

30. Fifty years later Devin McKinney still has cause to echo the same sentiment, writing, "As much as anything, it is this grasp [of the consequences of violence] that distinguishes strong violence from weak." Appropriately, for this comparison with Agee's review, McKinney begins by observing that another Disney film—*Bambi*—succeeded in troubling an earlier generation with the murder of Bambi's mother. McKinney, "Violence: The Strong and the Weak," 101.

31. James Agee, review of *The City That Stopped Hitler—Heroic Stalingrad*, *Nation*, September 25, 1943; reprinted in Agee, *Agee on Film: Criticism and Comment on the Movies*, 34.

32. Fussell provides numerous examples of the way that demonizing the enemy was concomitant with a refusal to acknowledge injustices, even barbarities, perpetrated on the Allied side. See, for instance, chapter 9 of *Wartime*, 115–29.

33. James Agee, review of *The Eve of St. Mark*, directed by John Stahl, *Nation*, June 3, 1944; reprinted in Agee, *Agee on Film: Criticism and Comment on the Movies*, 80.

34. James Agee, "Prize Day," *Nation*, December 25, 1943; reprinted in Agee, *Agee on Film: Criticism and Comment on the Movies*, 50.

35. James Agee, review of *Bataan*, directed by Tay Garnett, *Nation*, July 3, 1943; reprinted in Agee, *Agee on Film: Criticism and Comment on the Movies*, 28.

36. James Agee, review of *Air Force*, directed by Howard Hawks, *Nation*, February 20, 1943; reprinted in Agee, *Agee on Film: Criticism and Comment on the Movies*, 9–10.

37. James Agee, "A Great Film," review of *The Story of G.I. Joe*, directed by William Wellman, *Nation*, September 15, 1945; reprinted in Agee, *Agee on Film: Criticism and Comment on the Movies*, 162.

38. Agee, "A Great Film"; reprinted in Agee, *Agee on Film: Criticism and Comment on the Movies*, 163.

39. James Agee, review of *The City that That Stopped Hitler*; reprinted in Agee, *Agee on Film: Criticism and Comment on the Movies*, 34.

40. In general, Agee adopts a critical tone toward documentary commentary: "In this country the spectators are treated as fools, more often than not by other fools. Or call them misled. The proof is in every commentator's voice, his phrasing, his abject mawkishness and political childishness" ("Prize Day"; reprinted in *Agee on Film: Criticism and Comment on the Movies*, 49.) Robert Warshow elaborates:

> A typical figure in our culture is the "commentator," whose accepted function is to make some "appropriate" statement about whatever is presented to his attention. "Grim evidence of man's inhumanity to man," he remarks of the corpses of Buchenwald. "The end of the road," he says as we stare at dead Mussolini on the newsreel screen. (And what can one do but agree?) Even in its most solemn and pessimistic statements, this voice is still a form of "affirmation" (its healthy tone betrays it); at bottom, it is always saying the same thing: that one need never be entirely passive, that for every experience there is some adequate response; at the very least, there is always—there must be—something to say.

"Paisan" (1948), in Warshow, *The Immediate Experience*, 225.

41. Agee, "A Great Film"; reprinted in Agee, *Agee on Film: Criticism and Comment on the Movies*,162–63.

42. James Agee, "A Great Film"; reprinted in Agee, *Agee on Film: Criticism and Comment on the Movies*, 161.

43. Agee's critical sensibility is distinct from the sensibility designated by Susan Sontag with the phrase "aesthetics of silence" in *Styles of Radical Will* (New York: Farrar, Straus and Giroux, 1969). John Huston does not reflexively interrogate film language to the extent that Sontag would require. But the taciturnity Agee describes is a step in that direction.

44. We can detect here a parallel with Bazin's praise of ellipsis in Rossellini's *Paisan*: "A baby cries beside its dead parents. There is a fact. How did the Germans discover that the parents were guilty? How is it that the child is still alive? That is not the film's concern." Bazin, *What Is Cinema?* 2:35.

45. Quoted in Fussell, *Wartime*, 67.

46. James Agee, review, *Nation*, September 30, 1944; reprinted in Agee, *Agee on Film: Criticism and Comment on the Movies*, 104.

47. James Agee, review of *A Tree Grows in Brooklyn*, *Nation*, February 17, 1945; reprinted in Agee, *Agee on Film: Criticism and Comment on the Movies*, 131.

48. James Agee, "Death Takes a Powder," *Nation*, May 6, 1944; reprinted in Agee, *Agee on Film: Criticism and Comment on the Movies*, 76.

49. Warshow, *The Immediate Experience*,221–22.

50. Warshow, *The Immediate Experience*,222.

51. Walter Benjamin, "The Story Teller," in *Selected Writings*, vol. 3, 1935–1938, ed. Howard Eiland and Michael W. Jennings (Cambridge, MA: Harvard University Press, 2002), 143–44.

52. Benjamin, "The Story Teller," 143.

53. Benjamin, "The Story Teller," 147.

54. In a footnote, David Bordwell writes of an "invisible college" linking Frankfurt School theorists to New York film critics such as Barbara Deming and Robert Warshow. *Making Meaning: Inference and Rhetoric in the Interpretation of Cinema* (Cambridge, MA: Harvard University Press, 1989), 290n.

55. Manny Farber, "The Gimp" (1952), in Farber, *Negative Space*, 73.

56. Farber, "The Gimp," 75.

57. Robert Warshow, "The Legacy of the 30's" (1947), in Warshow, *The Immediate Experience*, 8.

58. Warshow, "The Legacy of the 30's," 8.

59. Warshow, "Paisan," 225.

## Chapter 5

1. See Ernest Mandel's *Delightful Murder: A Social History of the Crime Story* (Minneapolis: University of Minnesota Press, 1985). Mandel analyzes the shift, in postromantic crime stories, from a focus on the murderer to a focus on the detective, arguing that it reflects the ascendancy of bourgeois rationalism and concern for the protection of property.

2. Roy Hoopes, *Cain* (New York: Holt, Rinehart and Winston, 1982), 350.

3. In the novel Mildred tries to throttle Veda in a similar scene, Monte stops her, and Mildred feels remorse. This is as close as the novel gets to murder. The screenplay went through several scripts and writers (Cain, Thames Williamson, Catherine Turney, Albert Maltz, Ranald MacDougall, and others) before taking final form. (Maltz also worked on *The Naked City*.) For the fullest account of the genesis of the script, see Albert J. LaValley, "Introduction: A Troublesome Property to Script," in *Mildred Pierce*, ed. Albert J. LaValley (Madison: University of Wisconsin Press, 1980), 9–53. See also Rudy Behlmer, ed. *Inside Warner Brothers (1935-1951)* (New York: Viking Press, 1985), 256–57; and Roy Hoopes, *Cain*, 348.

4. Hoopes, *Cain*, 339–40.

5. "It is certain that Wald did not get the idea of a flashback treatment of *Mildred Pierce* from seeing the picture, *Double Indemnity*, as *Double Indemnity* was released by Paramount on April 24, 1944. We know from Cain's letter to Wald, dated September 22, 1943, that the flashback idea was in Wald's mind at that time. [Here Behlmer inserts the following footnote: "It is possible, of course, that Wald was aware of the structure of *Double Indemnity* from a reading of the script, discussions with people involved in the project, an advance screening of parts or all of the film, or word via the industry grapevine."] It is, however, possible that the success of the motion picture, *Double Indemnity*, helped to confirm Wald's conclusion that this was the correct line of approach to *Mildred Pierce*." Tony Chapman, letter to Roy Obringer, February 12, 1950, quoted in Behlmer, *Inside Warner Brothers*, 260–61.

6. Hoopes, *Cain*, 314. According to Charles Higham, Cain objected to the changes made to his story—even if the changes were intended to please his fans. He objected primarily, however, not to the murder, but to the way the screenplay deprives Veda of her talent as a musician. Charles Higham, *Warner Brothers* (New York: Scribners, 1975), 184–85. Cited in LaValley, "Introduction,", 15.

7. Behlmer, *Inside Warner Brothers*, 260.

8. Pam Cook, "Duplicity in *Mildred Pierce*," in *Women in Film Noir*, ed. E. Ann Kaplan (London:British Film Institute, 1998), 69.

9. See Joyce Nelson, "*Mildred Pierce* Reconsidered," *Film Reader* 2 (January 1977): 65–70.

10. Parker Tyler, *Magic and Myth of the Movies* (New York: Henry Holt and Company, 1947), 218.

11. David Bordwell, "The Classical Hollywood Style, 1917–60," in Bordwell et al., *The Classical Hollywood Cinema*, 20.

12. LaValley, "Introduction," 38.

13. Tyler, *Magic and Myth of the Movies*, 211.

14. Eisenstein, *On the Composition of the Short Fiction Scenario*, 13. Tyler's essay on *Mildred Pierce* resonates with Eisenstein's discussions of metaphor, metonymy, and murder, discussed in chapter 2. Like Eisenstein, Tyler remarks the power of a murderer who appears, at once, guilty and innocent. He criticizes *Mildred Pierce* for its superficial transformation of Veda into guilty scapegoat, arguing that the film disavows its unconscious, where Veda is Mildred's double.

15. Bordwell, "The Classical Hollywood Style, 1917–60," 60.

16. Lev Kuleshov, *Iskusstvo kino: moi opyt* (Moscow: Tea-Kino-pechat', 1929), 100. Quoted in Eisenstein, *Selected Works*, vol. 1, *Writings, 1922-1934*, 143.

17. I take this noun-as-verb from Schwenger, "Corpsing the Image."

18. LaValley points to the same repetition: "Without undue stress, Curtiz often reminds us of important themes by a slight panning shot: for example, when Mildred enters the café with Wally in the opening sequences, the camera pans to the stage where Miriam [Veda Ann Borg] is singing. Later we learn that Mildred here found Veda doing the same." "Introduction," 45.

19. LaValley observes, "[Curtiz's] actors are always busy doing common actions and many of the script changes deal with these, for example, the mixing of drinks becomes a major motif for Mildred's worldliness and disillusionment." "Introduction," 45.

20. Mary Ann Doane interprets Veda's acquisitiveness as Hollywood World War II propaganda that tries to position women as threats to the wartime economy. Veda pursues luxury goods in order to appear as a stylish, seductive woman, which in turn enables her to increase still further her consumerism. Mary Ann Doane, *The Desire to Desire: The Woman's Film of the 1940's* (Bloomington: Indiana University Press, 1987), 81.

21. Bordwell et al., *The Classical Hollywood Cinema*, 18.

22. Stanley Cavell, *The World Viewed* (Cambridge, MA: Harvard University Press, 1979), 33.

23. Hoopes, *Cain*, 314.

24. Hoopes, *Cain*, 373.

25. James Agee, review, *Nation*, October 13, 1945; reprinted in Agee, *Agee on Film: Criticism and Comment on the Movies*, 165–66.

26. LaValley, "Introduction," 21.

27. Linda Williams, for instance, writes, "The failure of *Mildred Pierce* to offer either its female subject or its female viewer her own understanding of the film's narrative has made it a fascinating example of the way films can construct patriarchal subject-positions that subvert their ostensible subject matter." Linda Williams, "Something Else besides a Mother: *Stella Dallas* and the Maternal Melodrama," in *Feminism and Film*, ed. E. Ann Kaplan (Oxford: Oxford University Press, 2000), 480. See also Frank Krutnik, *In a Lonely Street: Film Noir, Genre, Masculinity* (London: Routledge, 1991): "At several points in the film, Mildred/Crawford is overtly sexualized: her bare legs captured in the 'gaze' of both a male character and the camera . . . serving to deny the woman a subjective centering within the text" (62).

28. Tyler, *Magic and Myth of the Movies*, 224–25.

29. Tyler, *Magic and Myth of the Movies*, 228. The observation that "both Mildred and Veda are too shallow as human beings to be conscious of their guilt roles" has, since Tyler, metamorphosed into a more pointed and specifically feminist criticism. See nn. 20 and 27.

30. Tyler interprets *Mildred Pierce* as the story of an Electra complex: "Mildred imagines herself as Veda, in love with her own father, Mildred's husband, as Mildred was in love with her father. The passionate desire to give Veda everything, to see her grow up happy and successful in every way, is an ordinary case of displacement; paradoxically Mildred wants to give her every charm and chance to accomplish that which she was prevented from accomplishing, union with her father. But the desertion of Mildred by Pierce, Veda's father, lends extra neurotic energy to Mildred's aim, and it is not till late that she realizes she must supply Veda with another 'father' to complete her own (Mildred's) incest pattern. This she

does by marrying Beragon; sure enough, this brings Veda and Beragon together, and Mildred duly surprises them in an incestuous embrace. But in the shock of the moment Mildred wakes up . . . from her complex." *Magic and Myth of the Movies*, 226. Contrast Tyler's concept of realism, which excludes *Mildred Pierce*, with Wald's, discussed above.

31. Hartman, *The Fate of Reading*, 204, 207.

32. Only forty-five years before *The Battleship Potemkin*, Dostoevsky published *The Brothers Karamazov* (1880).

33. "The female spectator is invited to witness her own commodification and, furthermore, to buy an image of herself insofar as the female star is proposed as the ideal of feminine beauty." As a result, "the film, in its commodity form promotes a certain mode of perception . . . which, for the female spectator, initiates a particularly complex dialectic of 'being,' 'having,' and 'appearing.'" Doane, *The Desire to Desire*, 24–25.

34. Tyler, *Magic and Myth of the Movies*, 229.

35. Bordwell et al., *The Classical Hollywood Cinema*, 16.

36. Quoted in Martin Jay, *The Dialectical Imagination: A History of the Frankfurt School and the Institute of Social Research, 1923-1950* (Boston: Little, Brown and Company, 1973), 214.

37. Jay, *The Dialectical Imagination*, 214.

38. Ray, *A Certain Tendency of the Hollywood Cinema*, 47.

39. Bordwell and Thompson, *Film Art*, 386–87.

40. Charles Musser, *The Emergence of Cinema: The American Screen to 1907* (New York: Charles Scribner's Sons, 1990), 354.

41. See, for instance, David A. Cook, "Ballistic Balletics: Styles of Violent Representation in *The Wild Bunch* and After," in *Sam Peckinpah's "The Wild Bunch,"* ed. Stephen Prince (Cambridge: Cambridge University Press, 1999),130–54; Prince, *Classical Film Violence*; and Richard Slotkin, *Gunfighter Nation: The Myth of the Frontier in Twentieth-Century America* (Norman: University of Oklahoma Press, 1998), 578–623. Charles Musser has pointed out that Porter did not consider *The Great Train Robbery* a Western. Instead, he counted his 1906 film *Life of a Cowboy* as the first Western. See Musser, "The Travel Genre in 1903–1904: Moving towards Fictional Narrative," in *Early Cinema: Space, Frame, Narrative*, ed. Thomas Elsaesser (London: British Film Institute, 1990), 123–32.

42. Warshow, *The Immediate Experience*, 123 (my emphasis).

43. Jane Tompkins, *West of Everything: The Inner Life of Westerns* (Oxford: Oxford University Press, 1992), 57.

44. Tompkins, *West of Everything*, 153.

45. Owen Wister, *The Virginian, a Horseman of the Plains* (Oxford: Oxford University Press, 1998), 313.

46. D. A. Miller, *Jane Austen; or, The Secret of Style* (Princeton, NJ: Princeton University Press, 2003).

47. Laura Mulvey, "Visual Pleasure and Narrative Cinema," in *Feminist Film Theory: A Reader*, ed. Susan Thornham (Edinburgh: Edinburgh University Press, 1999), 63. Originally published in *Screen* 16, no. 3 (1975): 6–18.

48. Melvin Van Peebles, "Audio Commentary," *Sweet Sweetback's Baadasssss Song*, Laserdisc, directed by Melvin Van Peebles (New York: Criterion Collection, 1997).

49. Miller, *Jane Austen*, 17.

50. Miller, *Jane Austen*, 28.

51. Miller, *Jane Austen*, 46.

52. Lee Clark Mitchell, "Violence in the Film Western," in *Violence and American Cinema*, ed. David Slocum (New York: Routledge, 2001),176–91.

53. Mitchell, "Violence in the Film Western," 178. We also see men made into objects of the gaze in the story world (and not simply through their costuming). Gaylyn Studlar, for instance, observes the objectification of Michael O'Rourke (John Agar) by Philadelphia Thursday (Shirley Temple) in *Fort Apache* (John Ford, 1948). "Sacred Duties, Poetic Passions," in *John Ford Made Westerns*, ed. Gaylyn Studlar and Matthew Bernstein (Bloomington: Indiana University Press, 2001), 59.

54. Mitchell, "Violence in the Film Western," 185.

55. Miller, *Jane Austen*, 49.

56. See, for instance, Luis J. Rodriguez, *Always Running: La Vida Loca: Gang Days in L.A.* (Willimantic, CT: Curbstone Press, 1993). "There is an aspect of suicide in young people whose options have been cut off. They stand on street corners, flashing hand signs, inviting the bullets. It's either *la torcida* or death: A warrior's path, when even self-preservation is not at stake. And if they murder, the victims are usually the ones who look like them, the ones closest to who they are—the mirror reflections. They murder and they're killing themselves, over and over" (9). The intricate ties between murder and suicide are also a Dostoevskian theme.

57. Miller, *Jane Austen*, 28.

58. Anti-Christian and antifeminist, Westerns, according to Tompkins, actively mock the social values—temperance, peaceful conflict resolution, spirituality, and so on—upheld in Christian and/or domestic narratives. *West of Everything*, 39–44. Gaylyn Studlar takes issue with Tompkins's generalizations concerning gender and Westerns—specifically John Ford's Westerns—in "Sacred Duties, Poetic Passions," 44–46, 55, 61–62, 65,and 69.

59. Perez, *The Material Ghost*, 240.

60. Musser adds, "The term 'realism' can also be applied to the entire film. . . . The careful attention to the details of robbing a train, the emphasis on process as narrative, almost takes *The Great Train Robbery* out of the realm of fiction and suggests a documentary intent." *The Emergence of Cinema*,354–55.

61. Tom Gunning, "The Cinema of Attractions: Early Film, Its Spectator and the Avant-Garde," in Elsaesser, *Early Cinema*, 56–62. Gunning writes, "What precisely is the cinema of attractions? First, it is a cinema that bases itself on the quality that Léger celebrated: its ability to *show* something. Contrasted to the voyeuristic aspect of narrative cinema analysed by Christian Metz, this is an exhibitionist cinema. An aspect of early cinema . . . is emblematic of this different relationship the cinema of attractions constructs with its spectator: the recurring look at the camera by actors. This action, which is later perceived as spoiling the realistic illusion of the cinema, is here undertaken with brio, establishing contact with the audience" (57).

62. G. W. F. Hegel, *The Phenomenology of Mind*, trans. J. B. Baillie (New York: Harper and Row, 1967), 233.

63. Hegel, *The Phenomenology of Mind*, 233.

64. Eric Sherman and Martin Rubin, *The Director's Event: Interviews with Five American Film-Makers* (New York: Atheneum, 1970), 49.

65. Hegel, *The Phenomenology of Mind*, 229.

66. Sherman and Rubin, *The Director's Event*, 49.

67. Sherman and Rubin, *The Director's Event*, 50.

68. Gilberto Perez emphasizes these underlying social tensions not only in his reading of Ford Westerns but in his criticism of Richard Slotkin's *Gunfighter Nation* (which also reads social conflict into the Western duel): "It little considers the history of America in relation to the history of other nations. It suffers from American exceptionalism not because it believes in American preeminence—rather the contrary—but because it nonetheless assumes the singularity of American history and American mythology." Perez implicitly alludes to the concept of class struggle that emerges from Hegel's dialectic between mastery and slavery when he continues, "An interesting if debatable case could be made—Slotkin almost makes it—that the Western portrays the violence of the ruling class and views it approvingly, whereas the gangster movie, whose hero is usually an immigrant, portrays the violence of the upstart lower class and views it disapprovingly." *The Material Ghost*, 245.

69. Warshow, *The Immediate Experience*, 110, 111.

70. Warshow, *The Immediate Experience*, 108, 109.

71. Tompkins, *West of Everything*, 12–13.

72. Tompkins, *West of Everything*, 57.

73. See Mitchell, "Violence in the Film Western"; and D. A. Miller, "On the Universality of *Brokeback Mountain*," *Film Quarterly* 60, no. 3 (Spring 2007): 50–60, who also "decodes" this violence as a part of his subtle and complex analysis.

74. André Bazin, "The Western; or The American Film *Par Excellence*," in Bazin, *What Is Cinema?* 2:140–48. See esp. 140, 141, 148.

75. Warshow, *The Immediate Experience*, 116.

76. Piotr Hoffman, *Violence in Modern Philosophy* (Chicago: University of Chicago Press, 1989), 146.

77. Sam Peckinpah uses a mirror in a murder scene to similar effect in *Pat Garrett and Billy the Kid* (1973). Stephen Prince writes, "The film's climactic image of Garrett, after he has killed the Kid, shooting his mirrored reflection and then gazing at himself through the shattered glass, is Peckinpah's most poetic image of the mutilation of human potential by violence." "Introduction: Sam Peckinpah, Savage Poet of American Cinema," in Prince, *Sam Peckinpah's "The Wild Bunch"*, 30. In *Mildred Pierce* we also see bullet holes in the mirror after Monte is shot, but the glass does not reflect the killer, since Veda's violence is not at issue but functions, instead, as a structuring device.

78. See Jean-Pierre Oudart, "La Suture," *Cahiers du Cinéma*, nos. 211 and 212 (April–May 1969).

79. Robert Ray writes, "American history's major crises appear in American movies only as 'structuring absences'—the unspoken subjects that have determined an aesthetic form designed precisely to conceal these crises' real implications." *A Certain Tendency of the Hollywood Cinema*, 31.

80. Ralph E. Friar and Natasha A. Friar, *The Only Good Indian . . . : The Hollywood Gospel* (New York: Drama Book Specialists, 1972). For an overview of criticism of the book, see Angela Aleiss, *Making the White Man's Indian: Native Americans and Hollywood Movies* (Westport, CT: Praeger, 2005), xvi, 175n.

81. The literature on Native Americans in film is vast. Here I will simply mention a few important book-length studies, all of which demonstrate that Hollywood representations of Native Americans tell us more about Hollywood and the culture in which it exists than they do about Native Americans and their history. In *Regeneration through Violence* (Norman: University of Oklahoma Press, 2000), Richard Slotkin analyzes the ways in which Native Americans have been made to fit into the mythology of the American frontier. Angela Aleiss looks not to myth but to Hollywood history to explain why certain key representations of Native Americans happened in her recent *Making the White Man's Indian*. Armando José Prats focuses on the various rhetorical processes of "othering" Native Americans in *Invisible Natives: Myth and Identity in the American Western* (Ithaca, NY: Cornell University Press, 2002). And Jacquelyn Kilpatrick traces Hollywood representations of Native Americans through the double framework of Hollywood and U.S. history in *Celluloid Indians: Native Americans and Film* (Lincoln: University of Nebraska Press, 1999).

82. See, for instance, William Tsutsui, *Godzilla on My Mind: Fifty Years of the King of Monsters* (New York: Palgrave Macmillan, 2004); David J. Skal, *Screams of Reason: Mad Science and Modern Culture* (New York: W. W. Norton and Company, 1998),166–94; and Peter Biskind, *Seeing Is Believing: How Hollywood Taught Us to Stop Worrying and Love the Fifties* (New York: Henry Holt and Company, 1953).

83. See Ray, *A Certain Tendency of the Hollywood Cinema*,247–95. See also John G. Cawelti, "*Chinatown* and Generic Transformation in Recent American Films," in *Film Genre Reader II*, ed. Barry Keith Grant (Austin: University of Texas Press, 2003), 243–61; also in Gerald Mast and Marshall Cohen, eds., *Film Theory and Criticism*, 2nd ed. (New York: Oxford University Press, 1979),559–79.

84. Frederic Jameson, *Signatures of the Visible* (New York: Routledge, 1992),82–84.

85. Jonathan Rosenbaum, *Dead Man* (London: British Film Institute, 2000), 21.

86. See, for instance, Viktor Shklovskii, "Poeziia i proza v kinematografii," in *Poetika kino* (Moscow: Kinopechat', 1927; reprint, Berkeley: Berkeley Slavic Specialties, 1984), 139–42. See also Herbert Eagle, "The Poetic Cinema of Yuri Ilyenko," paper presented at the American Association for the Advancement of Slavic Studies Annual Conference in Toronto, November 23, 2003, 3.

87. See, for instance, James Steffen's detailed discussion of Parajanov's work in relation to the Poetic School in "A Cardiogram of the Times: Sergei Parajanov and the Politics of Nationality and Aesthetics in the Soviet Union" (doctoral thesis, Emory University, 2005).

88. *Dead Man*, DVD, directed by Jim Jarmusch (New York: Miramax, 1996).

89. Cathy Caruth, *Unclaimed Experience: Trauma, Narrative, and History* (Baltimore: Johns Hopkins University Press, 1996), 91–112.

90. Jameson, *Signatures of the Visible*, 95.

91. In addition to Fredric Jameson, critics who have located a social critique implicit in *The Shining* include Frank Manchel and David Cook. Manchel argues that the film re-

veals patriarchy as oppressive to Jack as well as to his wife and son ("What About Jack? Another Perspective on Family Relationships in Stanley Kubrick's *The Shining*," *Literature/ Film Quarterly* 23, no. 1 [1995]: 67–78); Cook interprets job-stressed Jack Torrance's murderous roar, "I'm right behind you Danny!"as "psychologically descriptive of the man behind every boy, generation on generation, passing down . . . the violence which is the natural by-product of our economic system" ("American Horror: *The Shining*," *Literature/Film Quarterly* 14, no. 2 [1986]: 4). In response to interpretations of the film as social critique, John Brown cautions, "Like no other movie I know, it both necessitates and defies the critical act" ("Reflections on *The Shining*," in *Cinema and Fiction: New Modes of Adapting, 1950–1990*, ed. John Orr and Colin Nicholson [Edinburgh: Edinburgh University Press, 1992], 120).

92. An emphasis on undecidability of meaning also occurs in films without murder. But it is telling that films that most rigorously, and, now, canonically, insist on the impossibility of meaningful narrative knowledge, such as *Un Chien Andalou* (Luis Bunuel and Salvador Dali, 1929) or *Last Year at Marienbad* (Alain Resnais, 1961), both have murder tableaux.

## Conclusion

1. Godard, *Histoire(s) du cinéma*, 3:33. (I am transcribing from the books accompanying the CDs, which Godard published in conjunction with the films.) For a catalog of all the meanings Godard gives to the claim that cinema is dying, see Michael Witt, "The Death(s) of Cinema According to Jean-Luc Godard," *Screen* 40, no. 3 (1999): 331–46.

2. Chapter 4 (a), "Control of the Universe," in Godard, *Histoire(s) du cinéma*, 4:43.

3. In *Histoire(s)*, Godard explains Hitchcock's "mastery" as follows:

we've forgotten
why Joan Fontaine leans over
the edge of the cliff
. . .
and what was it that Joel McCrea
was going to do in Holland
we don't remember why
Montgomery Clift was maintaining eternal silence
or why Janet Leigh stopped at the Bates motel
or why Teresa Wright
still loves Uncle Charlie
we've forgotten what it was that Henry Fonda
wasn't entirely guilty of
and why exactly
the American government had hired Ingrid Bergman

but
we remember a handbag
but
we remember a bus in the desert

but
we remember a glass of milk
the sails of a windmill
a hairbrush
but
we remember a row of bottles
a pair of spectacles
a sheet of music
a bunch of keys
because through them
and with them
Alfred Hitchcock succeeded
... by taking control of the universe
...
and the reason why Alfred Hitchcock became
the only poète maudit to meet with success
was that he was the greatest creator of forms
of the twentieth century

(Godard, *Histoire(s) du cinéma*, 4:42–43)

4. Paul K. Saint-Amour, "Modernist Reconnaissance," *Modernism/Modernity* 10, no. 2 (April 2003): 350–52.

5. For a recent theoretical consideration of these practices, see Bernstein, "Intact and Fragmented Bodies."

6. In his interview with Truffaut, Hitchcock recounts how he rejected Saul Bass's breakdown of the scene into fragments in favor of a single shot with a fairly tight framing of Arbogast's face:

> One day during the shooting I came down with a temperature, and since I couldn't come to the studio, I told the cameraman and my assistant that they could use Saul Bass's drawings. Only the part showing him going up the stairs, before the killing. There was a shot of his hand on the rail, and of feet seen in profile, going up through the bars of the balustrade. When I looked at the rushes of the scene, I found it was no good, and that was an interesting revelation for me, because as that sequence was cut, it wasn't an innocent person but a sinister man who was going up those stairs. Those cuts would have been perfectly all right if they were showing a killer, but they were in conflict with the whole spirit of the scene.... We needed to show a staircase and a man going up that staircase in a very simple way. Alfred Hitchcock and François Truffaut, *Hitchcock/Truffaut* (New York: Simon and Schuster, 1983), 273.

That Hitchcock felt the fragmented body to be a murderous body suggests the powerful association of murder with such a montage breakdown.

7. William Rothman, *Hitchcock: The Murderous Gaze* (Cambridge, MA: Harvard University Press, 1982), 316.

8. Hitchcock's is a lyrical eye. Robert Kaufman, borrowing from Adorno, defines the lyrical I as "that which, by dint of aura's dynamic of charged distance, can break down

the hardening of subjectivity . . . and hence can allow the subject to 'catch . . . the slightest glimpse beyond that prison that it [the "I"] itself is,' thus permitting 'the "I,"' once 'shaken, to perceive its own limitedness and finitude' and so to experience the critical possibility of thinking otherness." Robert Kaufman, "Aura, Still," *October* 99 (Winter 2002): 49. Kaufman is quoting from Theodore W. Adorno, *Aesthetic Theory*, ed. and trans. Robert Hullot-Kentor (Minneapolis: University of Minnesota Press, 1997), 269, 245. "Limitedness and finitude" are precisely what Hitchcock's overhead shots of Arbogast and Jonathan convey in Rothman's interpretation.

9. Jean-Luc Godard, *The Future(s) of Film: Three Interviews, 2000/2001*, trans. John O'Toole (Bern: Verlag Gachnang & Springer, 2002), 64.

10. I am building, here, on Ray's wonderful discussion of reverse shots in Ford and Huston in *A Certain Tendency of the Hollywood Cinema*, 233–36.

11. Kaja Silverman and Harun Farocki, *Speaking about Godard* (New York: New York University Press, 1998), 10–12.

12. Silverman says of the scene, "The second time, that word ['death'] is available only to us; it is thus Godard, not Nana, who insists upon the relation between her and Jeanne." Silverman and Farocki, *Speaking about Godard*, 11.

# Bibliography

Abel, Richard, ed. *French Film Theory and Criticism: A History/Anthology, 1907–1939*. Vol. 1, *1907–1929*. Princeton, NJ: Princeton University Press, 1988.

Adorno, Theodore W. *Aesthetic Theory*. Edited and translated by Robert Hullot-Kentor. Minneapolis: University of Minnesota Press, 1997.

Agee, James. *Agee on Film: Criticism and Comment on the Movies*. New York: Modern Library, 2000.

———. *Agee on Film: Reviews and Comments*. London: Peter Owen, 1963.

Aleiss, Angela. *Making the White Man's Indian: Native Americans and Hollywood Movies*. Westport, CT: Praeger, 2005.

Andrew, Dudley, and Steven Ungar. *Popular Front Paris and the Poetics of Culture*. Cambridge, MA: Harvard University Press, 2005.

Arvidson, Linda. *When the Movies Were Young*. New York: E. P. Dutton and Company, ca. 1925.

Aumont, Jacques. "Griffith: The Frame, the Figure." In *Early Cinema: Space, Frame, Narrative*, edited by Thomas Elsaesser. London: British Film Institute, 1990.

Bakhtin, Mikhail. *Problems of Dostoevsky's Poetics*. Edited and translated by Caryl Emerson. Minneapolis: University of Minnesota Press, 1984.

Balázs, Béla. *Theory of the Film (Character and Growth of a New Art)*. Translated by Edith Bone. New York: Roy Publishers, 1953.

Barthes, Roland. *Camera Lucida: Reflections on Photography*. Translated by Richard Howard. New York: Hill and Wang, 1981.

Bassinger, Jeanine. *The World War II Combat Film: Anatomy of a Genre*. New York: Columbia University Press, 1986.

Bazin, André. *Bazin at Work: Major Essays and Reviews from the Forties and Fifties*. Edited by Bert Cardullo. Translated by Alain Piette and Bert Cardullo. New York: Routledge, 1997.

———. *The Cinema of Cruelty: From Buñuel to Hitchcock*. Edited by François Truffaut. Translated by Sabine d'Estrée. New York: Seaver Books, 1982.

————. "Death Every Afternoon." In *Rites of Realism: Essays on Corporeal Cinema*, edited by Ivone Margulies. Durham, NC: Duke University Press, 2003.

————. *Jean Renoir.* Translated by W. W. Halsey II and William H. Simon. New York: Simon and Schuster, 1973.

————. *Jean Renoir.* Paris: Editions Champ Libre, 1971.

————. "Mort d' Humphrey Bogart." *Cahiers du Cinéma* 68 (February 1957): 2–8.

————. *Orson Welles: A Critical View.* Translated by Jonathan Rosenbaum. New York: Harper and Row, 1978.

————. *Qu'est-ce que le cinema?* Paris: Éditions du cerf, 1958.

————. *What Is Cinema?* Translated by Hugh Gray. 2 vols. Berkeley: University of California Press, 1967.

Behlmer, Rudy, ed. *Inside Warner Brothers (1935–1951).* New York: Viking Press, 1985.

Benjamin, Walter. *The Origin of German Tragic Drama.* Translated by John Osborne. London: New Left Books, 1977.

————. *Selected Writings.* Vol. 3, *1935–1938.* Edited by Howard Eiland and Michael W. Jennings. Cambridge, MA: Harvard University Press, 2002.

Bernstein, Jay M. "Intact and Fragmented Bodies: Versions of Ethics 'after Auschwitz.'" *New German Critique* 33, no. 1 (Winter 2006): 31–52.

————. "Suffering Injustice: Misrecognition as Moral Inquiry in Critical Theory." Paper presented at Emory University's 10th Annual Graduate Student Philosophy Conference, Atlanta, GA, March 25, 2005.

Bilinsky, Boris. "Le Costume." *L'Art Cinématographique* 6 (1929): 33.

Biskind, Peter. *Seeing Is Believing: How Hollywood Taught Us to Stop Worrying and Love the Fifties.* New York: Henry Holt and Company, 2000.

Bonitzer, Pascal. "The Silences of the Voice." In *Narrative, Apparatus, Ideology,* edited by Philip Rosen. New York: Columbia University Press, 1986.

Bordwell, David. *The Cinema of Eisenstein.* Cambridge, MA: Harvard University Press, 1993.

————. *Making Meaning: Inference and Rhetoric in the Interpretation of Cinema.* Cambridge, MA: Harvard University Press, 1989.

Bordwell, David, Janet Staiger, and Kristin Thompson. *The Classical Hollywood Cinema: Film Style and Mode of Production to 1960.* New York: Columbia University Press, 1985.

Bordwell, David, and Kristin Thompson. *Film Art: An Introduction.* 8th ed. New York: McGraw-Hill, 2008.

Branigan, Edward R. *Point of View in the Cinema: A Theory of Narration and Subjectivity in Classical Film.* New York: Mouton, 1984.

Bronfen, Elizabeth. *Over Her Dead Body: Death, Femininity, and the Aesthetic.* Manchester: Manchester University Press, 1992.

Brown, Bill, ed. "Thing Theory." Special issue, *Critical Inquiry* 28, no. 1 (Autumn 2001).

Brown, John. "Reflections on *The Shining.*" In *Cinema and Fiction: New Modes of Adapting, 1950–1990,* edited by John Orr and Colin Nicholson. Edinburgh: Edinburgh University Press, 1992.

Brunelin, André-G. "Jacques Becker, ou la trace de l'homme." *Cinéma 60,* no. 48 (July 1960): 97.

Burch, Noël. *Theory of Film Practice.* Translated by Helen R. Lane. New York: Praeger Publishers, 1973.

Bush, Lyall. "Feminine Narrative and the Law in Renoir's *Le Crime de M. Lange*." *Cinema Journal* 29, no. 1 (Fall 1989): 54–70.

Caruth, Cathy. *Unclaimed Experience: Trauma, Narrative, and History.* Baltimore: Johns Hopkins University Press, 1996.

Caveing, Maurice. "Dialectique du concept du cinema." *Revue Internationale de Filmologie* 1, no. 1 (July–August 1947): 71–78.

Cavell, Stanley. *The World Viewed.* Cambridge, MA: Harvard University Press, 1979.

Cawelti, John G. "*Chinatown* and Generic Transformation in Recent American Films." In *Film Genre Reader II*, edited by Barry Keith Grant. Austin: University of Texas Press, 2003. Also in Gerald Mast and Marshall Cohen, eds., *Film Theory and Criticism*, 2nd ed. (New York: Oxford University Press, 1979), 559–79.

Cook, David. "American Horror: *The Shining*." *Literature/Film Quarterly* 14, no. 2 (1986): 2–4.

———. "Ballistic Balletics: Styles of Violent Representation in *The Wild Bunch* and After." In *Sam Peckinpah's "The Wild Bunch*," edited by Stephen Prince. Cambridge: Cambridge University Press, 1999.

Cook, Pam. "Duplicity in *Mildred Pierce*." In *Women in Film Noir*, edited by E. Ann Kaplan, 69–80. London: British Film Institute, 1998.

Crisp, Colin. *The Classic French Cinema, 1930–1960.* Bloomington: Indiana University Press, 1993.

*Dead Man.* DVD. Directed by Jim Jarmusch. New York: Miramax, 1996.

Deleuze, Gilles. *Cinema 1: The Movement Image.* Translated by Hugh Tomlinson and Barbara Habberjam. Minneapolis: University of Minnesota Press, 1986.

Doane, Mary Ann. *The Desire to Desire: The Woman's Film of the 1940's.* Bloomington: Indiana University Press, 1987.

———. *The Emergence of Cinematic Time.* Cambridge, MA: Harvard University Press, 2002.

———. "The Object of Theory." In *Rites of Realism: Essays on Corporeal Cinema*, edited by Ivone Margulies. Durham, NC: Duke University Press, 2003.

Donnell, Dorothy. "I Remember When." *Motion Picture Classic*, November 1925.

Durgnat, Raymond. *Jean Renoir.* Berkeley: University of California Press, 1974.

Eagle, Herbert. "The Poetic Cinema of Yuri Ilyenko." Paper presented at the American Association for the Advancement of Slavic Studies Annual Conference, Toronto, November 23, 2003.

———. "Yugoslav Marxist Humanism and the Films of Dušan Makavejev." In *Politics, Art and Commitment in the East European Cinema*, edited by David W. Paul. London: Macmillan, 1983.

Eikhenbaum, Boris. "Problems of Cinema Stylistics." In *Russian Formalist Film Theory*, edited and translated by Herbert Eagle. Ann Arbor: University of Michigan Press, 1981.

Eisenstein, Sergei M. *Film Form: Essays in Film Theory.* Edited and translated by Jay Leyda. New York: Harcourt, Brace, Jovanovich, 1949.

———. *Izbrannye proizvedeniia v shesti tomakh.* Moscow: Izdatel'stvo iskusstvo, 1964.

———. *Metod.* Edited by N. I. Kleiman. 2 vols. Moscow: Muzei kino/Eizenshtein-tsentr, 2002.

———. *Nonindifferent Nature: Film and the Structure of Things.* Translated by Herbert Marshall. Cambridge: Cambridge University Press, 1988.

———. *On the Composition of the Short Fiction Scenario.* Translated by Alan Y. Upchurch. Calcutta: Seagull Books and Eisenstein Cine Club, 1985.

———. *Selected Works.* Vol. 1, *Writings, 1922–1934.* Edited and translated by Richard Taylor. London: British Film Institute, 1988.

———. *Selected Works.* Vol. 2, *Towards a Theory of Montage.* Edited by Michael Glenny and Richard Taylor. London: British Film Institute, 1991.

Eisenstein, Sergei M., and Ivor Montagu. First Treatment of *An American Tragedy.* Eisenstein Collection. Museum of Modern Art, New York.

Emerson, Ralph Waldo. "Nature" (1836). In *Selected Essays,* edited by Larzer Ziff. New York: Penguin, 1982.

Epstein, Jean. "Grossissement." In *Bonjour cinéma,* 93–108. Paris: Editions de la sirène, 1921.

———. "Magnification." In *French Film Theory and Criticism: A History/Anthology, 1907–1939.* Vol. 1, *1907–1929,* edited by Richard Abel. Princeton, NJ: Princeton University Press, 1988.

———. "Magnification and Other Writings on Film." Translated by Stuart Liebman. *October* 3 (Spring 1977): 9–15.

———. "On Certain Characteristics of *Photogénie.*" In *French Film Theory and Criticism: A History/Anthology, 1907–1939.* Vol. 1, *1907–1929,* edited by Richard Abel. Princeton, NJ: Princeton University Press, 1988.

Farber, Manny. *Negative Space: Manny Farber on the Movies.* New York: Praeger, 1971.

Faulkner, Christopher. *The Social Cinema of Jean Renoir.* Princeton, NJ: Princeton University Press, 1986.

Ferguson, Otis. *The Film Criticism of Otis Ferguson.* Edited by Robert Wilson. Philadelphia: Temple University Press, 1971.

Fofi, Goffredo. "The Cinema of the Popular Front in France (1934–38)." *Screen* 13, no. 4 (Winter 1972–73): 5–57.

Friar, Ralph E., and Natasha A. Friar. *The Only Good Indian . . . : The Hollywood Gospel.* New York: Drama Book Specialists, 1972.

Fussell, Paul. *Wartime: Understanding and Behavior in the Second World War.* Oxford: Oxford University Press, 1989.

Gebhardt, Myrtle. "The Unknown Quantity." *Picture Play,* July 1926.

Gerould, Daniel. "Russian Formalism and Theories of Melodrama." In *Imitations of Life: A Reader on Film and Television Melodrama,* edited by Marcia Landy. Detroit: Wayne State University Press, 1991.

Gish, Lillian. *The Movies, Mr. Griffith, and Me.* Englewood Cliffs, NJ: Prentice-Hall, 1969.

Godard, Jean-Luc. *The Future(s) of Film: Three Interviews, 2000/2001.* Translated by John O'Toole. Bern: Verlag Gachnang & Springer, 2002.

———. *Histoire(s) du cinéma.* 4 vols. Munich: Jean-Luc Godard and ECM Records, 1999.

Gunning, Tom. *D. W. Griffith and the Origins of American Narrative Film.* Urbana: University of Illinois Press, 1991.

———. "The Cinema of Attractions: Early Film, Its Spectator and the Avant-Garde." In *Early Cinema: Space, Frame, Narrative,* edited by Thomas Elsaesser. London: British Film Institute, 1990.

Habermas, Jürgen. *The Future of Human Nature.* Translated by Hella Beister and Max Pensky. Cambridge, MA: Polity Press, 2003.

Hartman, Geoffrey. *The Fate of Reading and Other Essays.* Chicago: University of Chicago Press, 1975.

Hegel, G. W. F. *The Phenomenology of Mind.* Translated by J. B. Baillie. New York: Harper and Row, 1967.

Higham, Charles. *Warner Brothers.* New York: Scribners, 1975.

Hitchcock, Alfred, and François Truffaut. *Hitchcock/Truffaut.* New York: Simon and Schuster, 1983.

Hoffman, Piotr. *Violence in Modern Philosophy.* Chicago: University of Chicago Press, 1989.

Hoopes, Roy. *Cain.* New York: Holt, Rinehart and Winston, 1982.

Jameson, Frederic. *Signatures of the Visible.* New York: Routledge, 1992.

Jay, Martin. *The Dialectical Imagination: A History of the Frankfurt School and the Institute of Social Research, 1923–1950.* Boston: Little, Brown and Company, 1973.

———. *Downcast Eyes: The Denigration of Vision in Twentieth-Century French Thought.* Berkeley: University of California Press, 1993.

Jesionowski, Joyce. "Performance and Characterization in *Intolerance*." In *The Griffith Project*, vol. 9, *The Films Produced in 1916–1918*, edited by Paolo Cherchi Usai. London: British Film Institute, 2005.

Judson, Hanford C. "What Gets Over." *Moving Picture World*, April 15, 1911.

Kaufman, Robert. "Aura, Still." In *October* 99 (Winter 2002): 45–80.

Kepley, Vance. *The End of St. Petersburg: The Film Companion.* London: I. B. Tauris, 2003.

———. *In the Service of the State: The Cinema of Alexander Dovzhenko.* Madison: University of Wisconsin Press, 1986.

Kilpatrick, Jacquelyn. *Celluloid Indians: Native Americans and Film.* Lincoln: University of Nebraska Press, 1999.

Kozintsev, Grigorii. "A Child of the Revolution." In *Cinema in Revolution: The Heroic Era of the Soviet Film*, edited by Luda Schnitzer, Jean Schnitzer, and Marcel Martin, and translated by David Robinson. London: Secker and Warburg, 1966.

Kozloff, Sarah. "Humanizing 'The Voice of God': Narration in *The Naked City*." In *Cinema Journal* 23, no. 4 (Summer 1984): 41–53.

Kracauer, Siegfried. *Theory of Film: The Redemption of Physical Reality.* Princeton, NJ: Princeton University Press, 1997.

Krutnik, Frank. *In a Lonely Street: Film Noir, Genre, Masculinity.* London: Routledge, 1991.

Kuleshov, Lev. *Iskusstvo kino: moi opyt.* Moscow: Tea-Kino-pechat', 1929.

———. *Kuleshov on Film: Writings of Lev Kuleshov.* Translated and edited by Ron Levaco. Berkeley: University of California Press, 1974.

———. *Selected Works: Fifty Years in Films.* Translated by Dmitri Agrachev and Nina Belenkaya. Moscow: Raduga Publishers, 1987.

———. *Sobranie sochinenii v trekh tomakh.* Vol. 1, *Teoriia, kritika, pedagogika.* Edited by R. N. Iurenev. Moscow: Iskusstvo, 1987.

LaValley, Albert J. "Introduction: A Troublesome Property to Script." In *Mildred Pierce*, edited by Albert J. LaValley. Madison: University of Wisconsin Press, 1980.

Leaming, Barbara. *Grigorii Kozintsev.* Boston: Twayne Publishers, 1980.

Leenhardt, Roger. "Le Cinéma: Le Crime de M. Lange." *Esprit* 4, no. 42 (March 1, 1936): 977.

Levinas, Emmanuel. *Totality and Infinity: An Essay on Exteriority.* Translated by Alphonso Lingis. Pittsburgh: Duquesne University Press, 1969.

Leyda, Jay. *Kino: A History of the Russian and Soviet Film* Princeton, NJ: Princeton University Press, 1960.

Lichtheim, George. "Introduction to the Torchbook Edition." In G. W. F. Hegel. *The Phenomenology of Mind*, translated by J. B. Baillie. New York: Harper and Row Publishers, 1967.

Lukács, Georg. *History and Class Consciousness: Studies in Marxist Dialectics*. Translated by Rodney Livingstone. Cambridge, MA: MIT Press, 1968.

Manchel, Frank. "What about Jack? Another Perspective on Family Relationships in Stanley Kubrick's *The Shining*." *Literature/Film Quarterly* 23, no. 1 (1995): 67–78.

Mandel, Ernest. *Delightful Murder: A Social History of the Crime Story*. Minneapolis: University of Minnesota Press, 1985.

Marx, Karl. *The Poverty of Philosophy*. New York: International Publishers, 1963.

McKim, Kristi. "The Astounded Soul: Cinematic Aesthetics of Time and Love." PhD dissertation, Emory University, 2005.

McKinney, Devin. "Violence: The Strong and the Weak." In *Screening Violence*, edited by Stephen Prince. New Brunswick, NJ: Rutgers University Press, 2000. First published in *Film Quarterly* 46, no. 4 (Summer 1993), 16–22.

Merleau-Ponty, Maurice. *Phenomenology of Perception*. Translated by Colin Smith. London: Routledge, 2001.

Metz, Christian. *Essais sur la signification au cinema*. Paris: Éditions Klincksieck, 1978.

———. *Film Language: A Semiotics of the Cinema*. Translated by Michael Taylor. Chicago: University of Chicago Press, 1974.

Miller, D. A. *Jane Austen; or, The Secret of Style*. Princeton, NJ: Princeton University Press, 2003.

———. "On the Universality of *Brokeback Mountain*." *Film Quarterly* 60, no. 3 (Spring 2007): 50–60.

Mitchell, Lee Clark. "Violence in the Film Western." In *Violence and American Cinema*, edited by J. David Slocum. New York: Routledge, 2001.

Mitry, Jean. *The Aesthetics and Psychology of the Cinema*. Translated by Christopher King. Bloomington: Indiana University Press, 1997.

Moore, Rachel O. *Savage Theory*. Durham, NC: Duke University Press, 2000.

Morin, Edgar. *Le Cinéma ou l'homme imaginaire*. Paris: Éditions de minuit, 1956.

Mulvey, Laura. "Audio Essay." *Peeping Tom*. DVD. Directed by Michael Powell. New York: Criterion Collection, 1999.

———. "Visual Pleasure and Narrative Cinema." In *Feminist Film Theory: A Reader*, edited by Susan Thornham. Edinburgh: Edinburgh University Press, 1999.

Münsterberg, Hugo. *Hugo Münsterberg on Film*. Edited by Allan Langdale. New York: Routledge, 2002.

Musser, Charles. *The Emergence of Cinema: The American Screen to 1907*. New York: Charles Scribner's Sons, 1990.

———. "The Travel Genre in 1903–1904: Moving towards Fictional Narrative." In *Early Cinema: Space, Frame, Narrative*, edited by Thomas Elsaesser. London: British Film Institute, 1990.

Naremore, James. *Acting in the Cinema*. Berkeley: University of California Press, 1990.

Nelson, Joyce. "*Mildred Pierce* Reconsidered." *Film Reader* 2 (January 1977): 65–70.

Nesbet, Anne. *Savage Junctures: Sergei Eisenstein and the Shape of Thinking*. London: I. B. Tauris, 2003.

Neuberger, Joan. "Multimedia Essay on the History of *Ivan the Terrible*." *Ivan the Terrible Parts I and II*. DVD. Directed by S. M. Eisenstein. New York: Criterion Collection, 2001.

Nizhny, Vladimir. *Lessons with Eisenstein*. Edited and translated by Ivor Montagu and Jay Leyda. London: George Allen and Unwin, 1962.

Orwell, George. "Appendix 2: Notes from Orwell's Last Literary Notebook." In *The Complete Works of George Orwell*, vol. 20, *Our Job Is to Make Life Worth Living, 1949–1950*, edited by Peter Davison. London: Secker and Warburg, 1998.

———. "A Hanging." In *The Complete Works of George Orwell*, vol. 10, *A Kind of Compulsion, 1903–1936*, edited by Peter Davison. London: Secker and Warburg, 1998.

O'Shaughnessy, Martin. *Jean Renoir*. Manchester: Manchester University Press, 1988.

Oudart, Jean-Pierre. "La Suture." *Cahiers du Cinéma*, no. 211 (April 1969): 36–39; no. 212 (May 1969): 50–55.

Pappas, Peter. "Jean Renoir's *The Crime of M. Lange*." A Second Look. *Cineaste* 10, no. 3 (Summer 1980): 28–31.

Pearson, Roberta. *Eloquent Gestures: The Transformation of Performance Style in the Griffith Biograph Films*. Berkeley: University of California Press, 1992.

Perez, Gilberto. *The Material Ghost: Films and Their Medium*. Baltimore: Johns Hopkins University Press, 1998.

Pippin, Robert B. "Hegel." In *The Cambridge Dictionary of Philosophy*, edited by Robert Audi. Cambridge: Cambridge University Press, 1995.

Prats, Armando José. *Invisible Narratives: Myth and Identity in the American Western*. Ithaca, NY: Cornell University Press, 2002.

Prince, Stephen. *Classical Film Violence: Designing and Regulating Brutality in Hollywood Cinema, 1930–1968*. New Brunswick, NJ: Rutgers University Press, 2003.

———. "Introduction: Sam Peckinpah, Savage Poet of American Cinema." In *Sam Peckinpah's "The Wild Bunch,"* edited by Stephen Prince. Cambridge: Cambridge University Press, 1999.

———. *Savage Cinema: Sam Peckinpah and the Rise of Ultraviolent Movies*. Austin: University of Texas Press, 1998.

Pudovkin, Vsevolod Illarionovich. *Film Technique and Film Acting*. Translated by Ivor Montagu. New York: Bonanza Books, 1949.

*¡Que viva México!* DVD. Directed by Sergei Eisenstein. Reconstructed by Grigory Alexandrov and Nikita Orlov. 1931/1979. New York: Kino Video, 2001.

Ray, Robert B. *A Certain Tendency of the Hollywood Cinema, 1930–1980*. Princeton, NJ: Princeton University Press, 1985.

Reader, Keith. "Renoir's Popular Front Films: Texts in Context." In *La Vie est à nous! French Cinema of the Popular Front, 1935–1938*, edited by Keith Reader and Ginette Vincendeau. London: British Film Institute, 1986.

Renoir, Jean. "Introduction to the Film by Jean Renoir." *The Rules of the Game*. DVD. Directed by Jean Renoir. New York: Criterion Collection, 2004.

Rodriguez, Luis J. *Always Running: La Vida Loca: Gang Days in L.A.* Willimantic, CT: Curbstone Press, 1993.

Ropars, Marie-Claire. "L'Ouverture d'*Octobre* ou les conditions théoriques de la Révolution." In *Octobre: Écriture et idéologie*. 27–66. Paris: Editions Albatros, 1976.

———. "The Overture of *October*." Translated by Larry Crawford and Kimball Lockhart. *Enclitic* 2, no. 2 (1978): 50–72; 2, no. 3 (1978): 35–47.

Rosen, Philip. *Change Mummified: Cinema, Historicity, Theory*. Minneapolis: University of Minnesota Press, 2000.

Rosenbaum, Jonathan. *Dead Man*. London: British Film Institute, 2000.

Rothman, William. *Hitchcock: The Murderous Gaze*. Cambridge, MA: Harvard University Press, 1982.

Sadoul, Georges. *Histoire d'un art: Le Cinéma des origines à nos jours*. Paris, 1949.

Saint-Amour, Paul K. "Modernist Reconnaissance." *Modernism/Modernity* 10, no. 2 (April 2003): 349–80.

Schwenger, Peter. "Corpsing the Image." *Critical Inquiry* 26, no. 3 (Spring 2000): 395–413.

Serceau, Daniel. *Jean Renoir, l'insurgé*. Paris: Le Sycomore, 1981.

Sesonske, Alexander. *Jean Renoir: The French Films, 1924–1939*. Cambridge, MA: Harvard University Press, 1980.

Seton, Marie. *S. M. Eisenstein*. New York: Grove Press, 1960.

Sherman, Eric, and Martin Rubin. *The Director's Event: Interviews with Five American Film-Makers*. New York: Atheneum, 1970.

Shklovskii, Viktor. "The End of the Baroque: A Letter to Eisenstein." In *Za sorok let*. Moscow: Iskusstvo, 1965.

———. "Poeziia i proza v kinematografii." In *Poetika kino*. Moscow: Kinopechat', 1927. Reprint, Berkeley: Berkeley Slavic Specialties, 1984.

Silverman, Kaja, and Harun Farocki. *Speaking about Godard*. New York: New York University Press, 1998.

Simmel, Georg. *The Sociology of Georg Simmel*. Translated and edited by Kurt Wolff. Glencoe, IL: Free Press, 1950.

Skal, David J. *Screams of Reason: Mad Science and Modern Culture*. New York: W. W. Norton and Company, 1998.

Slotkin, Richard. *Gunfighter Nation: The Myth of the Frontier in Twentieth-Century America*. Norman: University of Oklahoma Press, 1998.

———. *Regeneration through Violence: The Mythology of the American Frontier, 1600–1860*. Norman: University of Oklahoma Press, 2000.

Solomon-Godeau, Abigail. "Male Trouble." In *Constructing Masculinity*, edited by Wallace Berger, 69–76. New York: Routledge, 1995.

Sontag, Susan. *Styles of Radical Will*. New York: Farrar, Straus, Giroux, 1969.

Spivak, Gayatri Chakravorty. "Translator's Preface." In *Of Grammatology*, by Jacques Derrida. Baltimore: Johns Hopkins University Press, 1997.

Stanislavsky, Konstantin. *My Life in Art*. New York: Theatre Arts Books, 1987.

Steffen, James. "A Cardiogram of the Times: Sergei Parajanov and the Politics of Nationality and Aesthetics in the Soviet Union." Doctoral thesis, Emory University, 2005.

Stewart, Garrett. *Between Film and Screen: Modernism's Photo Synthesis*. Chicago: University of Chicago Press, 1999.

Studlar, Gaylyn. "Sacred Duties, Poetic Passions." In *John Ford Made Westerns*, edited by Gaylyn Studlar and Matthew Bernstein. Bloomington: Indiana University Press, 2001.

————. *This Mad Masquerade: Stardom and Masculinity in the Jazz Age*. New York: Columbia University Press, 1996.

*Sweet Sweetback's Baadasssss Song*. Laserdisc, Directed by Melvin Van Peebles. New York: Criterion Collection, 1997.

Tall, Emily. "Eisenstein on Joyce: Sergei Eisenstein's Lecture on James Joyce at the State Institute of Cinematography November 1, 1934." *James Joyce Quarterly* 24, no. 2 (Winter 1987): 133–42.

Taylor, Greg. *Artists in the Audience: Cults, Camp, and American Film Criticism*. Princeton, NJ: Princeton University Press, 1999.

Taylor, Richard, and Ian Christie, eds. *The Film Factory: Russian and Soviet Cinema in Documents, 1896–1939*. London: Routledge, 1988.

Thompson, Kristin. *Eisenstein's "Ivan the Terrible": A Neoformalist Analysis*. Princeton, NJ: Princeton University Press, 1981.

Tompkins, Jane. *West of Everything: The Inner Life of Westerns*. Oxford: Oxford University Press, 1992.

Tsivian, Yuri. *Early Cinema in Russia and Its Cultural Reception*. Translated by Alan Bodger. Chicago: University of Chicago Press, 1998.

————. "Homeless Images: D. W. Griffith in the Eye of Soviet Filmmakers." *Griffithiana* 16, nos. 60–61 (October 1997): 50–75.

Tsutsui, William. *Godzilla on My Mind: Fifty Years of the King of Monsters*. New York: Palgrave Macmillan, 2004.

Tyler, Parker. *Magic and Myth of the Movies*. New York: Henry Holt and Company, 1947.

————. *The Three Faces of the Film* . South Brunswick, NY: A. S. Barnes and Company, 1960.

Vannercook, John W. *Black Majesty: The Life of Christophe, King of Haiti*. New York: Harper and Bros., 1928.

Virilio, Paul. *War and Cinema: The Logistics of Perception*. Translated by Patrick Camiller. London: Verso, 1989.

Vygotsky, Lev S. *Thought and Language*. Edited and translated by Eugenia Hanfmann and Gertrude Vakar. New York: MIT Press, 1962.

Wald, Malvin. "Afterword: The Anatomy of a Hit." In *The Naked City: A Screenplay*, edited by Matthew J. Bruccoli. Carbondale: Southern Illinois University Press, 1948.

————. "Commentary." *The Naked City*. Laserdisc. Directed by Jules Dassin. New York: Roan Group, 1995.

Warshow, Robert. *The Immediate Experience: Movies, Comics, Theatre, and Other Aspects of Popular Culture*. Cambridge, MA: Harvard University Press, 2001.

Willemen, Paul. *Looks and Frictions: Essays in Cultural Studies and Film Theory*. Bloomington: Indiana University Press, 1994.

Williams, Linda. "Of Kisses and Ellipses: The Long Adolescence of American Movies." *Critical Inquiry* 32, no. 2 (Winter 2006): 288–340.

————. "Something Else besides a Mother: *Stella Dallas* and the Maternal Melodrama." In *Feminism and Film*, edited by E. Ann Kaplan. Oxford: Oxford University Press, 2000.

Wister, Owen. *The Virginian, a Horseman of the Plains*. Oxford: Oxford University Press, 1998.

Witt, Michael. "The Death(s) of Cinema according to Jean-Luc Godard." *Screen* 40, no. 3 (1999): 331–46.

Wollen, Peter. *Signs and Meaning in the Cinema*. London: British Film Institute, 1998.

Woloch, Alex. *The One vs. the Many: Minor Characters and the Space of the Protagonist in the Novel*. Princeton, NJ: Princeton University Press, 2003.

Wood, Robin. *Sexual Politics and Narrative Film: Hollywood and Beyond*. New York: Columbia University Press, 1998.

Woods, Frank. "Spectator's Comments." *New York Dramatic Mirror*. November 13, 1909.

Yampolsky, Mikhail. "Death in Cinema." In *Re-entering the Sign: Articulating New Russian Culture*, edited by Ellen E. Berry and Anesa Miller-Pogacar. Ann Arbor: University of Michigan Press, 1995.

———. "Kuleshov's Experiments and the New Anthropology of the Actor." In *Inside the Film Factory: New Approaches to Russian and Soviet Cinema*, edited by Richard Taylor and Ian Christie. London: Routledge, 1991.

# Index

Page numbers in italics refer to illustrations.

Griffith, D. W. (*cont.*)
238n52; *Corner in Wheat* (1909), 9; *The Fatal Hour* (1908), 9–10, 183, 228n22; *Intolerance* (1916), 9, 28; *The Lonedale Operator* (1911), 9, 28–29; *The Lonely Villa* (1909), 9; *The Mothering Heart* (1913), 81; *Orphans of the Storm* (1921), 9; *Thou Shalt Not Kill* (1913), 28; *An Unseen Enemy* (1912), 9, 28, 37, 79–80; *Way Down East* (1920), 238n52
gun: close-up of, 24–25, 28–29, 120; close-up of hand on, 24–26, 29–33; in film theory, 25–29; parallels with camera, 17, 230n39; as stylistic flourish, 184; in Western film, 186, 232n23. *See also* weapon
*Gunfighter, The* (King, 1950), 200
Gunning, Tom, 9–10, 11, 183, 194, 228n22, 253n61

Habermas, Jürgen, 51
Hansen, Miriam, 2, 95
Hartman, Geoffrey, 150, 164, 181, 183
Hatch, Robert, 140
Hawks, Howard, 135; *Air Force* (1943), 18, 155–56; *The Big Sleep* (1946), 136; *His Girl Friday* (1940), 183; *Red River* (1947), 185; *Rio Bravo* (1959), 192
Hegel, Georg Wilhelm Friedrich: "Absolute Spirit," 40; dialectic of lordship and bondage, and Western showdown, 18, 19, 188, 193–202; narrative of individual self-consciousness, 196, 201; *Phenomenology*, 193; seeing self in other, 196; sharing of other's desire, 195; staking of one's life as crucial phase in development of self-consciousness, 194–95
Hegelians, left and right, 231n44
Heidegger, Martin, 106
*Heir of Genghis Khan, The* (Pudovkin, 1928), 7, 11, 29–36; close-up as negating device, 36; close-up of hand on revolver, 29–33; dialectic of loss and retrieval, 30; effect of murder scene as exclusion and presence-in-absence, 36, 39; parallel

structure, 30, 31–33; surgery sequence of close-ups, 33, *34, 35,* 57
*Heller with a Gun* (L'Amour, 1955), 197–98
Hellinger, Mark: as producer of *Naked City*, 244n9, 245nn10–11; voice-over narration of *The Naked City*, 141–46, 147, 150–51, 246n14
Hemingway, Ernest, 219
*His Girl Friday* (Hawks, 1940), 183
histrionic code, 79, 80, 235n18
Hitchcock, Alfred, 168–69; aerial views, 218–23, 257n8; *Bon Voyage* (1944), 218; classical continuity editing, 95, 98, 106; *Lifeboat* (1944), 218; *Murder!* (1930), 219; *North by Northwest* (1959), 219; *Psycho* (1960), 215, 219, 220–21, 257n6; *Saboteur* (1958), 219; *Stage Fright* (1950), 220; *Vertigo* (1958), 219
Hoffman, Piotr, 201, 254n76
Hollywood classical découpage, 63, 134, 167–68, 225n3; Bazin and, 95, 105, 135; and *Mildred Pierce* (Curtiz, 1945), 170, 177, 183; and murder mystery, 168; reifying effect of, 178; and temporal segments of life, 182
Hollywood genre films: abstraction of persons into types, 179, 181; aestheticization of Western violence, 184; expendability of individual in murder scenes, 134; formalism, 169; "male genres," 135–40; and montage, 133–35, 182–83; portrayal of Native Americans, 203; problem of representing murder, 202; psychoanalytic concepts as new realism, 167–68; scenes of killing, 17–18, 133; tension between individual scene and series of scenes, 17–18; and uniformity, 134–35. *See also* Western film; Western hero; Western showdown
Hollywood murder mystery: and city symphony, 142–43, 147–48, 152; formalism, 169; and psychoanalysis, 168, 181, 183; template for other narrative structures, 167–68, 169. *See also* murder; murder scene